$2-

D0958376

NEVERTHELESS, SHE PERSISTED

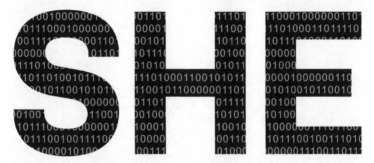

TRUE STORIES OF WOMEN LEADERS IN TECH

PRATIMA RAO GLUCKMAN

 FriesenPress

Suite 300 - 990 Fort St
Victoria, BC, V8V 3K2
Canada

www.friesenpress.com

ISBN
978-1-5255-1210-0 (Hardcover)
978-1-5255-1211-7 (Paperback)
978-1-5255-1212-4 (eBook)

1. BUSINESS & ECONOMICS, WORKPLACE CULTURE

Distributed to the trade by The Ingram Book Company

NEVERTHELESS,  PERSISTED

TRUE STORIES OF
WOMEN LEADERS IN TECH

01010100 01101000 01110010 01101111 01110101 01100111 01101000 01101111 01110101
01110100 00100000 01110100 01101000 01101001 01110011 00100000 01100010 01101111
01101111 01101011 00101100 00100000 01110100 01101000 01100101 01110010 01100101
00100000 01100001 01110010 01100101 00100000 01110100 01110111 01101111 00100000
01100011 01101111 01101110 01110011 01101001 01110011 01110100 01100101 01101110
01110100 00100000 01101111 01100101 01110011 01110011 01101111 01101110 01110011
00101110 00100000 01000110 01101001 01110010 01110011 01110100 00101100 00100000
01110000 01100101 01110010 01110011 01101001 01110011 01110100 00101110 00100000
01010010 01100101 01100111 01100001 01110010 01100100 01101100 01100101 01110011
01110011 00100000 01101111 01100110 00100000 01110111 01101000 01100001 01110100
00100000 01110011 01101111 01100011 01101001 01100101 01110100 01111001 00100000
01100101 01111000 01110000 01100101 01100011 01110100 01110011 00100000 01101111
01100110 00100000 01111001 01101111 01110101 00100000 01101111 01110010 00100000
01110100 01101111 00100000 01100100 01101111 00101100 00100000 01110000 01110010
01100101 01110010 01110011 01101001 01110011 01110100 00100000 01110111 01101001
01110100 01101000 00100000 01111001 01101111 01110101 01110010 00100000 01101111
01110111 01101110 00100000 01110110 01101001 01110011 01101001 01101111 01101110
00100000 01101111 01100110 00100000 01110111 01101000 01100001 01110100 00100000
01111001 01101111 01110101 00100000 01110111 01100001 01101110 01110100 00100000
01110100 01101111 00100000 01100001 01100011 01101000 01101001 01100101 01110110
01100101 00100000 01101001 01101110 00100000 01111001 01101111 01110101 01110010
00100000 01101100 01101001 01100110 01100101 00101110 00100000 01010100 01101000
01100101 00100000 01110100 01100001 01101001 01101100 01110111 01101001 01101110
01100100 01110011 00100000 01101111 01100110 00100000 01100101 01101100 01110010
00100000 01111001 01101111 01110101 00100000 01110011 01101111 01100001 01110010
00101110 00100000 01010100 01101000 01100101 00100000 01110011 01100101 01100011
01101111 01101110 01100100 00100000 01101100 01100101 01110011 01110011 01101111
01101110 00100000 01101001 01110011 00100000 01110100 01101000 01100001 01110100
00100000 01110111 01100101 00100000 01100001 01101100 01101100 00100000 01101000
01100001 01110110 01100101 00100000 01110100 01101000 01100101 00100000 01110100
01101111 01101111 01101100 01110011 00100000 01110100 01101111 00100000 01100011
01101000 01100001 01101110 01100111 01100101 00100000 01110100 01101000 01100101
00100000 01110111 01101111 01110010 01101100 01100100 00100000 01100110 01101111
01110010 00100000 01110011 01101111 01101101 01100101 01101111 01101110 01100101
00100000 01100101 01101100 01110011 01100101 00101110 00100000 01001001 01100110
00100000 01100101 01100001 01100011 01101000 00100000 01101111 01101110 01100101
00100000 01101111 01100110 00100000 01110101 01110011 00100000 01101101 01100001
01101011 01100101 01110011 00100000 01101001 01110100 00100000 01100001 00100000
01110000 01101111 01101001 01101110 01110100 00100000 01110100 01101111 00100000
01101001 01101110 01110100 01100101 01110010 01110110 01100101 01101110 01100101
00100000 01101001 01101110 00100000 01101111 01101110 01100101 00100000 01110111
01101111 01101101 01100001 01101110 11100010 10000000 10011001 01110011 00100000
01101100 01101001 01100110 01100101 00101100 00100000 01110111 01100101 00100000

In loving memory of my mom, Chitty (1947–2016),
who nurtured me to find my own place in this world.

can get there, slowly but surely—one woman at a time.

My long term hope for the tech world is to have equal representation of men and women as CEOs, board members, executive leaders, middle managers, and engineers. I hope that by telling these women's stories, I will encourage new generations of women to develop the skills and determination to make this a reality. Let's go change the world.

ABOUT THE AUTHOR

Pratima Rao Gluckman knew she wanted to be an engineer from a young age. When she took her first programming class, she fell in love and began on her career path. She attained a master's degree in computer science (University of Texas at Arlington), a master's degree in chemistry, and bachelor's degree in instrumentation engineering (BITs Pilani India). After a few years working in the industry as a software engineer, she made the decision to move into engineering management. Leading came naturally for her, and currently, in her field of enterprise software, she manages a team of engineers.

During her time in the industry, she has grown aware of the gender bias and related imposter's syndrome that makes it challenging for women—including herself—to achieve their desired potential. From this realization, *Nevertheless, She Persisted* was conceived. It is Gluckman's hope that this book contributes meaningful changes in the tech world so that many more women can enter careers as engineers and thrive to become effective leaders in their organizations.

She currently resides with her husband and three children in the San Francisco Bay Area.

TABLE OF CONTENTS

FOREWORD

In 1997, my computer science degree in hand, I walked through the doors at Pixar. The first thing I learned was not some interesting piece of technology that I would use for my little corner of the computer animation pipeline. Rather, I learned that nothing matters more than story, and imbuing those stories with heart. Pratima Rao Gluckman has done enormous work in bringing together these stories told by tremendous women who show not only unwavering determination but also deep heart. Their honesty about their experiences pulls back the curtain and shows what it is truly like to be a woman leader in technology. The stories, along with sage morsels of advice, are made all the stronger by the range of personalities and traits these women exhibit, especially interesting are the ones we don't always think of as typical leader, or female, traits. It is refreshing to see the many and varied pathways that these women have taken to success. Their words and experiences teach us that we don't have to ram ourselves into some specific box in order to succeed. Success lies in each of us finding strength in who we are, where we came from, and the things we are passionate about (with a touch of butt kicking thrown in for good measure).

This book will serve as a wonderful guide for young women just starting out, as well as for women who are further along. We can all use the advice given here, wherever we are in our careers. I think these stories will also be a great touchstone for men who want to be our allies but are still learning to recognize the moments when their support could change the cultural tides of boardrooms and companies. We live in a time of massive innovation, a time in which technology is alleviating and solving some of our hardest problems. Imagine the things we will achieve when every young girl has this guidebook in her hand. It will lead her to a seat at the table at which she will help shape products and devise solutions. And those tables will be in boardrooms and conference rooms where a diversity of people and ideas is no longer a novelty.

Danielle Feinberg
Director of Photography, Lighting
Pixar Animation Studios

~ ~ ~

What do you want to be when you grow up? So many of us grapple with the multitude of decisions and turning points along the way as we answer this question. For the women and men considering a career in technology, there is nothing more powerful than worthwhile role models. How do you decide to study computing or engineering? What are the important inflection points you will encounter? What decisions will you have to make? How do you ask for what you want? How do you know what you want?

Pratima takes you into the lives of the extraordinary women she features. Their stories are personal, but they include relevant life and career lessons for all of us. As I read each story, I found myself feeling their pain, cheering on their successes, and learning from some of their difficult choices. Each story brings insight into career trajectories and highlights the importance of mentors and sponsors. In addition to sharing these women's candid lessons, Pratima has included valuable references to books through which the reader can learn more, including *Women Don't Ask*, *Through the Labyrinth*, and *Emotional Intelligence*.

The perspectives and stories she provides are global. The stories begin in Israel, Taiwan, Argentina, China, and the US, as well as in her own country of origin, India. The choices that the women make are different. They study computing, engineering, and history; they join start-ups and large companies. But each story provides thoughtful context for the decisions they make and the consequences of those decisions.

Technology is changing our world. Many of the most important revolutions that will take place over the next fifty years have technology at their heart. Women, 50% of the population, still only make up between 20–25% of the technology work force. As we look to change the landscape, role models can have a lasting impact for many young women and men. Pratima brings to life extraordinary role models, sharing their stories, their aspirations, and their fears. One of the most important aspects of this book is Pratima's own story; her background helps her bring to life the stories of all the women she features.

I encourage you to embark on a journey of discovery. As you read this book and get to know these remarkable women, find your own answers as you discover what is possible in the world of creating technology.

Telle Whitney
Former CEO, Anita Borg Institute
Co-founder, Grace Hopper Celebration

INTRODUCTION

"I alone cannot change the world, but I can cast a stone across the waters to create many ripples."

— Mother Theresa

~ ~ ~

On February 7, 2017, on the floor of the U.S. Senate, Senate Majority Leader Mitch McConnell of Kentucky used a procedural rule to silence the objections of Senator Elizabeth Warren to the confirmation of Senator Jeff Sessions to become attorney general of the U.S. After the incident, McConnell said, "Senator Warren was giving a lengthy speech. She had appeared to violate the rule. She was warned. She was given an explanation. Nevertheless, she persisted."[1]

The Internet exploded after this incident. The phrase "Nevertheless, she persisted" quickly became a meme and a rallying cry of the feminist movement. On Twitter, this incident was characterized as a man of influence unfairly muzzling the voice of a woman.[2]

---

[1]   163 Cong. Rec. S855 (daily ed. February 7, 2017) (statement of Sen. McConnell), https://www.congress.gov/crec/2017/02/06/CREC-2017-02-06-bk2.pdf.

[2]   Daniel Victor, "'Nevertheless, She Persisted': How Senate's Silencing of Warren Became a Meme," *New York Times*, February 8, 2017, https://www.nytimes.com/2017/02/08/us/politics/elizabeth-warren-republicans-facebook-twitter.html.

Setting the partisan politics of this incident aside, I think the phrase "Nevertheless, she persisted" can inspire women not to let bias quiet their voices. The stories of women shared in this book are saturated with clear evidence of their persistence, whether through a grueling education or going back to ask for a promotion after being rejected before. For these reasons, I decided that *Nevertheless, She Persisted* was an apt title for this book. Persistence is so important because gender bias is so insidious and powerful, affecting how things will go in our families, our schools, our communities, and our corporations.

~ ~ ~

In my work as a mother, a writer, and a female leader in the high-tech field, I feel as though I am casting stones into turbulent waters by telling the stories of nineteen women who hold senior positions in the high-tech world of Silicon Valley. Why do I want to do this? I want to cast a stone representing limitless possibilities, the concept that anything is achievable, for my daughter and all the daughters out there. I want to cast a stone representing acceptance of female leaders for my sons, and all the sons out there, so they know how to accept, embrace, and love living in a world that is supportive of female leaders.

Too many media stories have been breaking lately about how both subtle bias and overt sexism play out in high-tech companies, which creates challenging work environments for female technologists. Ever in search of a big, salacious story, the media tends to focus on the negative rather than on the positive. As I interviewed the contributors for this book, however, many hopeful stories of success and persistence emerged. The media doesn't often highlight hopeful stories; I believe they need to be told.

One further stone is also being cast with this book. In a sense, the book as a whole forms a chapter of my experience as a woman in tech. My thoughts and reactions, interwoven with the other women's observations, offer further insights that have been awakened by the experience of talking with these remarkable women.

~ ~ ~

I knew at an early age that I wanted to be an engineer. I am the first female engineer in my family; I can't say that with pride, because we probably should have had more female engineers before me, but that's how it was. When I took my first programming class at age fourteen, I fell in love with engineering. I set a goal to become an engineer, and I had a fairly well-laid-out path to achieve it. The few senior girls in my school who had the same aspirations were my role models. Although becoming a software engineer was hard work, I knew I could do it. And I wasn't the only one who believed in myself; so did my parents, siblings, friends, and teachers. I believed I could become an engineer, so I did. I persisted, no matter what obstacles came up.

After a few years in the industry as a software engineer, I made a conscious decision to aim for moving into management. Being a leader had always come naturally to me. As a child, I organized a team to play neighborhood cricket. When I entered the workforce as an individual contributor, I consistently rallied other employees in my company to follow a vision. In 2013, after being an engineer for thirteen years, I achieved my first promotion to management at VMware. I like organizing teams to run with a concept that could have an impact on people's lives. I found that being on the management track suited me.

However, it has not been straightforward for me. When I look for female role models along this path, I see few. The lack of gender diversity at every level of leadership prevents many women from advancing in their careers. We need female role models in every employment sector, not just high tech; we need to diversify the workplace and offer guidance and inspiration to all younger women.

Throughout my technical career, my bosses and peers told me that I had a steep growth trajectory and that I was a change agent. Though I was flattered to hear that, I felt stuck, not knowing how to leverage that potential. At a certain point, when I moved into a new group, I realized that many of the challenges that were confronting me were the result of my being a female in a male-dominated industry.

Prior to that realization, I had been oblivious to the effects of gender bias, but something about the new group made it very evident to me. It was a business unit primarily run by men, with few women in senior positions. So, I set out to look for female role models. I went to a few conferences that offered networking and support opportunities, such as Silicon Valley Women in Engineering and the Grace Hopper Celebration of Women in Computing. There I met women in senior positions at various companies, which started to satisfy my desire to meet female role models.

One day, I chanced upon a YouTube video by Jessica McKellar, then an engineering director at a Silicon Valley startup. It captured a fascinating talk she gave, titled "How the Internet Works."[3] It is a technical discussion in which this female leader describes what happens at a networking level when a person browses the internet. In the talk, she exudes expertise and presents the topic confidently, with style and humor. I can't remember why, but I asked my husband to watch it with me. After the end of the video, he walked away saying, "Interesting. I wonder what her childhood was like." As I reflected on my husband's point, I grew curious to know what influences would help encourage a young girl like her to grow into someone who was a confident, knowledgeable leader in her field.

The more I thought about it, the more I got a palpable sense that there was a need for a book that shows how women become senior

---

3   Jessica McKellar, "How the Internet works," filmed March 15, 2013 at PyCon US 2013, video, 29:34, http://pyvideo.org/pycon-us-2013/how-the-internet-works.html

leaders in the tech industry. Women who are senior leaders are a rarity, even a curiosity—we often don't hear their stories and learn how they arrived at their perspectives. It occurred to me that others would want to know these women's stories as well.

~ ~ ~

To share the stories of female technical leaders, my first step was to interview them. Although I would have liked to talk to women CEOs, I realized they were few in number, and I knew it would be hard to get onto their busy schedules. So, my interview focus began with senior vice presidents (SVPs) and general managers. I started with my network at VMware, where I found only one SVP. That pushed me to interview VPs as well. With that, I found a few more women, but still not a substantial number. With the intention of recruiting senior women for my project, I also went to conferences, which led me to women who were willing to share their stories in this book. Some of them introduced me to other possible interview candidates. I also reached out to my broader work network, asking them to introduce me to others. Within six months, I had more than twenty successful women to interview.

Once I enlisted sufficient women, I came up with a list of questions. I started each interview by discussing childhood influences because I felt that was key to the success of these women tech leaders. What experiences in their childhoods determined the direction of their careers? What were their dreams when they were young? In school, how did they perform in math and science (subjects that are considered foundational for careers in tech)? What helped them become accomplished in those subjects? As young people, what were the perceptions of their family, friends, and teachers regarding their intellectual capacities? Did people have expectations that these girls could make significant contributions?

In their professional lives, who were their mentors? What were some of their failures? Their successes? How had they advocated for themselves in a male-dominated industry? How had they negotiated for what they wanted? Did they ask for promotions and raises? Did they experience gender bias? Did they collide with a glass ceiling that unfairly limited their growth based on their gender? And what about the glass cliff—did they achieve their success only when their companies were experiencing a downturn? Yes, I had many questions for these female technical leaders, and they were very gracious in their willingness to share their thoughts with me.

These stories are filled with invaluable perspectives on topics such as mentors, sponsors, work–life balance, and negotiation. There is a wealth of information here that you could use to affect your own life, as well as the lives of others. Certainly, there is no one right way to navigate a career in technical management. The personal stories that these women share about how they approached their career struggles can give you valuable information to better navigate your career path.

I realized that though each of their journeys is unique, some patterns emerged. There are often many glass ceilings, not just one; when one is shattered, another immediately emerges. Often a career intervention needs to happen to keep a woman's career moving forward. Also, the path to leadership is not straight, but more like an intricate jungle gym. Yet all these women persist as they make their way through.

~ ~ ~

As part of my research for this book, I found that many companies today are pledging diversity; however, it is unclear whether their commitment is being translated into action or results. The progress on gender diversity, for example, is not regularly shared across organizations. Measuring progress is something that needs to happen; companies and organizations must be accountable for change. We need to have metrics to quantify a business's ability to counter the effects of gender bias, and when the business doesn't achieve those metrics, we should persuade our senior leaders to follow best practices in this area.

My research also indicates that most companies don't invest in enough training for their employees around the subject of gender diversity; those that do, don't make it mandatory or high priority. Many companies fail to train managers properly on how to maintain objectivity to counter any bias during the hiring process and performance reviews. Sure, it is important to hire the right talent, but the recruitment process can be unfair when companies fail to mandate the use of diverse interview panels or don't require the selection of diverse candidates in final interview rounds. These are just a few examples of the many policy changes companies can adopt to improve in this area.

Although there are many suggestions in this book for both individuals and companies, there still isn't a perfect recipe for success. All too often, professional women bear the burden of changing and performing better than men to become successful. I believe society must be asked to do its part in accepting women the way they are and working toward changing the status quo. Creating a world where female leaders can thrive is everyone's concern, and everyone can work toward finding a solution.

~ ~ ~

The two primary audiences for this book are young women who are considering careers in technology and established women in the technical field. If you are a female technologist, I hope you will realize that your struggles are not unique and that you have what it takes to be as successful as the women interviewed.

I believe this project will be of interest to many people from other walks of life, as well. For example, educators could get a sense of how to help promising female technologists to thrive in our schools and universities.

I also hope that men will enjoy my book and be open to the idea that the world will be a much more exciting place when women technology leaders are prominent in our companies. I want to encourage men to become aware of their often unconscious bias toward accomplished women technical leaders. I believe it is vital to have men in this conversation, because we need them to advocate for real change in our world. We all have biases, whether it's regarding gender, age, race, or other forms of prejudice. Some manifest as overt bias, which can be easy to overcome because you can speak up to confront it directly. Unconscious bias, on the other hand, can be much more insidious, as we are often not aware of it. Unconscious bias can prevent the hiring, retention, and promotion of high-growth women.

This book is for parents too. They could get ideas about how to support their daughters to be confident in their technology and leadership skills. Hearing the profound influences these women experienced during their childhoods has given me ideas about what to do as a parent myself. Parents have a responsibility, not only to their children but also to their communities. They say it takes a village to raise a child. I say it takes a small group of enlightened people to raise awareness of the unconscious bias toward women technical leaders that we all harbor.

Throughout the chapters, the acronym "CS" is used in place of "computer science." Other commonly used acronyms are BS for bachelor of science; CMO for chief marketing officer; IPO for initial public offering; P&L for profit and loss; and STEM for science, technology, engineering, and math—one set of fields being encouraged in colleges.

~ ~ ~

While I was writing this book, I experienced a personal tragedy when my mom unexpectedly passed away. My relationship with her was one of the most important in my life. By no means did she have an easy life. An ambitious and talented woman, she never got the support she needed to realize her dreams. Though she wanted to be independent and have a career, she was forced to be a stay-at-home mom at the behest of my dad. For a short time when my father allowed her to work, she was a head cook at a few schools and colleges in India and eventually founded a preschool for local children from low-income families.

Though my mother wasn't able to attain a higher degree, education was of paramount importance to her. She made sure that her four kids got excellent educations—even when she didn't have the money to pay for them. In her eyes, education was not only necessary for her children, it was also important for her to assist with the education of neighborhood kids whose parents couldn't afford preschool. Though the school she founded wasn't profitable in the financial sense and didn't last long, her value of education was a huge motivating force for me. It helped me develop the drive to be accepted at one of the top-tier technical universities in India: the Birla Institute of Technology and Science in Pilani (BITS Pilani). In turn, the education and personal experiences I had there laid a strong foundation for my career in technology. It was challenging to write this book while mourning my mother's passing, but I am grateful for all she did to set me up for an enjoyable and rewarding career.

~ ~ ~

Interviewing this collection of women was certainly one of the highlights of my professional career. I found the answers to these questions illuminating. I heard some amazing stories. All the women featured in the book were eager to talk, and to help me in any way they could. I am so appreciative of their generosity with their time and willingness to share their personal stories publicly.

Spending time with these fascinating women, reflecting on their stories as well as their perspectives, has made a huge difference for me both personally and professionally. In the past year, I made several interventions in the lives of my female peers and direct reports. I advocated for them. I raised awareness in my organization about gender diversity and inclusion. I was successful in influencing my senior leadership team to make some changes within the organization. Through this journey, my world has shifted, and I wish the same for you. I know that we can learn, and we can adapt. I hope that this book casts stones that cause ripples in your own life.

CHAPTER 1: TELLE'S STORY

BIOSKETCH: *Telle Whitney's strongest role models have always been women, starting in her youth with astronaut Sally Ride. By happenstance in college, she discovered her affinity for programming, which provided the direction that has guided her from then on. In her early career as a technologist, her mentors and sponsors tended to be men. After meeting fellow CS professional Anita Borg, her profession took an unexpected turn toward becoming a mentor herself, in a big way, to the many women in tech who have been touched by their creation of the Grace Hopper Celebration of Women in Computing and subsequently the Institute for Women in Technology. Telle's success arose from her intensive pursuit, not just of science, but also of building the skills required to grow this nonprofit from a dream to a powerful and respected technology organization.*

"Women leave the technology field at twice the rate of men, so it's not just about getting women into the pipeline—it's about creating cultures where women thrive, which means, compared to today, the culture of the future is going to look significantly different."

— Telle Whitney, former President and CEO, Anita Borg Institute for Women in Computing

~ ~ ~

Telle's mother, her primary parent, influenced her life profoundly. She had moved Telle from Salt Lake City, Utah, to California when Telle was seven. "She thought I could do anything, and she communicated that to me," said Telle. Her mother's encouragement fostered a strength in Telle's character that has served her well throughout her career. Sadly, her mother passed away from multiple myeloma when Telle was fifteen.

Telle's return to Salt Lake City to live with her dad and stepmom marked the beginning of difficult times for her. "I was very good at math, but no one talked to me about math, either at school or at home," she said. "I was sort of a 'know-it-all' kid, and I thought I knew what to do, so I stopped taking math midway through high school—I figured it wasn't useful for anything."

In college, Telle felt lost. She started studying theatre, moved to political science, and then came close to dropping out. At this time, Telle received an unwelcome yet much-needed prod: her stepmom suggested that she take a career interest inventory test.[4] "Because the suggestion came from my stepmother, it was the last thing on earth I wanted to do, but I had run out of options, so I did it." The results of the inventory test identified an aptitude for computer programming. She tried a programming course and discovered a

---

4   For information on this test, see http://careerassessmentsite.com/tests/strong-tests/about-the-strong-interest-inventory/.

great fit. "I fell in love—it was immediate; I felt like I had found what I wanted to do."

In 1970, Telle graduated with a BS in computer science from the University of Utah. Female faculty taught her first class. While Telle was completing her undergraduate degree, a CS faculty member introduced her to Ivan Sutherland, a computer scientist famous for his work in graphics. Ivan and others were starting the CS department at the California Institute of Technology (Caltech). This connection led to Telle's second important career boost. "I had never considered going to graduate school. It was Ivan's interest in me and the support of the Utah faculty members that really led me to take a risk. It made such a difference."

Thus, Telle ended up attending graduate school at Caltech at an auspicious time. The VLSI (very-large-scale integration) revolution had just begun. Caltech had inaugurated the Silicon Structures Project, where circuits consisting of tens of thousands of transistors were being placed on single chips in a systematic way. Companies had the opportunity to spend a year at Caltech working on developing new semiconductor software and technology. Key people from Sun Microsystems (before Sun existed), IBM, Intel, and DEC were doing research there; Apple Xerox PARC staff visited. This lively environment fueled Telle's passion for technology.

Ivan left Caltech just a year after she started studying there, presenting Telle with the opportunity to work with Carver Mead, a pioneer in the field of VLSI. Carver became Telle's PhD thesis advisor, and a crucial factor in her career. "He didn't tell his students what to do—he'd ask questions so we all learned how to think. This helped me with my thinking process and taught me how to approach problems. And he really believed in me." Throughout her career, Carver helped her with connections that led her to all three of her first significant jobs.

As much as she loved being at Caltech and working with the people there, only 13% of Caltech students were female. "Most of the men there didn't know how to behave around women, so it was not a comfortable place to be. My thesis advisor did have other women students, but I just felt awkward."

When she finished her doctoral work in 1985, she decided to work in Silicon Valley. She began there as a researcher at the Schlumberger Laboratory of Computer Science. With that as her starting point, Telle built a successful technology career through the early 2000s. In small companies, she could stay involved with the technical side while also moving rapidly into management. After working as a researcher for two years, she joined Actel in 1987 and stayed there for eleven years, ending as software director. From there she went to Malleable Technologies as its vice president (VP) of engineering from 1998 to 2000, when Malleable Technologies was sold to PCM-Sierra.

Throughout the 1990s, Telle made an effort to network with other female technologists. "That first year, I systematically looked for other women in tech. Some of those women I met in the early years I'm still friends with. That's how I met Anita Borg: through mutual friends."

Her collaboration with Anita, a fellow computer scientist in the Silicon Valley orbit, brought about something amazing for women. In 1992, Anita told Telle about her dream: a conference center for women in tech, and a national conference that would spotlight the interests of women technologists. "I said YES, I'd like to help!"

Although neither woman had experience organizing a national conference, the two devised a plan and made it happen. That vision became the Grace Hopper Celebration of Women in Computing (GHC). The first gathering was held in Washington, DC, in June 1994; five hundred women attended. Telle recalls walking into the conference and being surrounded by technical women as a life-changing experience. Keynote speakers for their inaugural conference included Fran Allen and Barbara Liskov, the first and second female Turing Award winners. Shari Goldwasser, the third female Turing Award winner, was scheduled to speak, but was too far along in a pregnancy and ultimately couldn't attend. This successful celebration created more momentum for women technologists to network and support each other in their technology careers.

During the late 1990s, Telle continued her involvement in organizing the GHCs. In 1997, Anita founded the nonprofit Institute for Women in Technology. Sadly, Anita Borg was diagnosed with terminal brain cancer in 1999. By 2002, she could no longer fulfill her institute responsibilities. Supporting this project that was so close to her heart, Telle stepped up as interim president and CEO. The following year the organization was renamed in Anita's honor and memory as the Anita Borg Institute for Women and Technology (ABI).

Telle thrived in the role and remained for fifteen years, shepherding ABI's tremendous success, including making the decision to bring GHC in as a cornerstone of ABI. Starting in 2007, the biannual GHC advanced to an annual event. Attendance at GHC has grown from a few hundred people in the early to 2000s to 18,000 attendees in 2017, and from being a fledgling nonprofit to a hugely successful organization that supports the careers of female technologists. As of this writing, ABI has sixty employees, a great board of trustees, and a huge list of corporate partners. "The impact of ABI has just been amazing," Telle reported. In October 2017, Telle retired from this position.

~ ~ ~

Consider an alternate universe, one in which Telle didn't get the nudge that led her to CS. She would never have had professional successes in the field of CS, and she wouldn't have met Anita Borg and helped start the Grace Hopper Celebration. Fortunately, Telle *did* receive that strategic intercession. Unfortunately, however, the universe we live in is one where there often isn't an intercession.

~ ~ ~

Several people helped Telle to thrive in her profession. Her most important mentor was her PhD advisor, Carver Mead. As mentioned earlier, his belief in Telle made a world of difference. "A lot of what mentors offer is demonstrating that they believe in the people they are working with, and my mentor was well-known at the time. But he made sure to spend a lot of time in the lab, and we always had access to him, which was incredible."

Carver advised her on her first job. In 1988, when Telle was ready to leave Schlumberger Laboratory, he introduced her to some of his former students who were starting a company called Actel, which was only thirty people at that time. It was a semiconductor company, and Telle worked there for eleven years. At her next company, Malleable Technologies, he introduced her to the founder. He became a good friend as well.

Notably, Telle is one of the few women profiled in this book who also has a female mentor. Maria Klawe, now president of Harvey Mudd College, was original chair of the Anita Borg Institute board; she served in that role through 2011. Five years after Telle began her tenure at ABI, Maria stood by Telle during one of the most difficult times in her life.

In the space of those five years, Telle had moved ABI from financial instability to a well-respected organization. But as the institute grew, the needs of the organization inevitably changed. Telle's great strengths as a technologist in the start-up arena were no longer a best fit. Nevertheless, when several board members suddenly asked Telle to resign, she felt shocked, angry, frustrated—and hurt.

Maria stepped in as both board chair and a friend of Telle's. After many closed-door sessions with the board, she was able to mentor Telle through this experience. "Part of her being my mentor was to tell me some hard truths about what was going on," Telle confided. "At that point, I took on a presentation coach, I worked really hard, and I turned things around. To this day, I appreciate her mentorship." Out of her discussions with Maria, Telle developed a plan to improve herself and grow the institute, and gained approval of the plan from the board. She proceeded to work with a team of advisors, two professional coaches, and other CEOs, incorporating tangible metrics to evaluate her success. She described it as an exhilarating, albeit sometimes overwhelming, experience.

One thing that struck me about this story was the feedback Telle received in the fifth year of her presidency at the institute. This was her board's first assessment—and they wanted to replace her. Giving feedback is often hard, but should be done early and often; people need to know how they are doing in their careers. It's a disservice not to, because this denies people the opportunity to grow.

~ ~ ~

I asked Telle why she thinks most women have few or no female mentors. "As you move into the technology world, the mentors who are going to be the most effective are the people who are already being successful in areas you want to be successful in. Today, unfortunately, most of them are still men, so I think it's far more important to have the right mentor—the one who has the skill set you are looking for—than to have a woman mentor just because she's female. That's why many of the women you've talked to have men as their mentors: men have the power."

Where Telle most values women is as her role models. Sally Ride—the first American woman to fly in space, in 1983—was one. Sally founded a nonprofit, Sally Ride Science, and was actively supportive of the Anita Borg Institute. Another is Martina Navratilova, a fierce tennis competitor. "We need to have female role models, because role models are those people who you aspire to be. That's a lot of what Grace Hopper is based on."

~ ~ ~

"Women in particular need to have someone who believes in them. I've certainly had mentors all along the way, as well as sponsors. There's a great quote: 'Women are typically over-mentored and under-sponsored,'"[5] Telle said. Then she asked me, "Do you know the difference?" Luckily, I did.

Mentors coach and guide you with career advice, and they provide a perspective. Sponsors are senior-level people in an organization who have the reputation and credentials to put you forward for positions. They believe in your potential and advocate for your career; they risk their reputation when they back you. They are your ticket to the top.

Telle agrees. "I've never really worked in big companies, but my thesis advisor was a famous man who introduced me, through his connections, to the first three companies I worked at. Having someone who believes in you can make a huge difference."

Telle has also witnessed what happens when a woman is put under the supervision of someone who is inexperienced. Telle recalls Julie,[6] a young woman who was elated to start her first job as an engineer at a company she had always wanted to work for. However, an inexperienced manager supervised her. Julie ended up hating her job but didn't have enough experience to realize that the problem was her manager's shortcomings, not hers. Because Telle had the opportunity to mentor Julie, she and other women in that company helped Julie find a role where she fit much better.

~ ~ ~

Julie left that company after ten years to attend medical school. Why? Maybe the tech world wasn't her thing, or maybe her experience with that poor manager marred her for the rest of her tech

---

5   The full quote is: "Our interviews and surveys alike suggest that high-potential women are over-mentored and under-sponsored relative to their male peers—and that they are not advancing in their organizations." From "Why Men Still Get More Promotions Than Women" by Herminia Ibarra, Nancy M. Carter, and Christine Silva, in *Harvard Business Review* 88, no. 9 (September 2010).

6   "Julie" is a pseudonym.

career. It's hard to tell. Telle notes that women leave tech at twice the rate of men for several reasons: because of family demands, workplace resistance to women's leadership styles, or gender bias in general. To combat this trend, Telle says, "It's not just about getting women into the pipeline; it's about creating cultures where women thrive."

One way we can keep women in the tech pipeline is by providing guidance on their career choices early on. Telle's own story: "I didn't mind going to school, but I also didn't know what I wanted to be when I grew up. In high school, I was just unconsciously doing well, I nailed my studies, but I got no real advice about what that meant. I didn't take science. I had no guidance about what my choices were."

Telle attributes her confusion to her personal situation, losing her mother when she was young and being raised by her father and stepmother. But it's also true that many girls just don't receive any counsel about career options. Telle had no exposure to science and technology, and started college as a theatre major—which was an inappropriate choice for her. It took her stepmother's idea, right before Telle gave up on college altogether, of that career inventory test to discover her aptitude for computer science. From then on, she became a straight-A student. Her success boiled down to finding the right match academically.

In addition to offering young women guidance to get into college CS programs, women then need support in sticking with their CS majors. Today in the United States, only 18% of CS graduates are women.

Harvey Mudd College is one of the rare exceptions, boasting a 50% average of women students in their CS department.[7] Telle explained this to me. Harvey Mudd offers an introductory CS class specifically designed for students unfamiliar with programming. Once these students have gained some expertise in programming,

---

[7]   Taken from https://qz.com/730290/harvey-mudd-college-took-on-gender-bias-and-now-more-than-half-its-computer-science-majors-are-women/.

they enter the regular curriculum with the advanced students. This is one of the innovations that lead to low dropout rates.

Telle also told me about Stanford University, where "those who've had no exposure to computer science take an intro course that's for *all* students, and develop a love for it. Other universities that allow students to move into a CS major during their first year see huge upticks in female participation."

She then contrasted the program at Purdue University. "One of our ABI board members is the dean of engineering at Purdue, where you have to declare your major before you enter. That means all the students have to have been exposed to rigorous engineering or CS coursework in high school—but the level of exposure to computing in most high schools is scant." This is one of the situations that ABI is working to change, because they know what works to increase the participation of women in high tech, both in schools and in companies.

~ ~ ~

Telle felt like an imposter when she went to Caltech because her studies had not prepared her for the rigor or the school. "I spent that first year sure that someone would find me out, and that I didn't belong." She had the same feelings when she first took over the institute. "I felt I wasn't good enough. I think I live with that feeling today. In our field, you are making huge decisions about taking that next step, and you're also trying to take on more; it's easy to feel that you just don't belong."

However, how women overcome imposter syndrome makes all the difference in how that impacts their lives. How does Telle overcome these feelings today? "The strength that has served me well over the years is just showing up," she explained. "I just put one foot forward. It's just perseverance. I have a great network, so I don't have to go it alone. But for others, when they hit that wall, they just give up. And most women have to balance family and work." Work–life balance is a struggle for women because much of the burden of running the home falls on the woman. When work starts to suck, or there isn't a clear path ahead, women tend to leave. If work were fulfilling, women would stay, even if they didn't have a great work–life balance.

When we talk about imposter syndrome, we often attribute it to women. Telle remarked, "I think that if you look broadly at women, lack of confidence is the thing they suffer from the most, and the imposter syndrome goes to the heart of confidence," she said. "It's that feeling of thinking you are not good enough. Many women won't apply for a job unless they meet all the criteria, whereas men will apply for that same job if they meet 50% of the criteria. At Google a few years ago, women weren't putting themselves forward for promotion. In that sense, I think that women struggle with lack of confidence more than men." She added that she believes everyone, regardless of gender, "has that feeling of not being good enough."

~ ~ ~

This feeling of inadequacy often means that women are good negotiators for others, but not for themselves. Telle agreed: "I think it's hard to ask for a promotion. When I went to Malleable Technology—remember, it's a four-person start-up—I was VP of engineering, so I was one of the top three on the management chain." The founder and CEO gave her a lot of stock, and he matched her salary. Telle had a peer and colleague who was a man. When the company was bought by PMC-Sierra, stock holding became public information, and Telle found out that her peer had more stock than she did. When she confronted the CEO, and asked him why she had less stock than her male VP peer, he told her that she never asked.

"And I didn't negotiate at all when I first came on; I felt like the CEO would take care of me. I didn't actually ask him for more; he gave me more money along the way. I realized in hindsight that I probably got more stock when my colleague was negotiating for more." Telle went on to confess that she is still a terrible negotiator. When she first came to the Anita Borg Institute, the organization was in dire straits. The board of trustees is responsible for organizational oversight, including CEO compensation, so it was years before she finally asked for a raise. They were responsive, but she had waited longer than she should have. "I know how important negotiation is, but I can't say it's my strongest suit."

Telle spoke of companies being secretive about their salaries. She learned she wasn't being paid fairly only when her holdings became public. But how do we know if we are being paid fairly? Luckily, a few companies,[8] such as Apple, Intel, GoDaddy, Microsoft, and VMware, are performing and publishing their internal salary audits and are now coming out fairly on compensation between the genders. According to Telle, "The best companies are doing pay audits and making adjustments, but it's very easy to unconsciously get way off track." For companies that claim equity as a core value, this practice should become standard practice.

~ ~ ~

I was curious to hear stories from Telle about gender bias. "I think it's just a fact of life," she admitted. "All of us suffer biases, both within ourselves and externally, and anyone who says they haven't just didn't realize it was happening. I think I was never stopped career-wise by bias because start-ups were so desperate for help—they hired whoever said they could do the work." But she does have a few choice recollections.

"At one of my earliest companies, a senior executive told me, 'Oh, you'll probably leave and have babies,' and others weren't necessarily that comfortable being around me. And at my first job out of college, before I went to graduate school, the site manager sexually harassed

---

8   https://www.glassdoor.com/blog/companies-equal-pay/

most of the women there. He left me alone. Everybody knew it, yet nobody called him out on it. It was mostly talk, but it was tolerated."

Today Telle works primarily with women at the Anita Borg Institute. "Even a group of fifty women can have some of the same problems as a group of men," she observed. A dear friend of hers was a retired senior executive. Quite successful, she had always been turned off by women's groups, and didn't want to be part of them. The people she was accustomed to interacting with were all men: in her mind, *they* were the successful people. However, one day, when speaking to a group of young women, she saw the impact she had on them and realized her own biases against women. That was a turning point for her, and she too began to get more involved supporting gender diversity and inclusion.

When I became aware of gender bias and started looking for women who were successful, I noticed that they acted like men in the workplace—the way they dressed, their short hair. I asked Telle what she thought about this. "If you take a step back and look at the field we work in, the few women there often take on male characteristics," she agreed. "There are many women who don't even realize they're doing that. I have some of that in me. When I first took over the Anita Borg Institute, I had to take a step back and look long and hard look at some of those characteristics." Telle had succeeded in a man's world, so it made sense that she would have taken on some of the characteristics of the men she had been working with.

While women may unwittingly adopt male coloration, men unconsciously assume an ethic of meritocracy in the high-tech world. Telle had an interesting take on meritocracy and illustrated how the absence of true meritocracy is invisible to men.

"In Silicon Valley, those who are in a significant position of power truly believe it's a meritocracy. I think that the idea of a meritocracy is a myth, and most women don't believe it. It's subtle; I mean, you go into a company as a woman, and the pattern matching[9] comes up, so you aren't necessarily given the same opportunities as your male counterparts. The decision makers don't even know they're doing that. This is particularly true in the start-up world, where venture capitalists are out to make a lot of money. When founders come in and talk to them, there's a lot pattern matching, and they don't invest in women. No, I don't believe it's a meritocracy."

"I was talking to the senior engineering VP at a large company quite a few years ago. He said, 'I love our culture—we're a complete meritocracy; we just need more women.' He didn't even realize the ridiculousness of what he was saying. What he really meant was that he wanted more women *who looked like men*. He just didn't realize he was saying that."

Telle also sees the glass ceiling. "I do think there are places where it's getting shattered. For example, hopefully we're about to elect a female president.[10] But certainly, every woman in my generation has hit her head on a glass ceiling. Sometimes I've bumped it up against it. The dream is to have a culture where women thrive, and that means it's going to look significantly different from today, where people can be who they are."

But what about the glass cliff, I wondered, which women encounter *after* they've shattered the glass ceiling? "Because there aren't as many leadership opportunities, it's more common to give women an opportunity only when things are falling apart. I don't think it's conscious. People just get so desperate that they finally give it to a woman. So yes, there are glass cliffs." Telle knew of several painful cases.

---

9   A method by which patterns are determined and associated with previous patterns. This technique is used to evaluate people and can easily lead to social stereotyping. For a recent overview, see https://thinkprogress.org/new-research-shows-how-our-brains-distort-faces-to-fit-stereotypes-d8399524cade/.

10   Telle's interview took place on August 19, 2016, before the US presidential election.

Despite all of this rather discouraging wisdom about gender bias, the lack of meritocracy, and bumping into glass ceilings and cliffs, Telle offered strongly positive advice for women. "Take risks. It's easy to see all the downsides of doing something, but if opportunities present themselves, take the risks anyway. It's very easy to get caught up in the what-ifs and not risk." She reminded me: "You learn so much from failures. You can find a way to transform a failure into a great future. That future may be in a different field or a new location, but if you fear to take on a tough assignment because you might fail, that's the wrong choice. You've got to try; at least you'll learn a lot."

~ ~ ~

TAKEAWAYS

- Telle stressed the need for support; women are often "over-mentored and under-sponsored." She has had many mentors and sponsors throughout her career.

- It's important to have a mentor that matches your skill set, even if that means choosing a male over a female mentor.

- Even more important than a mentor is a sponsor who advocates for your career growth.

- Telle described the difficulty of entering into the tech field: women have to compete with men "who've been programming since they were five years old," and universities can be inflexible regarding shifting one's major.

- Women in tech often "take on male characteristics."

- You can fight imposter syndrome by putting "one foot forward."

- Gender bias is a fact of life, and in Silicon Valley meritocracy is a "myth" that hides gender bias.

- Telle stresses the importance of taking risks, and of failures, because that's the way to learn.

CHAPTER 2: PAM'S STORY

BIOSKETCH: *As a serial entrepreneur, Pam Kostka seeks her highs by working for start-ups. She launched her career with a Harvard MBA, and is now the CEO of a stealth-mode mobile start-up. Prior to that, she was the CEO of Bluebox Security, which she successfully sold. She likes to work in environments that test her limits, taking on complex problems and tenaciously working her way through them.*

"I tend to have a direct communication style, which is penalized in women. Women are supposed to be more empathetic in their style, but I am more direct and logical. Maybe I am that way because I had to be, in order to get my voice heard."

— Pam Kostka, CEO, stealth-mode startup

~ ~ ~

Pam Kostka was driven to excel; she inherited a strong sense of conscientiousness from her father. Zealous to please her parents, Pam always strove to attain the top marks in her class. She signed up for, and then excelled in, the most challenging classes. Pam was second in both her high school and college academic class ranking. She recalled her feelings: "I was going to do the best job that I could, but I recall various activities I wanted to be in where I wasn't as good as I wanted to be and was ready to quit. My mom advised sternly, 'We are not a family of quitters.' While my dad gave me the work ethic, my mom never let me quit on myself, which was valuable as I got older."

Pam's propensity for pushing herself is a constant theme in her story. Her love of challenges and the sheer thrill she gets from overcoming them have motivated her to spend most of her career building start-ups.

Her first job out of college involved researching various tech industries, identifying qualified executive talent, and recruiting them—in essence, studying the industry that would become her own and building the start of a valuable network. Working with one mentor there, she received a precious and lasting gift. As a newly minted college grad, Pam was reticent about speaking up in meetings with people who were older and had much more work experience. This mentor told her that if she had a question in a meeting, she should ask it, because the chances were that other people are wondering about it too.

"He was instrumental in helping me speak up in a roomful of older adults. I was twenty-one years old, thinking 'What could I possibly contribute to this conversation?' He helped me find my voice— my literal and figurative seat at the table. We actually had a private hand signal that he would give me to make me sit up and engage! It was an invaluable gift to have so early in my career, to be told that regardless of age, experience, or gender, I was there because I had valuable contributions to make."

As for many of the other women in this book, her mentor was male. "There were not many women who worked in that field, but he invested in me." He gave her numerous business books to read and opportunities to work in nonprofits, which exposed her to things she normally wouldn't have discovered. "He was the one who put in my head that I would be an excellent candidate for Harvard. No one else in my family had done graduate level work, but he believed in me. I still keep in touch with him to this day." Pam was fortunate to have a mentor at the very start of her career—someone who guided her to pick a profession she was destined to love.

A defining moment came shortly after that, when she felt it had come time to go to business school. Which to choose: Stanford or Harvard? Stanford would make sense because she knew she wanted a career in tech. On the other hand, since she was raised on the east coast, she knew the value of Harvard's network, which is three times as big as Stanford's in terms of the number of people who graduate. In the end, she wanted to prove to herself that she could tackle what she felt was the more difficult path. "Harvard scared me more—it's a cutthroat atmosphere, that it was going to be hard for me coming from a less quantitative background, that I was going to fail out. I say that choosing Harvard was my pivotal moment, because in both start-ups and other ventures I gravitate toward the most challenging option, and just claw my way up through whatever is dished my way. I see it as, 'This is my challenge and I have to figure out a way to be successful at it.' So that was the most pivotal thing—the realization that I like challenges, and I like to do things that scare me, test my limits, test my boundaries."

Because Pam wanted to get into tech, after she received her MBA, she moved straight to Silicon Valley. Starting her professional life in the tech start-up world, Pam got lucky in those first couple of years. Soon after arriving in California, she landed a product management directorship in a company called Connect Inc. in Mountain View, which went public with an IPO while she was there. Even though she didn't yet have an in-depth knowledge about tech because she wasn't technically degreed, she threw herself into the job and kept rising in the product management ranks. As it happened, this was the sole position in which she had any form of female mentorship. "The only exposure I had was an exec at Connect, who took a personal interest in me. She gave me tremendous professional and personal guidance and was an incredible role model in what it meant to be tough and demand the best of people. She became a personal as well as a professional friend."

"I feel lucky that I fell into product management, because I see it as a 'general-manager-in-training' job, where you have to work through influence over others, as opposed to having direct control. It's *theoretically* easier, when you have hire and fire authority, to get someone to do something; it's entirely different when they don't report to you. All these people are pulling on you—if you do your job well, then the product sells, sales drive up, and the engineers are happy because they are building something meaningful that has been purchased in the marketplace. But if you fail, obviously you are pulling down the company and not contributing to the bottom line like you are supposed to."

Her second job was for a start-up called Extensity, which "pioneered one of the first massive Java applications that was out there," and was one of the first companies supported by the Kleiner Perkins' Java Fund.

Before she joined Extensity, she negotiated that the CEO would double her equity percentage if their first product got out by

Christmas. Once she was onboard, she assessed that the product was actually closer to alpha, whereas the company felt it was closer to beta. Taking a risk, she told the CEO, "I know we have a lot of money riding on this—and I've got a personal interest in getting this product out the door as planned—but I am telling we are not ready. If we push this product out the door in this timeframe, the customers won't adopt it, the market won't take it, and we will get a bad reputation." Her CEO appreciated that she was candid with him; in fact, he ended up giving her the bonus, even when the product launched later than originally planned. Evidently it wasn't a problem, as Extensity also eventually went IPO.

Pam's next move was to become vice president of marketing at a start-up called North Systems. She had long nurtured a goal of becoming vice president by age thirty: "I was gunning for that. That was a personal metric I had set for myself." Unlike her first two start-ups, which had amazing IPOs, North Systems was an early dot-com tragedy. However, Pam recalls that as difficult as it was, it was also an invaluable learning experience, because she learned how to shut down a company responsibly. "Statistically, most start-ups don't make it, and I got a front row seat for that experience. It was stressful and painful and draining, but a necessary and inevitable part of my start-up education."

From there, Pam founded her own company, Visiline, and next did another stint as marketing vice president at another start-up before taking a senior VP/CMO role with a company called Sabrix. There her role was to expand the business; she remained with Sabrix for five years. Over the following six years, she worked as CMO at VirtuOz, vice president of marketing for Nuance, and both marketing vice president and CEO at Bluebox Security. By April 2016, Bluebox Security was successfully acquired by Lookout, the global leader in securing mobility. Since that time, she has been developing an exciting stealth-mode mobile start-up company.

~ ~ ~

Pam's five-year tenure with Sabrix provided some "interesting gender moments," as she described them to me. "In all of my careers, I think I've worked with women only twice at the executive level. I grew up in a man's world, where I was always surrounded by men at the table, and honestly, I gave that little thought. Sabrix was the first time I became aware of a few things. The CEO was, and still is, an excellent mentor to me—I learned about being a fair and excellent operator under his tutelage. He has three daughters and is the least gender-biased person I know. He gave me and other women in the company wonderful career opportunities. Yet even with his leadership and culture setting, there was still gender bias."

"I learned that I was known as the 'dragon lady,' because I was a very forceful personality, and the CEO had empowered me to make big strategic and executional decisions. All the things a man would be applauded for, I was labeled for. It was fascinating, because my team members, those who reported to me, didn't call me that name and laughed when others called me that. They knew what it was really like to work with me. However, everybody around them was afraid of me. They were like, 'Here she comes, the dragon lady.'"

Women in positions of authority often get derogatory epithets, where men are tagged with positive or neutral bynames (often military in origin). We see that as well with Lily Chang in chapter 18, who won the "scary person" award in one of her work settings. This is another form of labeling women as aggressive at work. People often confuse assertive with aggressive. Even during Pam's time at Sabrix, during a formalized training course on communication, she recalls that "the trainer noted that women who use direct communication are always going to be labeled a 'bitch,' 'aggressive,' and other derogatory terms, whereas the same communication style from a man is not going to be labeled that way." Such labels can be used in support of women or against them, in my experience. Luckily, Pam says she has a thick skin, and being labeled "dragon lady" did not deter her from speaking her mind.

"Also, don't be sorry that you are an aggressive, direct communicator. Back in my Sabrix days, I coined the phrase 'candor without malice.' Kim Scott, the author of *Radical Candor: Be a Kick-Ass Boss without Losing Your Humanity*,[11] writes about the same concept: good managers have to be able to deliver painful messages, but you have to do it maturely and sensitively, motivated by genuinely caring about improving the person you are providing the feedback to."

When Sabrix was ultimately acquired, one of the acquiring company's first actions was to raise Pam's salary. Compared to her male peer executives, Pam had been underpaid. "They gave me a $15,000 pay raise because they worried about discrimination." This was definitely an aha moment for her.

Since Pam had spoken about gender bias in two start-ups, I was curious about whether she had encountered gender bias at Harvard Business School. "I don't know that I personally experienced gender bias, but there's kind of a built-in bias to the style at Harvard, which is that you are supposed to speak a lot in class. Classroom speaking is a significant component of your grade, and due to the forced grading curve, one third of *every* class will receive a low pass or failing grade. Many women were hesitant or slower to raise their hands and speak up in class, so women were at higher risk of getting what's known as a low pass in a particular class. They were not as proactive or assertive, and they often filtered themselves, worrying that what they had to say wasn't impactful enough. But the men would just jump in."

In short, Pam herself didn't necessarily face gender bias at Harvard, because she had an early mentor who had helped empower her not to be afraid of speaking in front of other people. However, Pam felt that the case study methods that Harvard conducted favored a male dynamic (where it's necessary to be assertive and speak up in order to succeed) over a more female dynamic, which

---

11   Kim Scott, *Radical Candor: Be a Kick-Ass Boss without Losing Your Humanity* (New York: St. Martin's Press, 2017).

is often more communal and collaborative. She noted that Harvard Business School has made subsequent efforts to invest in helping woman be more assertive in this type of case study dynamic.[12]

~ ~ ~

Pam has had to advocate for herself throughout her career. This has taken a variety of forms that will be familiar to many readers who are now senior women in their fields.

One of the lessons Pam honed from her post-college mentor is her forthright communication style. Over the years, she has worked to refine it, but she calls out bullshit when she sees it. "I never backed down from being aggressive or direct just because somebody was going to criticize me for it. I won't apologize for being a woman. I tend to have a direct communication style, which is also penalized in women. Women are supposed to be more empathetic in their style, but I am more direct and logical. Maybe I am that way because I had to be, in order to get my voice heard." However, Pam does not feel she is abusive or overly aggressive in her speech—the dragon lady, she was known as by some. Those who have worked with her know her as tough but caring. "I never ask more from anyone than I am personally willing to give. I believe good leadership comes partly from leading by example. And I challenge people to be the best they can be as individuals and as teams. It comes from a place of deep caring about people professionally and personally."

After her successful exit from Bluebox, of course Pam planned to continue her career as a CEO. However, even with her impressive background, she keeps being offered lower-level jobs. "There are still recruiters who call me and say, 'There is this amazing marketing job for you at an early-stage start-up.' I don't think people would

---

12   For an overview, see http://www.nytimes.com/2013/09/08/education/har-vard-case-study-gender-equity.html?pagewanted=all.

ever propose to a man that they step backward in their career, but recruiters are entirely comfortable saying that to me."

I have seen that happen time and again to women in technology careers: they are offered roles that either take them a step backward in their career path or that move them into support functions. The women who refuse are the ones who are already keenly aware of gender bias, some because they have made that mistake in the past. It's possible that our patriarchal society perceives it is okay for women not to advance in their careers. It's also true that men experience a lot of pressure from this society; they are supposed to be the leaders and the breadwinners. When a man chooses to take a step backward in his career, he gets flak for that too. Now, with more women being primary breadwinners, this mindset is changing—but we have a long way to go.

I was not surprised to hear Pam declare that she doesn't believe in meritocracy. "There is nobody who's going to naturally take care of you," she said. "Men, however, might get a little bit of an edge and more naturally be taken care of." That's because far more men possess powerful positions in society, and to some extent they look out for each other; the system is built to serve them.

"I wish it were a meritocracy," she said. "However, you have to ask for what you deserve." She underscored the point with one more story. She had negotiated her first job and was making $90,000; she was proud of brokering such a good salary. At the same time, her company hired a guy from outside who was her peer for a while. When she was promoted to a director position, she noticed that the company was intentionally hiding his salary from her, even though she had access to the salaries of everyone else who reported to her. It turned out that he was making $50,000 more than she was. "I was like, 'Guys, there can be some pay discrepancy, but I have the director title. He doesn't—and there is a significant wage disparity.' I went right into the CEO's office and told him, 'Fix it, or I am walking.'" The company fixed it.

~ ~ ~

As we began discussing imposter syndrome, Pam did not seem to be plagued by that, although she did describe moments of self-doubt where she asks herself, 'Can I do this?' "There is always the fear of the unknown," she told me. When she first faced running a sales team, she thought, "Gosh, I've never run a sales team before." But she countered those feelings of self-doubt by taking up the challenge, as she anticipated the flip side of that fear: her excitement at wondering if she could do it.

Then, when she became CEO, she not only had to carry the burden of her employees' welfare but also that of their families. "Being CEO is a lonely job. There are a lot of employees and their families who rely on me to make good, sound decisions," she said. "So that probably weighs heavily on me, especially at night—did I do a good job today, or did I *not* do a good job today?" Those worries felt like more than just imposter syndrome.

Pam proposed to me that imposter syndrome arises for women "because they wait longer to do things than men do." She recalled her own struggle with this.

"I thought, did I spend too much time as a CMO before becoming a CEO? For years, people kept telling me, 'You can be CEO.' When I left VirtuOz, I actually went around my network asking, 'Do you think I can be a CEO?' People looked at me cross-eyed and said, 'Of course you can be CEO. You are the only one doubting yourself.' So maybe I did have imposter syndrome. People said, 'You have been ready for two years now, so go for it.'"

Pam also recalled when she rejoined her Sabrix CEO friend, this time at VirtuOz. She told him, "I really want exposure to all the responsibilities you have as a CEO. There are certain things that only a CEO should know, but I really want to understand the finance part of it. I want to be able to answer all those questions. So, I'll come to work for you again, under the condition that you will give me that exposure." She was in essence asking him to mentor her, because at that point she believed she could only ride in the passenger seat of the CEO car. In fact, at that point she was ready to be *driving* the car. If Pam had been a man, she would have leaped directly into the driver's seat.

In some sense, I believe that women tend to sabotage themselves and get in the way of their own success. I've always wondered about the term "glass ceiling" as well. What if we said there is no glass ceiling—how would our lives change? Would our potential and dreams be limitless?

~ ~ ~

Some people manage to counter imposter syndrome by having a great support network they can reach out to when they begin to doubt themselves. Apart from that, most women in this book have had a single source of support, one person or individual who has been their rock. Pam enjoys a three-person support system, with her first mentor, her sponsor, and her husband. Her mentor helped her with her journey to Harvard and introduced her to the world of tech. Her sponsor has been her CEO and friend at VirtuOz and Sabrix. "I could go to either of those gentlemen and bounce any situation off them and feel like I could get a truthful, supportive answer," she remarked. "I might not like what they have to say, but they'll be direct and honest."

Her husband is her true rock, and is incredibly supportive. He is a start-up software executive, working as an engineering vice president. He challenges her by asking her tough questions when she is dealing with a situation at work. The two of them also have a rule: one can't tell the other what job to take. When Pam decided to become CEO of a start-up, her husband stepped up to do the lion's share at home. Her higher title comes with a higher salary and increased responsibility. "It's great to have a cheerleader who knows you well, and who says, 'Go do it.'" She pointed out that men sometimes have a problem when their wife makes more money, so it is constructive when a relationship doesn't suffer from that internalized sexism.

Though the concept of "marry well" traditionally meant marrying into privilege or wealth, the notion has had a feminist revision to mean marry a partner who will be supportive on the domestic front.[13] I have long believed that the best thing you can do for your career is to choose the right partner; I have seen this in my own life. I couldn't have written this book, worked full-time, and raised three kids without my husband's support and encouragement. Yes, I married well.

Pam agrees. She says when they wake up in the morning, she is often out of the house before anyone wakes up and her husband takes care of the morning routine with their daughter. Although Pam feels a bit sad to get only an hour and a half with her daughter every day, she is thankful that she *does* get that time. Sometimes when her husband is working late, she picks up the slack, but more often than not, he does, since she tends to work longer hours. "I get a lot of time for work, some time for my daughter, some time for my husband, and very little time for me."

Fortunately, Pam likes her job. "I get to be the person at work that I want to be. I have this sense of fulfillment in my job, so those ten to twelve work hours every day are my 'me time.'" How interesting that Pam strikes her work–life balance by enjoying the person she is at work.

Many women are becoming the breadwinners of the family. We can do it with a great support system, but the cultural expectation is that we'll also take care of the household, so guilt often accompanies us when we are out there changing the world with scant time for our families.

---

13   See Tracy Leigh-Hazzard's blog article, "If You Want To Be a Successful Woman, Find the Right Life Partner" https://journal.thriveglobal.com/if-you-want-to-be-a-successful-woman-marry-well-592d80e04315

Nevertheless, when I asked if Pam ever felt guilty about not spending time with her daughter, she quickly said, "No. Every parent wishes they had more time with their kids, but I always felt it's the quality of our time, not the quantity." She also knows that if she took a step backward in her career, she would be resentful, and not be the person she needs to be for her daughter. "I think we all work too much. I don't feel guilty about it, and my husband doesn't make me feel guilty about it. This is partly because he is in this industry, so he knows the demands, and partly because he just knows my personality. Frankly, he wanted a wife who wanted to go back to work while also having a family."

Pam does her best for her daughter, and seeks to be a good influence through her work and achievements. "Honestly, for my eight-year-old daughter, I want her to see powerful women in her life." Pam makes an important point here. Young girls need strong female role models, and often find their first role models in their moms. Many women interviewed in this book had mothers who significantly influenced their lives; some of them became career women because their mothers were. Pam mentioned Hillary Clinton as a good role model, and how thrilled she was to see Clinton running for president. Although Clinton lost the election, the dream of a woman president and the implications it holds for women everywhere remain.

~ ~ ~

As a societal step toward helping support women, Pam observed that gender bias has some parallels to racial prejudice: both are serious ongoing issues based on assumptions. Gender and race are discrete but intersecting issues. She said we need to bring gender bias to the forefront, just as the Black Lives Matter movement does for racial bias.

"I read a great article the other day where a white guy asked his black friend, 'Can you help me understand this white privilege that

I have?' The friend gave an example of a black girl who went to Harvard. Every time someone asks her, 'Where did you go to college?' and she says, 'Harvard,' they'd say, 'The one in Massachusetts?' As if there were any other Harvard! There will be a white kid in front of her who says, 'I am going to Princeton.' Nobody says, 'You mean the one back east?' I think awareness and willingness to do something about it has to be part of the equation, and that's for everybody."

Pam believes in shining a bright light on gender bias, rather than putting the burden on individual women to change their own behavior, to be more assertive, to lean in, to speak up for what they want, and on and on. For instance, other countries in the world have female presidents. The United States is the world leader and a supposedly progressive place, but we haven't had a female president yet. Gender bias is staring us right in the face, but we will not acknowledge the elephant in the room.

She further pointed out the need to have men be open to considering what they do unintentionally. Many white people don't recognize racism because they haven't had the negative experiences that people of color do. For example, white people often assume that everyone has the same access to education and work that they do. Similarly, men often don't recognize gender bias because they are not subjected to it; racism and sexism are interrelated in that way. The pay inequities that continue to exist today point to gender bias. There is an implicit assumption made that women are not as skilled as their male peers and therefore don't deserve the same pay.

"So, men must constantly be aware of that and ask themselves, 'How can I make a change today? In this meeting, how can I call out that person? How can I ask to make room for that woman at the table? How can I praise an assertive statement from a woman?'

"There are studies that prove it doesn't matter what you do to raise your children to be colorblind; they will absorb bias through ads, movies, and everyday interactions. If they never see a black lawyer or a black doctor, there is still a subliminal message telling them that black people are not as accomplished as white people.

And the same effect is true for women. That's why it's important for my daughter to see that I am an accomplished professional woman. I can't just tell her to reach for the stars, I have to show her what that looks like."

Pam's comments bring to mind that similarly, women are always judged on how they look, act, and behave. To counter that, some women in the workplace tend to dress and act like men in order to be taken seriously. Pam contributed few examples as we talked, where women had to act and look a certain way in order to be taken seriously. Pam herself tends to wear pants because she is comfortable in them. She cautions that at the end of the day, the whole package of what people see when you walk into a room matters, so she advises dressing professionally. "My advice is bend, but don't break. You have a certain style. Sift through the feedback you are getting. Accommodate within the boundaries of what feels comfortable for you. If you are dressed like a man and not comfortable, then be who you are and don't apologize.

~ ~ ~

At the time of our conversation, Pam was taking a break after successfully exiting her previous start-up. Today she is back as the CEO of a stealth-mode start-up. In a real sense, she's soared beyond glass ceilings. So, when I asked her if she thought she still perceived a glass ceiling, I was surprised by her response. She quickly responded, "Oh, hell yes. I do, unfortunately. Even once you arrive at the top, you still are going to be defending yourself in a way that a man doesn't have to." Also at that time, the US was in the midst of a fascinating 2016 presidential election cycle, so of course the topic of Hillary Clinton's candidacy came into the discussion. Pam said, "Hillary gets so much more pressure and so much more analysis because she is a woman. She is asked questions men wouldn't be asked. She gets called things men wouldn't be called. Even if you achieve the highest position, I think there is always this gauze or film of bias through which you get evaluated."

This led to acknowledging the glass cliff effect, where women are given tougher and almost impossible jobs more often than men. If a woman in such a situation succeeds, Pam remarked, "The men say, 'She succeeded' and pat themselves on the back, saying 'we gave this chance to this woman and she succeeded.' She failed? 'Well that was expected, she's a woman.'

"Studies show that women aren't going to be given the choicest opportunities. Statistically, men have better odds of succeeding, because of this internal bias that exists—that women should be at home, that they should be behind the scenes. Yes, there is a glass ceiling. We're often given harder tasks—that glass cliff—and have to prove ourselves over and over and over. And even if we break through, we are still going to be in a bubble where we're always going to be evaluated and second-guessed based on our gender— not based on the same merits that a guy would be evaluated on. One of the great ironies of gender bias is that this extra burden of proof makes us eminently qualified to do the job."

Pam concluded, "There is always going to be something hanging over a woman making it harder for her, which is just her gender. Even when you achieve success, there is still something holding you down. It doesn't matter where you are in your career—you are still going to hit that ceiling. The ironic upside of this is that this extra burden often makes us better performers, better operators, better managers."

Nonetheless, Pam is breaking the glass ceiling every day. She successfully sold the strongly valued Bluebox Security, is highly credentialed, and is passionate about the start-up world. She has a direct communication style: she asks for what she wants, and she stands her ground when it comes to her personal style. Pam is a force of nature that no glass ceiling can stop, making her an inspiration to women in the tech world and beyond.

~ ~ ~

TAKEAWAYS

- Like many of the other women interviewed, Pam had parents who motivated her. She, in turn, wanted to please them by getting good grades and being top of her class.

- Pam loves challenges and situations that scare her and test her limits. That thrill steered her toward start-up companies, where the stakes are typically high.

- Pam encountered gender bias in her ambition and was named a "dragon lady," simply because she is particularly direct and logical.

- She observes that there is a built-in bias in institutions. Though women can individually triumph in gender-biased institutions, there is a need for more systemic change. Harvard Business efforts to combat institutionalized gender bias should be both applauded and emulated in many more institutions and organizations.

- She coined the phrase "candor without malice," which means she is direct and open in her communication, making her message palatable to her audience.

- She advises that women should "ask for everything they want," because we will inevitably face gender bias at work.

- Her rock of support is her husband, who helps her achieve the form of work–life balance that suits her. She also considers her "me time" as the time she is at work.

- Pam wants her daughter to see powerful women in her life, and is happy to be her daughter's role model.

- Pam makes an interesting observation that racism and sexism are both serious ongoing issues based on assumptions.

MERITOCRACY

Meritocracy describes a system in which people attain advancement based on their proven success and achievement. It is the opposite of a system in which people are rewarded based on wealth, privilege, and family influence. Although the term meritocracy was originally used only to describe a form of government, it soon took on wider application. Now, any type of organization can be described as meritocratic, including business organizations. To some degree, entrance into higher education is a meritocracy. Good grades and strong test scores are necessary to gain admission to competitive colleges, but even higher education is not immune to those who use wealth and family connections to gain admission, regardless of their academic qualifications. This brings me to the myth of meritocracy.

Meritocracy is a fallacy that we continue to believe in. I grew up believing that I lived in a meritocratic world, and I felt confident that, if I did a great job, the world would naturally reward me. I lived more than half my life believing that meritocracy exists. Deep down, I still believe that. It is hard to break free of the belief because it is so ingrained in our society that everything is based on impact and merit. We want to believe that everyone truly has an equal opportunity.

Here is a good example. At an event at the 2014 GHC celebration, Satya Nadella was asked to offer advice to women who are reluctant to directly ask their bosses for raises.[14] His advice was, "It's not really about asking for the raise, but knowing and having faith that the system will actually give you the right raises as you go along." Without using the term, he was asking women to have blind faith in meritocracy. Fortunately, the interviewer, Maria Klawe, the president of Harvey Mudd College, immediately contradicted his statement. Nadella's viewpoint caused an uproar, and people were quick to judge him. He ended up retracting his statement on Twitter, saying "[I] was inarticulate

---

14   https://www.theguardian.com/technology/2014/oct/10/microsoft-ceo-satya-nadella-women-dont-ask-for-a-raise

regarding how women should ask for raise. Our industry must close gender pay gap so a raise is not needed because of a bias."

~ ~ ~

I grew up in Hyderabad, India, and went to a school that was close to the school that Nadella attended. I can relate to his mindset around meritocracy. Like me, he truly believed that the tech world was a meritocracy and that hard work and merit would naturally be rewarded by the system. At the GHC celebration, he had his aha moment.

My enlightenment came more gradually. The belief that I live in a meritocratic world kept slowly being chipped away at; it took me a while to accept the fact that meritocracy is mostly a myth—especially in the tech industry. We would all like it to exist, and we pretend that it does, but it doesn't. Why is it a myth? It's a myth because of the bias that we all harbor. A lot of this bias is unconscious, but it still affects our perceptions. Because we have these biases and are constantly judging the world around us, it is hard for us to be fair and provide the same opportunities for people so that we can truly judge them fairly.

All of the women I interviewed for the book agree that the tech industry is not a meritocracy. Growing up, most of us trusted that we would be rewarded based on our skills and our efforts. My experience, and the experience of the other women in this book, is that this is mostly not true. Our trust was misplaced.

Occasionally, there are women who, with a combination of skill and luck, are rewarded based on merit. In preparing this book, I heard a few such stories. Some talented women, although reluctant to advocate for themselves, had the good fortune to be managed by individuals who could see their worth and offered them promotions based on their merits. Unfortunately, such experiences are the exception rather than the norm. I have heard many stories where hard work and accomplishments doesn't result in promotions, strategic projects, and raises. It's difficult in these circumstances to figure out what is the obstacle, but it could be both conscious and unconscious bias in our organizations.

Fortunately, there are things we can do. First, work hard and be exceptional at your work. Second, recognize that chances are meritocracy alone will not reward your efforts. Finally, it is important to be savvy about your surroundings and take initiative in a variety of ways so as to showcase your work and impact. What this will look like varies from person to person.

Throughout this book, you will learn about interesting steps that women have taken to seize the initiative to help advance their careers. There is no one right one way to become a female leader in tech or any other field, but I hope the experiences of the women in this book will give you both practical ideas as well as inspiration to become a leader in whatever area you choose.

CHAPTER 3: YANBING'S STORY

BIOSKETCH: *Yanbing Li is senior vice president and general manager of the Storage and Availability Business Unit at VMware. As a leader, Yanbing has the whole package. She is smart, articulate, strategic, and poised. Although she has an impressive academic pedigree, she values problem-solving skills and results more than classroom knowledge. Raised in China with engineer and doctor parents, she loved and excelled at STEM subjects since a young age. Yanbing came to the United States for graduate studies, and started her career as a research scientist in Silicon Valley after graduating from Princeton University with a PhD in electrical and computer engineering. She later returned to China as a VMware employee for five years. China provided a fruitful environment for her to develop and hone her leadership abilities. Now back in the United States, Yanbing is both ambitious and confident; she considers confidence an important trait to be taken seriously as a woman leader in technology.*

"Both men and women struggle with career navigation. To be able to navigate your career is a universally important thing. But some factors work to men's advantage: since there are more men, there are more people they can relate to, more role models, and more networking support. That is a big advantage."

— Yanbing Li, Senior VP and GM, Storage and Availability Business Unit, VMware

~ ~ ~

Yanbing grew up in China. Her mother is a doctor, and her father is an engineer. Both her family and her Chinese culture place tremendous importance on academics, which motivated Yanbing to excel from an early age. She joked, "I went to school until there was no more school to go to." She got her bachelor's degree in electrical engineering (EE) from Tsinghua University in China and then moved to the United States for a master of science in EE/computer engineering (CE) degree from Cornell University followed by a PhD in EE/CE from Princeton.

Although Yanbing invested a lot of time in her education, she says excelling in school is not the primary factor in being successful. "Academics doesn't translate into problem-solving, and knowledge doesn't translate into results and outcome. Having high intelligence doesn't translate into high success," she said emphatically. Although knowledge gained through formal education is necessary, other crucial factors are personal motivation, aspiration, commitment, drive, and curiosity.

Yanbing's career started in 1998 at Synopsis, an electronic automation design company. "I got into a research group called the Advanced Technology Group, but then I made a decision to go into engineering. Even though I had a big dream of building my original research into something amazing, I quickly realized that few people are lucky enough to do that. Though research tends to look at areas that are more cutting edge, the real fun for me is in engineering." Yanbing spent nine years at Synopsis, and moved from research to engineering to engineering management. After her tenure at Synopsis, she moved to VMware and has been there ever since. She joined VMware at the company's headquarters in Palo Alto, but soon moved to China as a senior engineering manager in the newly established China R&D Center in Beijing.

To the casual observer, it might appear that Yanbing's career journey is straightforward—after all, she has worked at only two companies. However, she made some clever choices and solved some significant problems for VMware during her first few years with the company, which distinguished her as a high-potential leader. This helped her to rise from a senior engineering manager when she started, to the rank of senior vice president and general manager of the Storage and Availability Business Unit in just seven years. While many of the women profiled in this book got their big opportunities by joining a start-up at a stage of high growth, Yanbing took a different approach by joining a business unit overseas that had strong growth potential. That offered her a strategic opportunity to build leadership skills.

When she joined VMware in 2008, Yanbing had several reasons for relocating back to China. Although she had been in Silicon Valley for ten years and was married with three young children, she regretted that she was "settling down into a certain pace of life." Further, during the first phase of her career, she hadn't thought much about the direction of her career. "But when I decided to go back to China, it was a conscious decision: I was giving up a lot of things to gain something else. I was giving up a secure and promising job and a comfortable lifestyle in California to embrace an entirely new China whose economic growth was a rocket ship. I really felt that made me come alive." She had family reasons for the change, as well. "My kids were young, and I wanted to expose them to the language, culture, and their extended family," Yanbing explained.

Yanbing's career accelerated in China. She began as a senior manager, tasked to build and grow an engineering team in VMware's China R&D operation. While her role was to manage one of the China teams, she took the initiative to develop a strategic proposal on how VMware could leverage China's vast talent to build a strong R&D operation. When she presented the plan to VMware's top leadership, Yanbing's talent was noticed. The leadership team was impressed with her strategic way of thinking and her initiative in solving some significant challenges for the organization.

In 2009, when the need for a managing director for VMware's China R&D Center arose, Yanbing became a clear choice. Though she was a junior leader, management took a leap of faith. She grabbed the opportunity to lead all aspects of building the VMware R&D presence in China, taking responsibility for managing technology development, people, operations, and strategic partnerships with local universities and the government. After two years in this highly visible role, Yanbing was promoted to corporate vice president of Continuous Product Development (CPD) and Global Sites, which significantly expanded her charter. She led the CPD organization (which had engineers in China, India, and the United States) and VMware's global R&D efforts along with the China R&D Center. She became the first VMware engineering vice president to lead a company-level engineering organization from a location outside the US.

Yanbing shared a few elements which she felt contributed to her success in China. First, it was important that she took a proactive approach about building and sharing strategies for improving VMware's business in China. Second, she benefited from China being a strategically valuable country for VMware, which put her in a highly visible position, allowing upper management to see the positive results of Yanbing's leadership efforts. Third, she found the culture in China supportive of women in engineering roles, which helped her thrive as an engineering leader.

~ ~ ~

In our conversation, Yanbing spoke about cultural differences between China and the US regarding women and STEM education. She feels that her formative years in China offered a favorable environment in which to build her foundational skills in math and science. Her schooling gave her the confidence that she could be an engineer.

"When I grew up, there wasn't a lot of stereotyping around engineering in China. It was all merit-based and exam-based, and girls often did better than boys. There was a natural selection process. I became far more aware of the stereotyping after I came to the United States. For example, recently when I was at the Maker Faire,[15] I could see why the creative engineering demographics there did not fit the mainstream expectation for girls and women in this country.

"China has less stereotyping in engineering and technology because those subjects are not considered 'nerdy' or undesirable— they are considered a mainstream and highly desirable career choice. If you are a girl and you choose engineering, it doesn't make you an outlier. I benefited from that. I hear that the stigma starts as early as middle school, here. I never experienced that in China. In the United States, engineering is not a highly desirable profession for young women."

Early in her career, as an individual contributor, Yanbing found it relatively easy to push back against gender bias, but as she progressed, she became more aware of how unconscious bias could affect her ability to progress. She explained:

"In your early career, everything is much more merit-based. So much of what you do is measurable. For example, the code you develop, the products and features you build, and the direct business outcome generated: that is fairly measurable. As you move up the management chain, your results become less tangible and more subjective. Gender bias and unconscious bias tends to kick in more then."

~~~~~

15 "Part science fair, part county fair, and part something entirely new, Maker Faire is an all-ages gathering of tech enthusiasts, crafters, educators, tinkerers, hobbyists, engineers, science clubs, authors, artists, students, and commercial exhibitors." (https://makerfaire.com/makerfairehistory/)

When Yanbing asks junior women engineers about their number one challenge in the tech world, the most common answer she hears is that women often are not considered *technically* credible. A high-performing woman in a technical role needs to show the results of her work. However, as women progress higher in management ranks, performance evaluation tools are more susceptible to unwitting bias, and she can face more obstacles on the way.

At VMware, Yanbing had an accelerated career up to the vice president level, at which point she started to encounter challenges while trying to navigate into a different role. Was this the glass ceiling that is much talked about? Becoming more strategic in how she navigated her career was the only way for her to continue to make progress on her ambitious leadership goals. She faced such questions as, "What is my identity? What do I want for my future? Where is my north star? What path must I carve out to get there?"

"Early in your career, you have more room to grow, so you don't bump into the glass ceiling. But as you move higher, the measurement becomes more subjective and opportunities get more competitive, you feel it more strongly. For me, as I was trying to move from one VP role into another, I realized that I needed to consciously manage my career path, identity, and brand. I also needed to manage what type of leader I wanted to become. That's when I learned the importance of navigating my career."

Oddly, in her conversations with her peers, many have denied the existence of the glass ceiling. "I've talked to plenty of my friends—younger friends, peers who grew up with an engineering pedigree—and they told me there is no glass ceiling for them." That didn't match what Yanbing was experiencing.

Do male leaders have to deal with the same sort of glass ceilings that can block their way at various points on the career ladder? She noticed significant differences between how men and women experience career breakthroughs. There is a particular way that bias in tech leadership targets and limits the careers of women—by advantaging men. Yanbing goes on to observe that "it goes beyond how a woman is taking charge of her own career, or how capable she is—some things are out of her control."

At the same time, she agrees that some men experience similar challenges in moving up in leadership. "I do think both men and women struggle with career navigation," she told me. "Plenty of my peers don't know how to navigate their careers. I think it's a universally important thing. If men don't know how to navigate, they will be stuck as well."

"Because there are more men in the field, they have more people they can relate to, more role models, more of a support network. People tend to like people who are similar to them. It's not conscious; it's due to greater access and commonality in how they look at issues."

Yanbing offered helpful tips for getting past a glass ceiling and challenging limitations. Tip one is to foster mentoring and sponsor relationships, especially from "your manager or your manager's manager or your peer managers—people you observe on a regular basis."

Her second tip is related, yet in a surprising way. Yanbing says it also helps to have role models, which are not quite the same thing as either mentors or sponsors. She advises being strategic in these relationships.

"Reach out to *people who have something that you can learn from*: some that are more experienced, and less experienced, and regardless of their gender or background. If you are willing to make a connection with them in that way, they will respond back. I have been successful in building up and down, left and right relationships. Listen to them and model what *they* do, rather than synthesize from everyone around you."

Another of Yanbing's tips applies when you first bump into that glass ceiling. That bump alerts you that it's time to start paying attention to career navigation. Her advice is to take the initiative and consciously manage your career path and your brand. Think about what type of leader you want to be.

While she is highly successful, she also suffers from imposter syndrome. She explained that confidence is related to the syndrome, and therefore can be used to combat it.

"I do think building self-confidence is a constant journey. I have self-doubt all the time. What I have learned is to manage it to the point where I don't care about it as much. I constantly remind myself of the bigger outcome, and focus on that rather than on every little imperfection."

Yanbing has noticed how self-confidence and insecurity play out for her three children. "My girls are more reserved and not confident. 'I am so scared of this exam; I've done horribly,' they will say—when the score on the exam was 100%. My son, on the other hand, will say 'I've done a great job,' when his results are only okay. I think a big part of it has to do with personality, but I also think that gender plays a role, even at an early age. Girls tend to look at their every imperfection starting at a young age, rather than focusing on what they've done well. Boys are the complete opposite." Yes, it is true, and sad, that most young women have to deal with the roots of imposter syndrome even long before their professional careers have begun.

Identifying and embracing several of her personality traits has helped Yanbing counter the effects of her own attacks of imposter syndrome. In her career, she has always strived to project an air of confidence as she leads. Some might call this being overconfident. Her response? "This is what makes a woman successful: her intelligence and her confidence. Sometimes being overconfident is the only way to compensate, as women don't get as much attention or airtime. People already discount you." There is indeed a tendency to minimize woman's leadership just because she is female. "Being confident has certainly helped me," she said.

Another trait that has been useful is ambition, which people can be confused about. Yanbing supports the idea that *being* ambitious increases your self-confidence. On the flip side, if a woman is *labeled* as ambitious, it can have a negative connotation. This subject is also discussed in the book *Through the Labyrinth*. The theory is that stereotypically, men are viewed as "agentic" (having agency: confident, competent, assertive, ambitious, and directive), and women are viewed as "communal" (warm, helpful, and collaborative). A woman who is agentic is seen less favorably than a man who is communal. Because of these stereotypical views, being seen as ambitious as a woman can work against you.

Yanbing's advice is to disregard these societal messages completely. "Ignore what people think. Ambition and drive is the leading factor to success, and it shows up as confidence—ambition, confidence, and success are all connected." However, her encouragement comes with a stipulation: "Don't let your ambition get in the way of being a team player. You still need to support each other, rather than just batting for yourself. When people criticize an ambitious person, they assume that person is just ambitious for themselves, rather than for the team. But ambition itself isn't a bad thing. A person can be ambitious without being self-centered. I value collaborative leadership. I focus on winning *the outcome*, not winning at the moment, or winning an argument."

Yanbing has been openly communicating for years that she aspires to lead a company and become a CEO. However, she has received feedback complaining that she is too ambitious. Some commented that she has not yet mastered all the primary skills needed to function well in the CEO role. I appreciated her rebuttal to this criticism:

"If a boy says, 'I want to be a scientist,' I won't ding him that he doesn't know physics yet. Becoming a CEO is my career goal. When you have ambition, and people don't see you in that role yet, too often it creates a negative result. You do get dinged. Yet successful people are ambitious. Strong people view ambition as an excellent quality. When I see ambitious people, who haven't yet overcome their challenges to achieve their dreams, I see that as a strength, not as a deficit."

I appreciated hearing Yanbing's perspective on ambition. What we need is to nurture ambition in women as an excellent quality. If you want to see an ambitious, confident woman in action, look up Yanbing's portion of the Day One keynote address for VMworld 2015 on YouTube.[16] On the first day of VMworld 2015, she spent the better part of twenty minutes on stage in front of 23,000 conference attendees, thoughtfully explaining some fairly technical aspects of her company's products. Yanbing had spent nearly two months preparing for this presentation (while also managing her other leadership responsibilities), and executed the presentation brilliantly. She was a refreshing speaker who worked hard to make sure everything went flawlessly—and she received an overwhelmingly positive response.

Interestingly, one of Yanbing's male colleagues made an odd comment about her presentation: "You did not just do a cameo, right?" The comment indicated that he thought Yanbing's role at the keynote would be like an actor stepping onto a movie set for a few minutes for a small part. He seemed surprised to learn that her role was to do the heavy technical lifting during the keynote. Speaking to his remark, she said, "These are the undercurrents, when a female technology leader is on stage." She says that a man would not have been deemed insignificant like that when he was on stage.

One lesson to learn here is that honing public speaking skills is an important way for a female leader to be visible. "Coming back to female confidence, when you project a confident, outward-facing image, people are more willing to understand and trust your credentials," Yanbing said.

When you see her walk into a room, you can tell by her body language that she is someone important. Overall, Yanbing is the complete package to become a CEO, even in a male-dominated industry. She is confident, competent, and most of all, she is strong, persistent, and skillful. "Despite the dire reality of the loss of women at each level, it is very doable. I have a pretty long career ahead of me. Becoming a CEO is a plausible career for me."

---

16   View from minute 41 at https://www.youtube.com/watch?v=Ev6RjaM6rXw.

It's important that we follow Yanbing's inspiring example and believe we have everything it takes to shatter the glass ceilings above us. Women must nurture ambition as part of our "brand" as women technical leaders.

~ ~ ~

TAKEAWAYS

- Yanbing was raised in an academic environment. She was naturally good at school—but for her, education isn't everything; other important factors are personal motivation, aspiration, commitment, drive, and curiosity to learn, rather than just knowledge.

- China offered much less stereotyping and gender bias for girls and women interested in engineering and technology. Girls tend to thrive in STEM in their formative years if they have an opportunity to learn in a less biased environment.

- Yanbing prioritizes mentoring, sponsoring, and role-model relationships. She connects with people who have more experience as well as those who have less experience, when she finds people who have something to offer. One can learn from people both above and below on the corporate ladder.

- Men typically gain more support and more role models because there is a higher percentage of males in leadership roles. Female mentors and role models are therefore harder to find.

- For Yanbing, confidence is a constant challenge. Her advice: project overconfidence and focus on the bigger outcome rather than small flaws.

CHAPTER 4: ANNABEL'S STORY

BIOSKETCH: *Growing up in a small village in China, Annabel Liu saw how the Communist Party's effort to promote gender equality dramatically improved women's socioeconomic status. She remembers slogans like "Women hold up half the sky" as an illustration of how women should play an equal part in the economy and the society. Her family moved to the United States when she was fifteen, and she learned BASIC in high school. She immediately fell in love with programming. Now working at a stealth startup and previously as vice president of engineering at LinkedIn, Annabel calls herself a geek and still loves coding. Her ultimate career goal has always been to continue to push herself to be the best she can be.*

"When all things are said and done, your fears will come to pass. Through practice, you gain skills. You have to be brave and push yourself to go on. Don't go back to your comfort zone because of fear. The strongest force that's holding us back is our fear of being rejected, of feeling embarrassed, of making a fool of ourselves. So what? You have to focus on the longer-term goal. I take pride in myself for being courageous and willing to take risks. Focusing on the long-term self-betterment helps me get over these negative feelings."

— Annabel Liu, former VP of Engineering, LinkedIn

~ ~ ~

Annabel's parents were born as peasants and grew up during the Chinese Cultural Revolution. Despite the hardships, her father ventured out to start a construction company. As the Chinese economy blossomed, his business thrived, making him one of the first successful entrepreneurs in his village. For Annabel's mother, the revolution interrupted what little opportunity she might have had to get a formal education. Along with help from extended family members, she took care of the farming while her husband dedicated most of his time to the company. Although she didn't have to continue the farm work, Annabel remembers, "My mom wanted to have a sense of purpose, wanted to have independence, wanted to do something meaningful and interesting."

Even though her dad was well established in China, he grabbed an opportunity to come to the United States, without knowing the language, the place, or the people, to seek better education and opportunities for his three children. He had never cooked a single meal in China, but he started working at a dishwashing job in a Chinese restaurant, eventually becoming a chef. "He had to learn everything," Annabel recalls. "He would come home excited and share the different pork cuts he just learned." Annabel's mother contributed by working in a clothing factory, though it compromised her health. The risks her parents took and sacrifices they made still leave Annabel in awe. From their example, Annabel continues to derive her own independence, determination, and the ability to "always keep hope high," traits that she identifies as key to her career.

Annabel has fond memories of her carefree life as a girl in China. Seeing that she was able to manage her school work relatively independently, her parents didn't enforce many rules; they just wanted her to be happy. She was not raised with the idea that a woman needs to stay home, nor was she ever told that a woman couldn't do certain things. As early as grade school, Annabel was interested in STEM. "I was into building things. My favorite subjects were math and science. It was clear that was where my passion was," Annabel said.

Annabel's family immigrated to the United States just in time for her to enroll in high school. There she was introduced to computer programming, which she enjoyed, but just as a hobby. In college, CS was not on the top of her list as a major. Instead, she chose chemical engineering because she was good at chemistry. Once she began her chemical engineering studies, however, she realized that chemical engineering is very different from chemistry. She was not enjoying it, and she realized that she couldn't sustain a career without that sense of fun.

She took a Fortran class, and found she both loved it and was good at it. Annabel convinced her advisor that she wanted to switch her major to CS, even though she would need to do a lot of catch-up studying. When she did, she started to come alive. Finally, she was home!

When Annabel immigrated to the US, she realized that socially and culturally, the environment was not encouraging for a girl in computer science. "There were 'toys for boys' and 'toys for girls.' It's like boys and girls lived in two separate worlds," Annabel said. In China, Annabel did well in school, and she was well-liked; people there were not conscious of gender roles. Everyone goes to school and puts in the required effort to succeed. In the US, however, some of her high school classmates labeled her as a geek, and she felt ostracized and unpopular.

After graduating with a CS major from Stanford University, she went to work for a high-tech start-up in Santa Clara, California. "It was fun, a lot of work, and so chaotic. As I was building stuff in this chaotic world, I wasn't necessarily learning," she said. The hectic pace didn't allow her time to become better; she was too busy cranking out code. She wanted an environment where she could learn to be a better software engineer.

At that point, Ariba was a hot company in Silicon Valley. She interviewed with Ariba six months after its initial public offering (IPO) and was offered a job. Following some of her friends' advice, she turned it down, based on the conventional wisdom that it is better to work at a company before they go IPO for equity grants and rapid development (but that may not always be the case).

Instead, she chose another start-up. "That start-up didn't go well, however," she said. The same manager at Ariba who had originally offered her a job a year before found this out and asked her to reconsider. This time, Annabel jumped at the opportunity. She felt it had been a mistake to decline Ariba's offer the first time around, and she felt fortunate to get a second chance. Now, she was certain she'd made the right decision. "I learned so much from the people working at Ariba—system architecture, design, and leadership."

This was a critical decision for her, as it shaped the rest of her career. At Ariba, she finally found her place. She was among passionate people who lived and breathed technology. Annabel tends to get obsessed with a technical problem, and at Ariba, people embraced this sort of intensity and curiosity. "People were passionate about what they did; we would talk about work at the office, in meetings, and at lunch. I thought it was very cool."

She stayed with Ariba for nine years. During that time, Annabel built a social capital of friends and colleagues who mentor and support her to this day. In those nine years, Annabel transitioned from an engineer to management—a natural move for her. As an engineer, she mentored new hires and junior engineers, did code reviews, and coached her mentees on how to handle production bugs. Under her guidance, she saw college graduates go from newbies to competent and confident engineers within six months. It was gratifying to see how she played a part in the growth of these team members. That was an important factor in why her transition from technical lead to manager was organic. Further, managing a small team allowed her to continue writing code—something she still enjoys. Throughout her tenure at Ariba, she was very hands-on; she not only knew the design and architecture of her product intimately but also got her hands dirty by occasionally writing code.

After that long at Ariba, however, work started to get less challenging. "I wanted new challenges. A friend referred me to LinkedIn. After I interviewed there, I could see myself working there. At LinkedIn, people are intelligent, passionate, and engaged—you feel like you want to be part of the team." Annabel took the opportunity for a new environment, and joined LinkedIn as a senior manager.

~ ~ ~

In her journey at LinkedIn, Annabel gradually built her brand by increasing her self-awareness in response to feedback. As her team grew from four engineers to over two hundred, listening to people around her helped her understand what mattered the most and what she should focus on at different stages. When the team was small, everyone was pretty much on the same page all the time. As the team grew, the nature of how the team worked changed. The larger the team, the bigger the variations arose in level of experience and understanding of the system. People also had different strengths and worked at different pace and style. She shifted her focus to make sure team members could leverage each other's skills and run together toward a common goal.

Another tweak she discovered that she needed to make to become a more effective leader in the organization was her communication style. Annabel's brand at work was a go-getter, assertive, driven, and even authoritarian at times. Although Annabel was execution focused and kept charging toward her goal, she wasn't aware of her effect on others. Feedback from her mentors and team members helped her realize that her communication style was being perceived as authoritarian. While she was expressing her authentic, energetic self, others viewed that negatively. "I would give my opinion during technical discussions. Because you are a manager or director, however, people believe that opinions are actually orders."

"There are many ways you can deliver a message. I thought about how I could communicate more effectively and compassionately: it was removing the perception of being authoritative to becoming empowering. I'd been so focused on achieving a goal that I didn't pay attention to how people perceived me, or my image. The image is secondary, however; what I care about most is my team's perception of me," she said.

What Annabel did was remarkable. She did not let the criticism that she was perceived as authoritarian or aggressive bring her down. Instead, she used it as a learning moment, evolving her style without sacrificing her authenticity. Oftentimes, women have a strong desire to be likable and compromise on their capacity to be effective. Annabel changed her communication style, but did so in a way that allowed her to stay true to herself while remaining effective.

When she used to provide a technical opinion to her team, Annabel was often merely trying to play devil's advocate. She was just another engineer on the team who wanted to understand the different tradeoffs to a technical solution. She started to adjust her communication style to make herself more effective and her intentions better understood. She had to become clearer in her communication to her team that she was giving an opinion, not an order. "I don't want the perception 'she dominated the whole meeting, and she gave orders.' So, I started being explicit—not ordering or commanding, but saying, 'Here is my input.'"

She makes another important point here. We treat our managers and bosses as authority figures. Yes, they have the power to determine your promotions and raises, but they are also part of your team. When they provide an opinion on a technical issue during a discussion, that doesn't mean it's an order.

Annabel also needed to get visibility within LinkedIn for herself and her team. She had to figure out how to communicate and manage upwards. How do you showcase yourself and your team, and demonstrate that you are making an impact on the company and on the business as a whole? "When you are focused on execution, you tend to forget to focus on visibility. Advocacy and visibility are just as important as execution. You are representing the team, and you want to provide the right updates at the right level, solicit feedback, and ensure that the investment in your team is going well."

Recently, one principal engineer I worked with told me an important story. When he was a senior engineer at another company, his boss said to him, "You are doing all this great work, but nobody in the company knows you. Why don't you start by walking around the halls and introducing yourself?" He did just that. Slowly, people started to get to know him and his work. Within three short years, he went from a senior engineer to a principal engineer. I always encourage engineers on my team to do the same. Visibility and social capital are important for succeeding in the workplace.

Apart from improving her communication style and gaining visibility, Annabel started investing significantly more energy in mentoring and growing her engineers. She identified her high performers and actively guided their careers. She continuously propelled them forward and advocated for them. As people stepped up to take more responsibilities, she was able to scale her own work better. "When you invest time in growing the next wave of high performers and leaders in your team, you can spend more time on planning and product strategy."

~ ~ ~

As people go from being tactical to strategic in their career, they run the risk of losing their technical understanding of the product and company. Now that Annabel runs a team of over two hundred engineers, staying technical becomes a challenge.

"I enjoy being technical, for personal satisfaction. When I go through a day of meetings, it is calming and therapeutic for me to take two or three hours to do technical work. At work, I tend to context-switch all the time. I will carve out time at night or weekends to have that dedicated time where I can calm down and gain inner peace. I do technical work mostly for that purpose."

Personally, that advice doesn't quite work for me. I have three young children and a full-time job. I am exhausted after a long day of work. Writing this book was an extra challenge for me. So, what's her advice for women like me, who are stretched thin in both their professional and personal lives? Annabel's suggestion: "Set a small goal, perhaps a six-month goal. You can say 'in the next six months, I want to learn user interface technologies, and build an app using the new technology.' Buy a book, read it in two weeks, and start coding."

I did find a way to publish this book, even with my hectic lifestyle, so perhaps this method is feasible for me. It depends in part on how badly you want to achieve something. Because writing this book was imperative for me, I structured my entire life so that I could be successful at getting it into print. Perhaps that's the key. How badly do you want something? The more you want it the more likely you will work for it.

At the time of our interview, Annabel was studying artificial intelligence and machine learning. The last time she had studied this subject was back in college, but she wanted a refresher. She took her own suggestion, setting a six-month goal to learn the subject. "I have two young kids," she adds, "and I don't like to set aggressive goals and get demoralized. I set small, realistic goals—first, go through the book. That helped me."

Annabel also has a weekly to-do list. On it, she carves out time for enjoyment and time for learning, such as reading the design documents on the projects she is responsible for. "This is important information for me to know, such as what problems the engineers are running into." She also gets personal satisfaction from reading the technical documents and understanding how everything in her product works. But whatever you add to your to-do list as part of your goal-setting, the key is to be realistic. "Our lives are so hectic. Don't be too aggressive," Annabel advises. Instead of wearing yourself out, she takes a tip from her senior vice president: "Focus on things that give you pleasure—and for the things that *need* to get done, get some help." For instance, Annabel used to organize a lot of events for her team, but then she hired a good technical program manager and delegated the task of organizing team events to her.

She uses the same technique at home, delegating tasks to her husband and kids, and hiring outside help. Does this give Annabel enough time with her kids? How does she view her work–life balance? She told me regretfully, "I often feel guilty. I joke that I am a 'drive-by mom,' since I tend to work more. Do I feel guilty? Hell, yes. But would I have it any other way? Hell, no."

As we see in other interviews here, many women experience guilt while trying to strike this balance, which often makes women experience great pressure to sacrifice their careers for their children. Annabel continues, "I am pretty efficient at home and work. My kids are the best judge of that. However, I didn't get to volunteer at their schools as much I would have liked to. My husband was volunteering one day, and a girl who was sitting next to my son asked him if he had a mom—because she was never there. That was the worst I've ever felt. And here I thought I was doing a good job as a parent!"

Annabel was subsequently able to reconcile with her guilt when she realized that she is helping her kids in other ways than volunteering at school. She helps with their homework, reads books to them, and takes care of things at home so her husband has the bandwidth to volunteer. "I cannot score an A on every front. I don't feel bad anymore." Regarding her husband overhearing their son's conversation at school, Annabel went on to observe, "That question would not have been asked if the mom was doing the volunteering, and the man wasn't." She told me one further story:

"I live in Los Altos, where there are many stay-at-home moms. Sometimes my kids are invited to birthday parties with professional clowns, mini-zoos, that sort of thing. They come home and say, 'That was the best party ever!' I am straightforward with my kids. I tell them that their friends' moms are full time at home, and that is *their* choice. But your mom happens to love work, and I spend all my time outside of work with you, but working is *my* choice. My kids have come to respect that. I hope I am setting a good example for them: to pursue something you are passionate about, and try to do the best you can."

~ ~ ~

Annabel has a few mentors she meets with regularly. They serve as a sounding board for her and help her gain more self-awareness. She recommends finding a mentor who fits your style and understands your style, your strengths, and your areas of growth. "They can help you get better in those areas. You have to understand first how you fit in, what your strengths are, what the areas are you need to work at." When one mentor cautioned Annabel that her execution of projects was scaring people, she took that advice to heart.

Annabel also knows the importance of sponsors, and feels she has been fortunate in this regard. She has often appreciated the support of both her immediate managers and those at higher levels. "A board member sent me a LinkedIn meeting request saying, 'Annabel, we haven't met, but I've heard so many good things about your getting this project launched on time.'" She believes visibility is key for sponsorship. "If you don't create that visibility, people cannot sponsor you." Be sure to communicate your achievements to help build your reputation.

Annabel attributes the lack of women in leadership positions directly to lack of sponsorship. "Who is willing to invest in you, who is going to trust in you?" She believes she has been fortunate. "I came across a set of people who bet on me: both individual contributors and managers. One manager looked at the qualities I had displayed and also those I hadn't exhibited yet—and believed I could get there."

Apart from sponsorship, women need to build a deep network, plus the social capital[17] to attain those coveted leadership positions. Not a group of superficial connections—a network that goes beyond just friendly colleagues and acquaintances. Annabel challenges women to ask themselves: "How many people know you well? How many people trust you, and know your ambitions and dreams? You need a few really strong connections."

Annabel remarks that men tend to hang out together, smoking in a corner or socializing outside of work over drinks. Women aren't invited, and sometimes important decisions are made during those times. Women miss opportunities like these that can affect their careers. Her advice to women is to deliberately make strong connections and relationships that you trust, relationships that will empower you and help move you to the next level.

But what about that glass ceiling women keep bumping against as they move up in their careers? Annabel says, "I know we can shatter that. The glass ceiling is there—but not because people are intentionally and maliciously putting it there. Glass ceilings exist because of a lack of sponsorship. We don't have enough women or men who give us the opportunity."

~ ~ ~

---

[17]   Status gained from the well-connected people immediately around them.

Women tell ourselves stories that get in the way of our achieving what we want; imposter syndrome is one term for this phenomenon. "I suffer this from time to time," Annabel told me, "sometimes technically, or sometimes when I want to deliver a presentation with eloquence." Annabel pointed out that one reason imposter syndrome is so widespread in our work culture is that we set such a high bar for ourselves. "We want to score A's everywhere, but we can't." By contrast, she urges people to select what to excel in based on what they *want* to get good at, and whether they have the necessary time to invest in it. "Pick the areas that you want to score A's in, and for all the others, be comfortable with a passing grade. There will be time for improvement later."

~ ~ ~

The common attribution of imposter syndrome to only women is a form of gender stereotyping. One additional reflection of gender bias is in obvious pay inequities. "I have several examples where someone was brought in at the same level as I was, but got paid more than I did," Annabel told me. That made her feel bad, but she tried not to let it bother her. To overcome this, she focused on moving forward.

"I could prove that I could do a better job than that person. I could showcase that to my manager and the entire company. I tried to show this with my own growth and accomplishments, but the situation bothered me from time to time."

Unlike some other women profiled in this book, Annabel didn't ask a superior to fix the pay inequity. She believed in correcting the unfairness by using meritocracy. However, Annabel reiterates that we do not live in a meritocratic world and must advocate for ourselves.

"I believe in meritocracy, but it only takes you so far. The higher you go, the more other factors become more important. I believe that you need to manage your reputation, you need to communicate your achievements, knowledge, and passion. Let other people see you—do not hide in the corner and wait for people to find this hidden gem."

The gender pay inequity is exacerbated when women don't ask for what they're worth. We have to advocate for ourselves when it comes to compensation. Interestingly, Annabel says she is not great at negotiating. "This is something I am still learning," she admits. "But I did negotiate in my first job. Because I had multiple offers, I had leverage. I was not consciously negotiating, but I wanted to accept the higher offer, even though I liked the position and the team of the lower offer. The hiring manager said, 'We may not be able to beat all that, but we can come close.'" Annabel's thought process during her consideration of multiple offers helped land her the position that worked in her favor.

To women who struggle with negotiating salaries or asking for promotions or raises, she says, "Definitely ask. You might not get it right away, but you have planted a seed. Tell your manager in a friendly but firm tone, 'When you have time, take a look at what I have achieved and then compensate me fairly.'"

~ ~ ~

"I think I am fortunate. I am successful not because of my title, but because I am completely happy with who I am. That means being able to recognize both my strengths and my weaknesses; admitting things I don't know, being comfortable with who I am, and striking a good balance at home." Having achieved being comfortable with herself, she also feels fortunate to be a woman. As she points out, "By nature, we have the gift to be more empathetic. We multitask well. We are emotionally strong. I see it in my mom, in myself, and in my girlfriends. I am happy to be a woman." Listening to Annabel, I am reminded of Maya Angelou's poem "Phenomenal Woman." Maya was proud to be a woman, and she has uplifted many women with her poem. That's how I felt when I completed my talk with Annabel. She made me feel proud and happy to be a woman.

~ ~ ~

TAKEAWAYS

- It's crucial to find a company that is a right fit for you.

- Annabel believes in the importance of feedback in learning how to develop a team that works well together.

- Though Annabel's brand was perceived as authoritarian early in her career, she found ways to evolve her leadership style while still being effective.

- Her highly technical nature is an underlying factor in her success.

- She benefited from finding a mentor who fit her style.

- To resist imposter syndrome, she chose what to focus on based on what she wanted to excel at.

- Conquering one's fears can lay the groundwork for success.

- Sponsorship can be key to breaking the glass ceiling.

- Annabel urges women to manage their reputation and communicate their achievements, knowledge, and passion.

YOUR BRAND

Do you consciously manage your brand at work?

Companies pay a lot of attention not only to how their products are rated, but also to how their corporate brand is viewed as a whole. As more research in marketing of goods and services is done, it has become apparent that it is just as important to pay attention to how a corporation is perceived as it is to pay attention to the quality of the product or service it provides. The same is true for you at work. Of course, it is important to do good work, but it could be even more important how your brand is viewed.

When I think of brand, I am often reminded of Ivy League schools, such as Yale and Harvard. These schools have strong name recognition and are associated with high-quality education. Graduates of these universities are sought after in the job market because the trust in the rigor of the programs gives them credibility.

It's equally important for you, as an individual, to create your own brand. What's your brand? It's the set of qualities that people remember about you after you leave the room. It's more than your reputation, although your reputation at work is part of it.

Examples of what people might say that show awareness of a person's brand are: "She knows her stuff," "She's a go-getter," "She gets things done," "She's a team player." That's how people perceive that individual, and that becomes their identity at work. Your identity can make things easier or harder for you. For instance, would you be more likely to entrust a strategic project to someone about whom people say, "She delivers on her commitments," or to someone whose brand is "She isn't trustworthy" or "She is too political."

It's important to carefully manage your brand as you progress up the technical or leadership ladder, but it can be tricky. Say you do a great job on a project. If your manager, or your manager's manager, doesn't know about your contribution to the project, then your good work does nothing to build your brand. At the same time, you don't want to be viewed as someone who is always talking about their accomplishments; you could be perceived as self-centered and not a team player. Just as companies are careful about their messaging, you should be careful about how your actions help or hurt you.

In the process of interviewing women for this book and writing their stories, I learned quite a bit about managing one's brand at work. For instance, in chapter 15, Ana Pinczuk says that one of the important lessons she learned during her early years at Bell Labs was how to build a more professional persona. As she transitioned from a college student to a professional, she needed to establish herself as a serious person. Being intentional about her brand and taking on a bit of gravitas paid off for her.

On career development in general, Ana's advice is to "think two jobs ahead" and to be conscious of your journey. "One of the fundamental things you need to do is to know where you are and where you are perceived to be in your career—and then the journey is the difference. Understand your priorities so that you know how much you're willing to sacrifice, and understand where your brand is relative to the job that you want, and bridge that gap."

Establishing and maintaining a good brand is a lot of work. It also requires a lot of self-awareness. One of the first steps is to get what's called "360-degree feedback." Survey the people who report to you and your peer colleagues, as well as people outside of your direct chain of command. Find out what they perceive to be your strengths and weaknesses. It can be painful to get that feedback, but if you take the feedback and think about how you are viewed presently versus how you want to be viewed in the future, you can start to come up with actionable items on how to build your brand to further your career.

I think when women manage their brand well at work they can be more successful, and they find that it becomes easier to navigate the labyrinth. Consciously manage and build your brand, and the world becomes your oyster.

CHAPTER 5: JENNIFER'S STORY

BIOSKETCH: *Does it matter if you don't fit the mold of a stereotypical leader? Will it affect your aptitude as a leader or your chances of being promoted to a leadership position? Yes and no. Stereotypes of leaders do exist and can affect who is promoted. Though Jennifer Anderson doesn't have all the stereotypical traits of a leader—she admits that she is an introvert—her thoughtful and collaborative leadership style has made her a highly effective leader. She shatters the image of a leader we expect or envision. Formerly a vice president of research and development at VMware and currently the engineering director of the data team at Uber, she demonstrates that diverse leadership is possible and needed in the world of tech.*

"People who are aggressive and assertive are often seen as natural leaders, and they are the ones that tend to get promoted. Many women, such as myself, were not brought up that way, but it doesn't make me any less effective as a leader. There has to be a cultural shift in our understanding of what makes a good leader. Someone who gets people to cooperate is a better leader than someone who asserts their agenda to get what they want. We need to realize there are different personality types that can all contribute in different ways to making a great company."

— Jennifer Anderson, Engineering Leadership, Uber

~ ~ ~

Jennifer grew up in a Southern California suburb near the University of California (UC), Irvine, where she would eventually pursue her undergraduate degree. As a child, Jennifer excelled in math and science, and was recognized in these subjects by her high school. Her father was a "gadgets guy" and would buy many of the latest gizmos. When Jennifer was a teenager, her father bought an early version of a Commodore PET (personal electronic transactor), one of Commodore International's home/personal computers. Playing with the PET sparked Jennifer's interest in studying computers.

In her senior year of high school, Jennifer was interested in astronomy and was considering it as her college major. "My parents were not thrilled by my choice and urged me to reconsider, asking 'Do you really want to spend your life sitting in a dark room halfway across the world?'" As much as she loved astronomy, she agreed with her parents that it wasn't a great career choice for her. As she entered college, she didn't know what to major in, but given her aptitude for math and science—as well as her fascination with her PET—she decided to give the then-emerging field of CS a try.

Jennifer regards her decision to study CS as one of the best decisions in her life. After she graduated from UC Irvine with her CS undergraduate degree, Jennifer felt that there was much more to learn in the field, and decided to get an advanced degree. Although UC Irvine didn't have a master's program in CS, they offered a PhD program. Jennifer recalls, "A masters was what I really wanted, but UC Irvine had a PhD program, so I thought I'd go ahead and apply. Since I was applying for the PhD program at Irvine, I thought, 'What the heck, let me apply to a few more places.'" Jennifer was accepted by Stanford and MIT as well as UC Irvine. "I hadn't expected to get in anywhere besides UC Irvine, but I had to get out of my comfort zone and give it a shot. I chose Stanford and enrolled in the PhD program there even though it meant moving away from my friends and family and entering a challenging program where I wasn't sure if I'd be successful," Jennifer recalled.

Although Jennifer had excelled academically during her undergraduate years, things didn't come quite as easy at Stanford. "I felt unprepared. It took me a little while to get my bearings," she admitted. The students who went to Stanford came from all over the world, graduating from highly competitive schools. Jennifer, shy by nature, found herself thrown into a much more competitive environment than she was used to. To further complicate matters, though there had been many women in her undergraduate CS program at UC Irvine, Jennifer was the only woman in her class in the PhD program at Stanford.

To explain what helped her get through Stanford, she said, "I am stubborn. A certain amount of stubbornness is good for determination, and I wasn't going to give up. Part of me felt like I couldn't quit. Sometimes it is the right decision to say, 'This isn't for me'—it's okay to say, 'I quit.' For me, I tend to be too stubborn about things I should be giving up. But in this case, my stubbornness paid off."

Being the only woman in her class was an interesting experience for Jennifer. "Everybody treated me nice enough; I wasn't discriminated against, but I was a curiosity. I remember walking down the hall," she told me, "and I overheard somebody say, 'There is the woman,' while pointing at me. I really stood out. I felt like if I messed up, all eyes were on me. It was weird. Everyone knew who I was—for better or worse. But standing out helped me become more resilient."

I wondered why few women make it to graduate education in CS, and I asked Jennifer for her thoughts. "I believe that the perceived culture of CS scares a lot of women away," she replied. "Many women I knew at the time thought CS was for nerds who want to work by themselves, and they didn't want anything to do with it. They don't realize that CS is highly collaborative. Most projects require a great deal of interaction with others to succeed. It's also a very creative discipline, where you get the opportunity to solve problems in innovative ways. Lots of people don't realize that."

Jennifer graduated with her PhD in the area of parallelizing compilers. Her time at Stanford provided a solid foundation for her career, while toughening her up. With her work reviewed by people who were demanding critics, she had to develop a thick skin. Her Stanford degree also conferred the credibility, of a top-tier university. "Wherever I go, people assume a basic level of competence from me," she observed. "It's been an advantage throughout my career. It helped me grow as a person."

While at graduate school, Jennifer won a scholarship for women in the Stanford CS program from Digital Equipment Corporation's Western Research Lab (WRL). The esteemed Anita Borg, who already had a long history of advocating for women in technology, and who had started at WRL as a research engineer, founded the scholarship. Jennifer pointed out that there was a bit of irony in saying that she "won" the scholarship. "Since I was the only woman in my year at Stanford, there was no competition for the scholarship. I can't claim it was for any fabulous merits of my own."

After graduation, Jennifer joined WRL as a researcher working on profiling tools and compiler optimizations. After she had been there a few years, frustration began to grow within the lab. Digital Equipment was not successful in turning employee research into products, and people were starting to leave to seek opportunities in other companies. Around this time, Edouard Bugnion, one of Jennifer's classmates at Stanford and one of the co-founders of VMware, asked her if she would be interested in interviewing to join VMware.

Although currently VMware is a subsidiary of Dell Technologies and has some twenty thousand employees, when Jennifer joined, the company was still in start-up mode. It had only about twenty engineers and had just released the initial version of its first product, VMware Workstation.

Jennifer's daughter was one year old at that time, so Jennifer felt somewhat apprehensive about joining such a young venture. She wasn't willing to sacrifice her family life to work crazy hours and have no work–life balance. She was also worried that, as one of the few women in the company, she'd get pushback or be penalized for needing time to care for her child. However, when she learned that Diane Greene, who was one of the founders and the original CEO of VMware, also had a young child, Jennifer "took that leap of faith that her personal life would not be destroyed." She reasoned, "Diane Greene is in the same boat as I am. If there's any company that will be understanding about a woman with a young child, it is this company."

Jennifer had a couple of other thoughts about the advantages and disadvantages of joining VMware. One potential advantage was that because VMware had a woman CEO, there would be less gender bias than in the rest of the computer industry. She believed that, "having a female CEO would make a big difference. Anyone who is overly sexist won't join that company," she thought.

It turns out that VMware was the right environment for Jennifer. She spent thirteen years there, eventually moving from software development into management, and then working her way up to a vice president role. However, her transition to management wasn't seamless. She enjoyed development work, but as a manager, she needed to shift her focus to being a leader rather than an individual contributor. Her promotion to management came with a lot of self-doubt. "That year I had a crisis of confidence," she told me. "Did I make the right decision? Am I going to be able to move up successfully? Should I have stayed as a developer? At many companies, developers are much more respected and well regarded. In some ways, I felt like I had taken a step down."

Jennifer says that early in her transition to management she almost left VMware. She loved the team and the people in her group but she was having difficulty shifting her mindset from being an individual contributor to being a manager. I was curious to know what helped her acclimate to her new role. She said, "I decided I needed to give management more of a chance. I decided to keep at it and see how it played out. The people in the group were so great, and it was wonderful working with them. I stuck with it and ultimately decided to stay on the management track. It took some years, but after a while I felt I'd made the right decision."

The role of an individual contributor is very different from a manager's. Being the organizer of the team and the decision-maker requires a different mindset than writing code. I found it interesting that what helped Jennifer transition to the new role was deciding to take more time to get accustomed to the role and, indeed, with time, it became clear that becoming a manager was a good decision for her.

In 2003–2004, EMC Corporation acquired VMware, and Jennifer quickly received two more promotions as the company grew. Then in 2013, Jennifer decided it was time to move onto her next adventure. She joined a start-up in stealth mode that was founded by Diane Greene. The company was called Bebop Technologies. Her official role at Bebop was software engineer, a big change from her previous role.

After two and a half years with Bebop, Jennifer took a position as a director at Uber, because "they are changing the world in innovative ways—both in technology and in social and economic ways." Jennifer is now back to leading a team, and she's happy with her position. "My team is responsible for the data analytics infrastructure and platform at Uber."

~ ~ ~

When Jennifer wanted to move into a senior director position, and subsequently into a vice president role, she met a challenge. She had to hone some of her traits and rough edges as a manager. Remember her stubbornness? She explained, "There were times my manager wanted me to do something and I disagreed with it. Sometimes I felt like I knew better, but in retrospect I can see that my manager may have had more information than I did. That probably held me back; I was seen as not being cooperative and not putting the company's interests first," she concluded.

In addition, Jennifer was getting other feedback about how she was approaching her role as a manager. "Some of the feedback I received was, 'You need to be more assertive. You need to be more willing to make tough decisions and be willing to fire people.' As a manager, I try hard to respect every person I work with as an individual and to listen to their point of view. If somebody is underperforming, *why* are they underperforming?" When her reports were not meeting expectations, Jennifer would try to help sort out the challenges, so they could keep their job and become more of an asset to the team.

Jennifer also felt she was weak when it came to self-promotion, which probably set her back in her career. One way to influence how your manager perceives your work is to make sure they are aware of your accomplishments. "I am really bad at self-promotion," she admits. "I think that has hurt me. While I will readily promote my team members, I find it difficult to draw attention to myself. Other people have no problem doing that."

How did she overcome some of these barriers that held back her promotions? She replied, "I ended up taking management training classes. To be honest, at first, I was annoyed that I was supposed to take this training, but in retrospect, it was useful. It also showed me that the company valued me enough that they were willing to invest in my career." Jennifer was able to take feedback to heart and make positive changes in the areas that people were asking her to improve on, which directly led to her promotion to vice president.

I wondered whether, apart from her own personality traits, gender bias played a role in the rate at which she moved up the ladder. "Getting to the executive level is challenging in any company," she explained. "At VMware, I don't think I was held back because I am a woman. I believe some of my personality traits may have slowed me down." She says that there are men who are leaders whose leadership style is more stereotypically female, and they have the same problems with being viewed as viable candidates for promotions. Jennifer says, "It is not a man versus woman thing. There are plenty of women who are assertive and aggressive. There are plenty of men who are cooperative and social. But statistically, more women tend to be cooperative, social, and caring, and more men tend to be assertive types. I wouldn't say it was because I was a woman per se, but more because some of the personality traits I possess are not valued as highly."

Apart from the management training, Jennifer also worked on two other things. "First, I did learn how to come across more like a leader by speaking and writing with more confidence and being more decisive. I learned this by watching my peers and learning how they behaved in meetings and when communicating. I had to be really honest with myself about what areas were weak spots for me and what needed to change, and then I worked to improve those areas," she said.

She continued, "Second, I developed a lot of expertise over my time at VMware, and I like to think that I was valuable to the company. After a while, I think people realized that I was doing a good job, and that I was capable of taking on additional responsibility. I might have gotten promoted faster if I fit the 'leader' mold better, but ultimately I got there over time through my continued accomplishments." Jennifer made a conscious effort to attain that level of leadership.

~ ~ ~

Jennifer's move from VMware to Bebop is interesting and unusual from a strategy perspective. The traditional career advice is to avoid a step-down career transition. Many of the women featured in this book made such transitions, which have paid off in the long run. Of course, other factors make it advantageous to join a small start-up. Are you passionate about what the company is doing? Does the company have potential for high growth? Will there be learning opportunities in the new role?

Jennifer wasn't concerned about being promoted at Bebop. She had a completely different set of motivations for working there. She remarked, "I wasn't managing a team at Bebop, but I didn't feel that was a step back at all. I got to work with many talented, smart people. I was excited about what Bebop was doing. I didn't care what title I had. I just wanted to be part of it." She was also drawn to Bebop's innovation. "The goal was to develop a platform that would allow you to build a suite of business software, that included human resources, enterprise resource planning, financial—everything a company needs to run its business. There was a lot happening both in the platform as well as in the approach to building applications. If the platform was successful, it would have a huge impact in the industry."

Jennifer's Bebop experience exposed her to a completely different model of software development. Her VMware experience dealt with low-level infrastructure, but at Bebop, she was able to be part of building a business software platform and application. "It was a really interesting experience. I just jumped in and did whatever was needed. At Bebop, I was more like a project manager at first. I was working with PMs on decisions about what was going to be in the release, and keeping things on schedule. I did most of the engineering hiring. Later, I also learned about web development and wrote code," Jennifer said.

Jennifer took a calculated risk by stepping down in her career to work for Bebop, but in her estimation, the company had a high potential of being successful. Her instincts proved to be correct; Google eventually purchased Bebop in November 2015.

Looking back at her career, Jennifer feels she's been successful. "I had a personal goal of becoming a VP at VMware, and I achieved that. I am proud of what VMware did as a company and the impact it had on the industry. I can point to that and say I was a part of it." When she was at Bebop, the title didn't matter to her. She only cared about working with smart people and "building something innovative and cool." In her current position at Uber, Jennifer feels the same. "I am happy to be part of a ground-breaking company like Uber, instead of something small and incremental."

~ ~ ~

Jennifer told me that recruiting mentors wasn't one of her strengths. "I can't say I've had formal mentors. It's probably my own fault, because I am bad at networking. I keep telling myself I need to go out there and meet people. I do it to some extent, but I am an introvert by nature. It's hard. My networking skills are limited. I can't point to somebody and say they have been my mentor," she said.

For Jennifer, what worked well was to keep an eye out for role models—people who offered examples of positive characteristics that Jennifer desired to emulate. "I would look at what people above me were doing. I'd ask myself, 'What can I learn from that? What are they doing that I am not?' I picked up tips along the way looking at people in the positions that I wanted. I had to be self-critical and work on those things."

She continued, "I have also had some great managers in my career. I felt like I was listened to and respected." Jennifer mentioned that one of her favorite managers, who was one of her role models, ended up sponsoring her for the vice president promotion.

Jennifer mentioned the names of a couple of her role models. Anita Borg was one. "I knew Anita when I was at Digital Equipment," Jennifer said. "What I learned from her was that she was unafraid to be herself. She did not care whether she was different from others. She was just herself. She had fun doing her work, and her enthusiasm influenced those around her. I really looked up to her."

Another one of Jennifer's role models is Diane Greene. "What I like about Diane is she is really down to earth while still coming across as a strong leader. So many CEOs are just unapproachable. Diane is able to exude a certain warmth and empathy, so you felt like she was one of us. At the same time, she was an effective CEO of a world-class company."

I found it useful to consider how role models could work in a similar way to having mentors. Many of the people who have the leadership qualities that we would want to emulate may not have the time or inclination to sit down with us and be our personal mentors. But that doesn't mean we can't view them from afar and learn from them by example.

~ ~ ~

Jennifer credits having a supportive husband and a "family first" personal policy for her satisfying work–life balance. However, even with that, she acknowledged that work–life balance was a challenge, and her approach may have slowed her career. Jennifer observed, "Women have to do it all. It's a challenge for modern women. In earlier times, women rarely worked outside the home. It's wonderful that women can have careers now. But, now so many women have two jobs: they have to hold down a career *and* they are primarily responsible for the home and the kids."

Many of the women in the book have mentioned that the work interested them more than the pay and that made them gravitate more towards work. This meant that they struggled with having a good work life balance. I call this the curse of the modern women. Many years ago, women were only expected to be home makers. Over the years, women have fought that expectation and slowly but steadily they reached a place where they get to bring home the bacon. However deep down ingrained in our consciousness (both men and women), the expectation that women are still homemakers exists. Women are somehow expected to do it all.

"I am lucky because my husband works from home," Jennifer said. "It's an advantage for me because if the kids are sick he can be at home with them. For many women, if their kids are sick, they are the ones who stay home to care for them. When my husband was working outside the home, we would split the responsibilities. Still, I felt like I was doing two jobs sometimes. There are some things that always fall on the mom, no matter what."

Faced with having to prioritize between her work and her family Jennifer put her family first. "When I had my kids, I promised myself that I would never put my work before my family. If there was ever a conflict between work and family, I would always put my family first, especially when my kids were small. There were business trips I didn't go on. There were opportunities to go out and visit customers—but I didn't go. I would also leave promptly every evening so that I could pick up my kids from daycare."

"A lot of other people in my group would still be pounding away at their keyboards as I was leaving. This may have slowed down my career, but I made the right choice. At least now, I can look back and know that I put my family first, and I don't have any regrets about it. I was able to attend all the performances and events at my kids' school. These things only happen once. Small as they may be, I'm glad that I didn't miss any of those moments."

Jennifer shared with me another challenge she faced in raising her children. As Jennifer is an expert in the CS field, it was only natural that should would want to pass that along to her daughter. Jennifer recalled, "I tried hard to get my daughter interested in CS.

Unfortunately, she didn't want anything to do with it. When she was in middle school, she took an HTML class and did well, but when she entered high school, I suggested she take a Java class, and she refused. She told me, 'There's no way I am taking that class—the only people who take that class are nerds and those whose parents force them to.' I was disappointed, but I respected her decision. However, her attitude is indicative of the misconception that CS is only for a certain type of person. That perception is still there, though it's starting to fade. There are more shows, movies, and other references in popular culture that present computer science in a positive light. It's starting to become more mainstream and barriers are starting to come down."

How unfortunate that Jennifer's daughter excelled in her HTML class in middle school, but the perception that her high school's Java class is for nerds became a barrier to her willingness to continue with those studies. Programming computers is too often seen as just for nerdy boys. More needs to be done to show young women that coding can be very rewarding, with plenty of women who enjoy the field. The notion that somehow CS is not for women, doesn't just limit young girls; it also creates barriers for female technologists who are well established in their careers.

~ ~ ~

Jennifer discussed some of her thinking about how people's stereotypes of the qualities of a leader are biased toward men. "There are cases where women are being discriminated against subtly or not so subtly," she said. "That was not the case for me. I find that the biggest hurdle for myself, and for many other women as well, is that I don't naturally possess the personality traits that are valued in the world of tech. Specifically, the industry values people who are assertive and aggressive. People who are bold risk takers and fit the alpha male stereotype. That's who a leader is supposed to be: somebody who shuts down the opposition and forges ahead. I am not like that, but I'm still an effective leader. I get things done by listening to others, and being collaborative."

Jennifer is a gentle, thoughtful leader, which is generally not seen as an asset in the world of tech. She doesn't shut down the opposition and forge ahead with her agenda at the workplace. Despite her different approach, she has been successful. That gives me hope that we can allow different personalities to thrive in the workforce and that bringing your authentic self to work can be a rewarding experience.

~ ~ ~

TAKEAWAYS

- The early influence of her father and the gadgets he brought home helped spark Jennifer's love of technology.

- Don't assume that you won't gain admission to a top university program. When applying to PhD programs Jennifer was accepted by two prestigious schools, MIT and Stanford.

- Being a woman in STEM didn't deter Jennifer—even when she was the only woman in her PhD program.

- Jennifer developed a successful leadership style even as an introvert with few stereotypical leadership qualities, by taking some tough feedback and using it as a blueprint for change.

- Never rely too heavily on your comfort zone—Jennifer made the leap from VMware (where she was well established as a vice president) to a small start-up called Bebop. Here she took a very different position at a high potential start-up. She also had an opportunity to work on technology that was new and exciting to her. She then moved to an entirely different role at Uber again taking a chance to work at a fast-moving and ground-breaking company.

- Success isn't always defined by a title or role: Jennifer pursued what she thought was best for her, even though some would say that she took a step down mid-career.

- More thoughtful work needs to be done to counter the belief that CS is only for a certain type of person. As technology has become embedded in all aspects of modern life, we need people from all sorts of diverse backgrounds who feel that CS is right for them.

CHAPTER 6: ANNE'S STORY

BIOSKETCH: *Anne Holler was the first woman principal engineer at VMware. Prior to VMware, she worked as a software engineer at HP and other startups. She has a master's and a PhD in computer science from the University of Virginia and Duke University, respectively. Although she is a shy introvert, she is extremely driven and competitive in a quiet way. She rarely advocates for herself. Anne is all about teamwork and collaboration. One might say that she is a quiet force of nature.*

"In the field of technology, I wanted to be all that I could be. I didn't want to be feeling insecure about certain areas of my job, but the truth is, you are always not going to know about certain areas. But I wanted that credential that said, 'I actually looked at a lot of areas—and I looked at my area deeply."

—Anne Holler, Principal Engineer, VMware

~ ~ ~

When Anne was a child, her mother read to her frequently, so Anne learned to read on her own early in life. As she grew older, she felt she wasn't outstanding at math, but she was definitely competitive. When she realized that other kids knew more math than she did, she got all fired up and began to focus on that as well as her English classes. Her parents, both accounting majors, thought this competitiveness was great. They always encouraged Anne and her younger brother academically, expecting them to get good grades. "They didn't tell me I couldn't do something I set my mind to," Anne said.

In fifth grade, Anne was chosen to be part of a STEM (science, technology, engineering, and math) program in which college kids used software to teach science to selected grade-school kids. Anne eagerly worked through the self-paced lessons on her computer. "It was new, cool, and super-exciting," she recalled. Later, Anne's high school teachers began experimenting with teaching computer programming. In her junior year, Anne learned Basic programming in the first semester, and assembly language and Fortran in the second semester. She enjoyed programming so much that she spent the money she earned as a cashier to attend computer programming classes at a junior college while finishing her high school degree. "I was just a nerd. I was into programming. It resonated with me."

Anne chose to attend Duke University for college, following in the tradition of her parents. Coming from public schools, she felt she didn't have all the skills that prep school students had learned. "In most cases, I was playing catch-up," during those years, but in computer science, she was way ahead. "I had that advantage: the one thing I was better at, and I wanted to major in it."

Because Anne was so far ahead of other students in her major, she was able to take both undergraduate and graduate classes. After receiving her master's in CS from Duke, she had intended to pursue a PhD, but found she wanted a break from school.

She met her first husband at the CS department; he was a PhD candidate there. When he completed his degree, they moved to Charlottesville, Virginia, where Anne joined the factory automation products division of General Electric. There she worked on microprocessors that operated robot controllers and machine tools. "There is a big difference between your software running on a server and your software cutting metal in an industrial lab," she noted. "Really great place to work, and I loved it.

"But the problem was, it was the eighties. The industrialization of America was going down, and we had sold a lot of the machine tools to Detroit. The Japanese were coming in with machine tools and robot controllers that were much cheaper."

US businesses like those in Detroit had trouble competing, and their factories were reducing investment. Timing proved convenient for Anne, however, because by then she wanted to get back to school. She began taking individual classes at the University of Virginia in Charlottesville at night while working at General Electric. "The first class I took was on compilers—which I hadn't taken at Duke—and I loved it." Anne realized quickly that she needed to go full-time for that PhD, since the degree required a laser focus on research.

She took a big leap. Around the same time, her marriage was falling apart, so she quit working, sold all her belongings, bought a car, and moved into an apartment of her own. She completed her degree four years later.

Next, she spent a year teaching operating systems and programming at a nearby university, but by then she knew she wasn't interested in continuing as a college professor. "In the field of technology, I wanted to be all that I could be," she said, acknowledging that this pursuit of knowledge is why many people get an advanced degree in the first place. "I didn't want to be feeling insecure about certain areas of my job, but the truth is, you are *always* not going know about certain areas. But I wanted that credential that said, 'I actually looked at a lot of areas—and I looked at my area deeply.'" She moved to California in 1992 and started to work for Hewlett-Packard (HP).

"The microprocessor marketplace was pretty diverse at the beginning of the nineties, and a lot of people could work at different places," she said, "but as the nineties wore on, you could see that the number of microprocessor architectures was shrinking."

Although Anne had considered being part of a start-up when she first relocated to California, she was afraid it would crash and burn. But after several years of watching the market shift, she decided to take another risk and went to work for Transmeta, a semiconductor company.

Transmeta was fun and chaotic. She recalls, "I was just like, 'Wow, this is kinda cool, in a weird sort of way.'" It was often disorganized, but from the standpoint of engineering, it was extremely liberating. At HP, Anne had well-defined roles and responsibilities; at Transmeta, she did whatever was needed. Anne was excited to work at Transmeta, and wanted the sense she could influence the technology—and she had the opportunity to do just that: when she joined Transmeta, it had fewer than two hundred people.

While she was at Transmeta, a few people she had known from her HP days had rounded up $9 million to create a company called Omnishift Technologies. They asked her to join. On the new company's first week, the entire team went to Fry's Electronics and bought computers. Omnishift built everything from scratch, and the product they built worked, but unfortunately, it didn't have a working business model. Omnishift was running out of money, and within twenty months, they folded.

VMware at that time was a start-up with fewer than two hundred employees. Friends of hers were working there, and Anne was hired in 2002.

"VMware's model combined the best elements of the first two start-ups I had been at. It was organized, like the second one, but there was a lot of flexibility, like the first one."

VMware had the added element of a female CEO: Diane Greene, who personally interviewed anyone who wanted to join the company. Anne was impressed with that, and with the fact that Diane was a mother. "I felt like, 'Wow, here is a person who *does* have it all. She is a technical person, she is a CEO, and she has kids.'" Anne doesn't have children of her own; she believed that, for herself, she would have had to sacrifice her engineering work to have children.

Anne was part of the performance team reporting to Ed Bugnion, one of the VMware founders. VMware had impressive female representation in both technical and management areas, and Anne felt it was a great place to work. Once there, her primary quest was, "How can I keep doing something where I feel like I can make a contribution and can learn?" This desire to contribute and learn has been a theme throughout her entire career.

After a few years with the performance team at VMware, Anne switched to the resource management team in order to return to development. At the tail end of her tenure with VMware, Anne was given the exceptional opportunity to work for the CTO office on a purely exploratory "moonshot project," one that isn't expected to generate near-term revenue or profits.

At this point, she had been at VMware for over thirteen years and was ready to shift gears. Even over the weekends, she found herself always thinking about VMware work; there was never time to learn about anything else. "I think a part of working that hard is that you feel a sense of loyalty—like you owe the company something—so you have to convince yourself that 'I should be well-informed about my field; even if it's not directly related to my job, I should be keeping myself up to date with these other things.'"

Although Anne was ready to move to a smaller company, she first took five months off to learn the Go programming language and take an online machine learning class at the California Institute of Technology (Caltech). After this break, she went to work for VeloCloud Networks, a cloud networking services company that simplifies branch-office wide area networking (WAN). "It's a small, fun place," Anne told me. "Lots of diversity regarding age and background. I have had a perfect time doing technical stuff. I feel like software development is a great career in general. It's a great career for women."

~ ~ ~

Anne doesn't believe any career is a bias-free meritocracy. "There is no such thing," she said. "I think there are a lot of challenges for women in the technical area, and it's both pretty obvious *and* subtle, but it's there. But if you push past these challenges, tech is a great career for women. I also believe you can have an impact, and it doesn't have to be a 'good old boys' club.'" To show women that they *can* do the work, can *thrive* in this career path, she has given several tutorials for the nonprofit CodeChix organization on Go, NodeJS, and JS.

When she graduated from college with her master's degree, she perceived the ratio of men to women in the tech field as being about 65%–35%.[18] Women seemed to be storming into the workplace, getting degrees in computer science as well as in medicine and law. Anne recalls a 65/35 ratio of men to women in her first job at HP. But over her career, Anne has watched the percentage of women in tech

18   In 1980, approximately 33% of undergraduate STEM majors were women; by 2014, women STEM undergrads were 17%. Women comprised 31% of computing occupations in 1985, reached 36% by 1991, and fell to 25% by 2015, where it remains as of 2017. (Source: *Women in Tech: The Facts, 2016 update*, National Center for Women & Information Technology)

decline. "It's almost like the dot-com boom sent the message that this was a guy thing—that wasn't true when I was in college."

With the release of the Pac-Man game, which featured an engaging digital creature, more women gamers emerged, and this finally got women interested in becoming developers. However, for a decade or more, the "good old boys' club" witnessed the decline of women working in the computer science field, which was a travesty.

~ ~ ~

Anne made the bold decision to take five months off after she quit VMware to simply learn more "technical stuff." I asked about her approach to learning. She sighed. "This is a challenge for me. Women are so busy; they have a job, family obligations."

This is an important point: work often becomes routine, and one can go for days without pushing oneself to learn new things. Anne, however, reports that she gets "antsy" when she falls into a routine. When this happens, she makes it a point to learn something new, despite the challenges. "It could be better to be more disciplined about learning—to set aside a certain amount of time for it." One way she learns is by networking. She is active in conferences, and on program committees reviewing papers. There, she is forced to read around twenty-five papers annually. "It's sometimes valuable to be a dumb newbie in a team, as that will force you to learn," she points out. "You have to push through that discomfort. It's almost like you become so antsy that you are willing to be a newbie, because otherwise you get bored."

~ ~ ~

Although I never had the opportunity to work with Anne when we were both employed at VMware, I certainly knew of her—most of the engineering women there did. She was the first female principal engineer (PE) at VMware to rise up the ranks from software engineer. This is a difficult level to achieve, and Anne took longer than most to be promoted. She was a senior staff engineer for seven years before she became PE. Wondering why it had taken her so long to become a PE, I asked how she had managed her VMware career growth. She said she was clueless; she hadn't focused on the VMware process of being promoted.

HP had a clear promotion process. When she left HP, and joined her first start-up, she assumed that to get a promotion, "you just work as hard as you can, and you learn things, and everything kinda just works out." Which turned out to be true, even at VMware—for a while. When she joined VMware, everybody was MTS (a member of technical staff), and there was no technical ladder. Again, she figured she would just learn things, and would be given more responsibility.

In the mid-2000s, VMware introduced the technical ladder, and Anne was promoted to staff. At that point, "I felt a little lost, a little antsy," she recalled. "I was a little stuck, growth-wise, and I didn't know how to fix it. The way I fixed it was by changing teams." Right after she changed teams, her first manager made sure she was promoted to the senior staff level. Anne felt bad about that; her manager had done all the work to promote her, even though she had left the team. Then, when she moved, she keenly felt her lack of direct experience in the new team's field. She asked to be downgraded, explaining to her new manager that she didn't deserve to be at a higher level than the others in the team. She suggested to him that she preferred to work herself back up. He replied that he was planning to promote others on the team.

By now, this story has made clear that Anne is an introvert who doesn't step forward to take credit for her work. One notable fact is that she didn't have mentors or sponsors who could help her think differently and guide her. Thus, she stayed in that senior staff role for seven years. On the positive side, she knew that since they had promoted her to senior staff, they were queuing her up to become a PE. She watched as her peers made that transition, but Anne hadn't figured out what to do in order to take the leap to principal engineer.

Finally, Anne did discuss promotion with her manager, but realized the interpersonal dynamics within that team were working against her. But a reorganization changed the dynamics. Her new manager, who had also been her first manager there, asked Anne why she hadn't been put up for PE. Anne replied that she truly did not understand why not. This time, she had a manager who stood up for her. "I am putting you up for PE. There are no guarantees, and it's a complicated process, but whatever happens, you will get good feedback—which is better than no feedback." Anne subsequently became VMware's first female principal engineer. This action sent a message of hope to all the other technical women at VMware. We had a role model in Anne.

From her current perspective, Anne now says, "A technical person needs to manage their career" to resolve stagnation and achieve success. I would add that in my experience as well, this is so true. If you don't ask and don't keep persisting, you will not be able to move the needle forward when it comes to your career.

Between 2012 and 2015, Anne oversaw senior staff promotions in her role as PE. Only one female engineer was promoted during her tenure. Anne saw some instances of talented women not being nominated. "You want the managers to put these women up for promotion," Anne said. "On the other hand, you also need to make the women aware that they need to ask for the promotion. Guys will ask, and if the manager says 'No,' they will just keep asking every year. This plants a little seed in the manager's brain." Referring to her experience, Anne added, "I don't tend to ask 'til it's really late. I never asked before that time. Again, I had this feeling that I would do this great job, and a promotion would just be natural." *This is a meritocratic narrative.*

Anne also had a hard time taking credit for her work. She believes that engineering is a team effort, and found it awkward that a particular individual would be singled out to be promoted over the others. She was sensitive about one person being given special treatment, so she always gave credit to the team to avoid claims that she was appropriating the credit.

An incident she experienced at HP sparked her concern about this. She was presenting at a meeting and got feedback that one of her colleagues felt she had taken credit for his work. "I felt horrible about that, because I hadn't thought about the situation that way at all," she said. "My core value was to *not* take credit for other people's work, so I never thought about that before." She addressed that person: "I screwed up here, because I heard from these sources that you are concerned that I am taking credit for this work. I certainly recognize that you did these things." It was a harrowing experience for her, which drove her to the other extreme: she doesn't take individual credit for her work, attributing it all to her team. This was one of the factors for the delay in her promotion to PE. There was always a "we did it" message in her accomplishments and not an "I did it." Anne still believes that everything is a team effort and not about one individual. I have to agree with her, but at the same time, I do believe it's important to take credit when it is yours. I've noticed that men typically don't hesitate to do so and there is absolutely nothing wrong with that.

Anne has been in several promotion meetings in which a strong team has done impactful work, and the manager has decided to put up a particular individual from that team for promotion. Everyone knows that that person was not the only reason the project was successful. Of course, gender bias comes into play here. "I often feel that managers favor guys over girls in this situation, especially when the guy is always asking to be promoted."

On the flip side, Anne has also been in promotion meetings where people are questioning if a person *really* did do the work to get promoted, knowing full well that everyone in that room probably got promoted at one time for something where they got more credit than they were due. "It's kind of like bicycling, when you have that group of people and they are shielding the one person so that they can draft[19] and move ahead; you've got to make sure that this method doesn't just work for the guys and that sometimes, the drafting is for the gals."

Some of Anne's other roadblocks with promotions and growth stem from the ubiquitous experience of imposter's syndrome. She feels uncomfortable in situations where she perceives her knowledge of a subject to be far below where it needs to be.

"I would call it a certain amount of insecurity. What I have noticed is that when I feel insecure, I respond defensively. When you are defensive, it's tough to learn, and it makes teamwork difficult. If I feel I don't know enough to do this job, I try to go into a disciplined mode where I am just going to have to suck it up. I am going to have to ask a bunch of stupid questions, and I hate that, but there is just no way around it."

She tends to get quiet if she thinks she doesn't know enough, but she has seen other people successfully push through that situation. When people are often quiet in discussions or meetings, it gives the impression that they know little about the topic. Many women don't speak up in meetings, which sometimes reflects poorly on them. Anne thinks that men tend to figure out a way to be visible in meetings by speaking up, even if their knowledge on the subject is scanty.

"When I was a kid, I thought the way careers worked is that you learn stuff, become senior in your area, and then help other people. I saw that in my teachers and professors. I hoped that's how my career would go—that I would become an expert." When you become an expert at something, that area often becomes a "brownfield" or retread, which no one wants to invest in, so then you have to learn something new, making you a newbie again. "It has always been this period of profound ignorance. I never achieve the nirvana where, since I know everything about this field, I just dispense knowledge." That's not the way engineering works.

---

19   In bicycling, a bicyclist drafts by riding behind another cyclist to expend less energy; this yields up to a 27% reduction in wind for the drafter.

While she's fearless and always willing to try something new, Anne described one instance where she experienced acute imposter's syndrome. She was asked to be a manager at HP because they thought she was a conscientious team player. Anne spent a year managing three team members who were dealing with serious personal problems. She told me it was "the worst time of my life. I felt concerned for these people's careers, and the challenges they faced. I felt like a fraud. I thought, 'I am here to help people develop their career. I am supposed to be motivating them.' It was a struggle. The whole thing was very stressful, and I felt like an imposter."

What about her experience with her technical peers? "I feel like there is an unconscious bias, that guys are assumed to know more than girls in the same situation," Anne notes. "Many times, when I would say something, people would act like they hadn't heard. Ten minutes later, a guy would say the same thing and everybody would glom onto it. I would be really pissed." She wondered if people really couldn't hear her, or something else was going on. It was challenging for Anne to deal with. Sometimes she would speak louder, but didn't want to sound resentful (even though she was). "You don't want to shut everything down to the point where people think, 'she's so hard to deal with.' Sometimes people will point the situation out to the others, and that is more effective."

This concern about not being heard is a widespread fear among women; a phenomenon deeply rooted in gender bias and the threat of stereotyping—it's ingrained in our society. Women's usual style of speaking is often viewed (by men) as not conveying confidence, which leads (men) to believing women are not competent. When women do speak up, either they are talked over or are perceived as aggressive. Thus, women learn not to speak up until they know a subject inside out, likely due to fear of the bias against women, as well as a learned fear of failure.

If you notice a woman's voice is not being heard, intervene. As Anne reminds us, that woman probably has something meaningful and impactful to say.

~ ~ ~

TAKEAWAYS

• Anne had supportive parents, was good at math as a child, and was encouraged in the competitive aspect of her nature.

• She made a conscious choice to prioritize her engineering career over becoming a mom.

• She witnessed a gradual decline in the percentage of women throughout her career, especially during the dot-com boom.

• She thinks about work a lot, which she attributes to a sense of company and team loyalty. She has to scramble to make time for learning on her schedule.

• She did not take deliberate steps to manage her growth and development for quite a while.

• Unconscious bias often meant that Anne felt her voice wasn't heard, or was valued less than those of a man.

SPEAK UP FOR YOURSELF

Some of the women profiled in this book are excellent negotiators for their company and their teams, but not for themselves. Women's reluctance to self-advocate is not so much a "classic female trait" as it is the way we are brought up to be. We are taught to think of ourselves as providers.

In the workplace, too many women feel it would be shameful to ask for more pay or to demand a salary commensurate with their worth. This stems from a tradition of discouraging women from feeling important, from "taking up space," and from not remaining passive. This is not an inherent predisposition.

I have seen that women often won't consider applying for a promotion until they have achieved 100% of the next position's requirements, whereas it's far more common for men to go after a new position, even when they meet only half the requirements. I fully support men who strive for promotions, but I feel that many women need to shift their mindset and begin asking for promotions sooner rather than later.

In the book *Women Don't Ask*,[20] Linda Babcock and Sara Laschever concluded that by not negotiating her starting salary for her first job, a woman leaves over half a million dollars on the table by the end of her career. Their research has revealed that men with the same qualifications are four times more likely to ask for higher pay. Often, women don't even realize they can ask. For most young women, graduating from school and landing a job is so exciting that they tend to not negotiate at all, for fear that they might lose the offer.

Women have been operating like this for years; they are reluctant to advocate for themselves. This behavior reflects societal training and gender stereotypes. Women are thought to be more oriented toward accommodating others. When women do ask for a promotion or a raise,

---

20 Linda Babcock and Sarah Laschever, *Women Don't Ask: Negotiation and the Gender Divide* (Princeton University Press, 2003).

they often are aware that they are deviating from the expectations ingrained in our society. Hence their reluctance.

However, things are improving. There is much more awareness of gender inequality and stereotyping, and professional women are starting to ask for what they deserve. Time and again, women are successful when they advocate for themselves and take a stand against injustices. Most times, these injustices are committed unconsciously. Each time women bring awareness to the inequality to correct it, they are helping other women.

~ ~ ~

To obtain what you deserve, defining exactly what you want is crucial. Pam Kostka (chapter 2) mentioned her personal goal of becoming a vice president by the time she turned thirty. Pam defined what she wanted, and it happened to her!

When I look back at my career, I didn't define what I wanted. I drifted along, taking whatever opportunity came my way, focusing only on doing the best job I could. I didn't think it was possible to define what I wanted. I didn't think I had possibilities. I now think that women and men who define what they want tend to be more successful, because the moment they define their goal and visualize it they can start to make it a reality. It also means they are taking charge of their career and holding themselves accountable.

Speaking up for yourself is the next critical component.

What I've observed, both throughout my own career and while conducting interviews with the women who contributed to this book, is that strong self-advocacy is often a challenge for women. When women negotiate hard for themselves, they tend to be labeled as aggressive. Yet, if a woman doesn't self-advocate aggressively, then chances are quite high that she will be offered less than she deserves. We are passed up for promotions and are paid less than our male counterparts, in part because we don't put our needs first. For many of us, it feels selfish to ask, even though taking care of ourselves allows us to take care of others too.

I often draw an analogy between self-advocacy and the required action during cabin depressurization on an airplane. In the event of depressurization, we are instructed to put our own oxygen mask on immediately, before helping others—even our own children. By doing so, the chances of effectively assisting others, and possibly saving a life—increase. The same thing goes with negotiating for yourself in terms of compensation and benefits. Placing your own needs first isn't selfish. It helps you to survive and thrive, and by doing so, it gives you more of an opportunity to help others.

I have my own story about traditional gender roles and self-advocacy. My husband is a stay-at-home dad to our three children. He thinks it's the best job he's ever had, and he loves it. One day he suggested that I pay him for taking care of our kids. He was serious. He feels that taking care of them is a full-time job. I can't argue against that, but I truly didn't know how to respond. My first thought was: *Has there ever been a woman on this planet who asked to be paid for taking care of her own children?* I am also sure that if the roles were reversed in our household, I would never have asked my husband to pay me for taking care of our kids; in fact, the thought would not have crossed my mind. Child-rearing would have been my unquestioned duty.

However, it would be great if more women thought as my husband did. His request wasn't selfish—it was fair. How many women dedicate their lives to their kids and family, only to have the partner leave, getting stuck with no money, no career, or worse, no education? If you are a stay-at-home mom, I suggest that you think about mustering the courage to ask your spouse for financial compensation. It's only fair.

CHAPTER 7: PATTY'S STORY

BIOSKETCH: *Patty Hatter is poised and confident. Rising through the ranks to become a senior vice president of Intel Security/McAfee, today she is a strategic advisor and investor to venture capitalists (VCs) and tech start-ups. She brings a Zen-like attitude to both her personal and professional life, recognizing a natural ebb and flow to work and family. When a situation at home comes up, she prioritizes it over her work life, and vice versa. "Everything is temporary," she says, so we shouldn't worry too much about things. She believes we have many interesting problems to solve, and we need both men and women to do so. "Different people just naturally bring different skills and insights to the table. That's the whole notion around diversity. That's what diversity is all about," says Patty, who supports diversity and believes in the value it brings to an organization.*

"Play broader, think bigger, get a bigger picture. It's incumbent on you to know more folks across the organization and play broader. It's going to make you better in whatever role you are in. I do think there are things in people's heads regarding the roles females should play, and how ready they need to be to move into different roles, but as we move through that as a society—instead of wringing your hands about it, and saying 'It's not fair'—it is what it is. You can take control and decide what steps you can take to keep moving forward."

— Patty Hatter, strategic advisor and
investor to VCs and tech start-ups

~ ~ ~

A lot of what made Patty the person she is today, and what enabled her to take risks early on in her career, has to do with her upbringing in a Pittsburgh suburb. Patty's dad is an engineer. Between Patty and her dad, they've earned four engineering degrees. Her mother stopped working as a secretary to raise Patty and her sister. Interestingly, her mother was better in math and science than Patty, and was one of the most brilliant people Patty has ever known. She always felt fortunate that she had encouragement from both her parents. Their message was, "Go. Go, you can do this." Patty's positive upbringing helped her grow into a confident person. Consequently, she has tremendous respect for people who are successful, despite discouragement from their family and society.

Her husband always jokes that she grew up in a bubble; however, Patty thinks of it as a "magical bubble," in which everybody was encouraged to do their best. Throughout her childhood, she never felt "girls do this, boys do that" from her parents or her community. In high school, she believed girls could do whatever they set their minds to. Gender never got in the way of her dreams and aspirations.

As a teen, Patty was an "all-rounder" who worked hard and was involved in many activities. Her mother had a rule: as long as Patty was busy with her studies, sports, and music (she played in the orchestra), she didn't have to get a job. But she always knew her first priority was to *finish* studying.

Patty's first experience with limitations on what "girls can do" was in her freshman year at Carnegie Mellon University, where she was working toward an engineering degree. She remembers this moment vividly. She met a young male student. At their first meeting, he said, "Patty, I consider you a friend of mine, so I am trying to help you here. You must not know this, but girls don't do engineering. Before you waste more money going down this path, you should think about your alternatives." Patty, who feels like she's had a lucky life because she was constantly encouraged, responded, "Thanks for the input. I think I'm good, but I appreciate your concern." Patty ended up on the dean's list, while her new male "friend" failed out of school by spring that year.

"I certainly wouldn't have gone through Carnegie Mellon University saying, 'I can do it' if I hadn't had my family's support. Some people are raised in families where there isn't time to be encouraging, or even worse, where females are explicitly discouraged—but they still rise through it. The will power that takes! It humbles me that people can succeed despite that situation."

"By the time you are in college, the die is cast. You are on whatever path you are going to be on," Patty says. Despite the cautionary concern of that young man, she had immense, unshakable confidence in herself. When you meet Patty, you can sense she is extremely sure of herself. "In grad school at Carnegie Mellon University, I was the only woman for miles in an engineering graduate program. But that didn't strike me as odd, because what I heard during my formative years was, 'You can do it.' So, it didn't occur to me that I couldn't do it."

Patty's first job right out of graduate school was at Bell Labs in New Jersey. As a rookie engineer, she was fortunate to be placed with a boss who turned out to be her sponsor. As Patty puts it, he "put me on a path." He wasn't tangled in office politics, but stayed focused on doing the right thing for the business. As he and Patty worked on numerous projects together, he tossed her any challenging problem to solve, regardless of how young or inexperienced she felt she was.

One moment with this boss that set the course for the rest of her career occurred when she arrived at work one morning. "I am living in New Jersey at the time. I come into work on a Monday, and he calls me into his office. 'Patty, I have this great idea. You go to Europe and build a business like this one we are building here in the US. You build it, you make money, you come back here. That's my plan.' I was so naïve. I figured I could figure it out."

Her boss's idea sounded like a good plan. He had faith in her, and most importantly, she had faith in herself, even though there were a few factors working against this venture. This business had only recently gotten started in the United States, so at such an early stage it would not be easily replicated in Europe. Moreover, her experience of Europe was composed of four days on vacation in Munich. But she took a huge risk and a leap of faith and said to her boss, "Okay, sure."

This opportunity was like a blank sheet of paper, with a big company brand like AT&T and Bell Labs backing her. The experience she gained in this endeavor, starting something from scratch, turned out to be fantastic and set the tone for everything else she's done in her career. For the next three years, she built Bell Labs offices in three different countries—the United Kingdom, the Netherlands, and Norway—gaining cross-functional experience by partnering with the sales teams in each office. She knew that after succeeding in that experience, nothing else would be as hard. Then it felt like time for her to return home.

But before she got back to the United States, she was offered a different role in Europe, and ended up staying for three more years. It was a great business opportunity and offered personal and career development in new markets. This new assignment gave her even more resources to continue to develop the business she started over the past three years. She was able to continue to scale the business, manage an increasingly large P&L, and grow the customer base. In this role, Patty's clients were all male, so it was an important developmental opportunity for her to find a way to work well with these customers, even with the gender difference and age difference. In this situation, it did help coming from a US-based company. There was a view that the US-based companies had different rules. Many European clients told her, "This isn't how we do it, but I respect the fact that your company sent you here to do this job, so let's get on with it."

"You have to take opportunities when they present themselves. You can't overthink everything. When I went to work on that Monday in New Jersey, was I thinking, 'Hey, I am moving to Europe'? No—if I had a million guesses of what I would be doing next, that would not have been one of them. But it was a great opportunity. I figured, 'What is the worst that could happen?' The worst is I learn a lot, and maybe we can't grow the business, but even that would still put me ahead. And it was a great experience, and I learned the connection of how to make something from very little. If you don't have a big base, how do you get creative on the resources? How do you network? How do you pull people with different skills together? How do you approach a business opportunity with an open mind?"

Patty has not made any career moves that she regrets. "You can always learn something," she says. "You're always moving forward in one way or another. It might not be exactly what you expected, but as long as you are learning, you are progressing. Whatever has happened in the past is done. It's all good. It got you to where you are. There is nothing to worry about."

What Patty says here is extremely important. Many opportunities come our way, and sometimes we shy away from them for reasons best known to us. The people who have the most success are the ones who jump on opportunities and take the big risks. Big risks yield big rewards. The opportunity to go to Europe and build a business at that young age helped Patty get to the place she is today.

Patty brings a glass-half-full perspective to her work environment. When she is thrown into a challenging situation, or forced out of her comfort zone, she figures that she just has more work to do. She works extremely hard and trusts herself to eventually figure things out. Patty also relies on her late mother's advice, listening to her mother's voice in her head, encouraging her to keep going and trust herself.

Knowing that not everyone has such a lucky childhood as she had, Patty gives back to the community through her nonprofit work. For example, she is on the board of the Silicon Valley Foundation, where she works to empower the next generation, either early in their careers or early in school.

~ ~ ~

"I would say the one thing about moving to different continents, and between East Coast and West Coast, is that you do lose a lot of your network. You have to start it up again, you have to keep building your network actively. I value mentors and a support framework. You have to figure out how to find them, even as you move from company to company and country to country."

Patty urges women to be proactive in consciously building connections, especially when in a new country or a new company. With so much change in her work life, Patty quickly honed her skills at reading situations and understanding the political landscape, so that she could jump right in and add value from the get-go.

When you are in the tech world and live in a hub like Silicon Valley, it's easier to keep your network, even when you move from one company to another, because your network is local to one area. For larger moves, her advice is to quickly find your center of gravity and build a network of people whom you can trust and reach out to for advice.

Many successful women have male mentors, because there are more men than women in high positions. It was not surprising to find that Patty had male mentors for the most part. "Most of the people I have worked with, and for, are men. Women need to get used to finding relationships and bonds not with just women, but also with the men they are working with."

Since awareness is growing among women about unconscious bias, and discussions about gender diversity are taking place in the workplace, more women are supporting other women. Patty had some good thoughts on this. "I do think there is something to the observation that women are used to being the only woman in the room. And suddenly when there are two or three women, you see some women struggle with the change in dynamics. I think we need women encouraging other women. You have to figure out how to make all boats rise together, in that case. But it's a journey. It's not how everybody naturally thinks."

~ ~ ~

Even though Patty has high confidence and doesn't suffer from imposter syndrome, she did leave some money on the table by not negotiating before her first job.

"Yes, women lose out on a lot of money. I still feel that women have to prove that they have already done the job they are moving into. And the same goes for salary. It's, 'Well, prove that you are worth more, and we will give you more.' It can be a crazy circle. You just have to be willing to have those conversations."

Over the years, Patty has gotten better at having those tough conversations. "I feel good as long I am willing to have the conversation with my boss about whether my compensation is appropriate for my role." Although it's hard to pinpoint the right compensation number, Patty says that just getting that conversation off your chest can make you feel good, regardless of the outcome.

"When I was starting out, I had zero sense of what people were getting paid. I grew up thinking that everything was fair and equal. It took me a while to realize that maybe life wasn't equitable. I hadn't thought about that before. It was so ingrained that 'everything is fair.' But once you are in the work world, you start to see that there are disparities, and you have to advocate for yourself in unexpected ways."

Many talented people do great work but are not getting the visibility they need to succeed. "You must get yourself in a position where you are recognized for your abilities, where you are advocating for yourself, where you have shown that you can do more. I guess it is a meritocracy, but a meritocracy where it takes advocating for yourself to get you where you want to be."

Patty advocated for herself in attaining promotions. Many women tend to shy away from promotion conversations with their bosses, but she approached it in an unusual way, by taking on more responsibilities. If a task needed to be done, she would collaborate and get it done. She didn't wait for permission. Before she knew it, Patty was operating at the next level. She kept moving along. The European experience at her first job helped her think big. Since the company was large and she was taking on challenges by building a business from scratch, she had to figure out how different parts of the organization fit together. Her close-knit career friends also thought big; many of them are women too. Patty explained: "Women tend to want to integrate things more. When you put a group of us together who were in that company at that time, all with the natural female inclination to synthesize, you get that mindset of thinking big."

~ ~ ~

It's hard to think big. Many people compartmentalize their job responsibilities when they are not thinking beyond them. Patty's encouragement to think big and play a broader role in one's organization is terrific, but it's hard for women to do that because typically we also have to shoulder a lot of responsibility at home. Work–life balance, as we all know, is often a struggle for women. "With family, there is always ebb and flow, times when things are a little more chaotic." When Patty's mom was sick in Pittsburgh, Pennsylvania, Patty flew from San Jose on a redeye flight once a week to visit her. That definitely introduced chaos, but it was necessary, and she knew that complaining wasn't going to help anything. To see herself through that time, she kept in mind that nothing is going to last forever. She wasn't her best at work during this difficult time, but she knew it was temporary.

"Now that I don't happen to have any odd family situations, I have doubled down on what I am doing here, so that means more work on nonprofits. And I just got appointed to a government subcommittee on security and privacy. Everybody has a certain number of hours that they can work in a day. Sometimes you are doing unusual things, like weekly flights back and forth to Pittsburgh, and that compresses what you can do at work, as well as outside activities."

During that period, Patty decided that her mom was her priority; work took a backseat. She has no regrets. "Decide what is important, be okay with that, and then prioritize." When an event occurs that is not in your control, and you need to pay attention to that situation, just do that. You can double down at work later. "One thing that I have gotten more comfortable with over the years is that nothing stays the same. You just have to go with the flow."

When she moved to California from the East Coast, Patty and her husband had no family in California except their five-month-old baby. Her husband was starting a company, and she was starting a job at a new company. They decided to get help. The truth is, if you want to succeed, you have to get comfortable asking for help. Patty joked that her best skill is asking for help. She and her husband found a live-in nanny, a huge relief for them. "You have to just to be honest with yourself as to where you need assistance. I do think women struggle with that."

She knows how to articulate her needs, but what about the glass ceiling? Too often, we have seen that women are judged on their performance, and men are judged on their potential. The bar is much higher for a woman. Patty agreed. "I still feel that there is a sense that women have to prove that they are already doing the job they are trying to move into. There is more of a natural inclination to give a little more leeway to male colleagues."

How do we overcome this? Patty offers several recommendations. First, play a broader role in your company, no matter what your current job is. She firmly believes that eventually things will start getting better and there will be equality. But today, women must frequently prove that we can already do a job or a role before we officially get it.

Networking is key. It's critical to keep building your network, and you should strive to know people across your organization.

Expanding on creating a network within your company, understand how all the pieces in your organization fit together and figure out how you can make the pieces come together differently. "I do think there are assumptions in everyone's mind regarding the roles women should play, and how ready they need to be to move into different roles. But as we progress as a society, instead of wringing our hands about it, and saying it's not fair, we must accept that it just is what it is and consider what steps we can take to move through that anyway. I just naturally spread out in an organization—that's how I like to work." When you do that, it helps you prove your competency, and you end up accelerating your career path.

"I've seen women quietly opt out of progressing their careers. Many women are highly educated, do well in school, have a lot to contribute. But after they have kids, many opt out. I feel that is bad for society. We have so many big problems we need to solve. We need everybody in the game. It pains me to see women who think, 'I am stuck at this level because I want to balance my kids and work.' Part of the problem is a real challenge, yes, but part of it is their own internal conflict."

Much of the internal conflict we experience occurs because we want to do everything perfectly. We want to be great mothers, and we also want to be successful at work. And we can't have both, right? No, we can have both. There just needs to be a give-and-take along the way. As Patty's story shows us, there is an ebb and flow to work and family. Sometimes work has to take the higher focus, and sometimes family needs to be made the higher priority.

"To boil it down to one thing I see all the time, especially among technical women: they talk themselves out of going after different jobs. This job requirement has maybe ten characteristics, and a woman thinks, 'I am just superlative at nine and a half of these characteristics. So, what I need to do, even before I apply for this job, is get another degree or study up on this characteristic; then, maybe, I can think about applying for a similar job in six months or a year.' This is craziness.

"Technical women are trained to be specific, particular, and exacting. These women want to be perfect. They are the ones who triple-checked their homework at school. At home, they make sure the laundry is perfectly done. When they get to work, they want things to be perfect. But what made you successful in school isn't going to make you successful at work. So be comfortable letting go, and tell yourself that you know enough and that you have the confidence to do whatever you are tasked to do.

"If there were one thing I could inject more of into the DNA of women, it would be: Just try."

~ ~ ~

TAKEAWAYS

- Patty is extremely confident; her parents and the community in which she grew up instilled this in her.

- Patty had a sponsor early on in her career: her boss, who believed in her and threw some challenging problems at her. He took a leap of faith that set the course for her career.

- The experience Patty had during her first three years in Europe, where she had to think big and start a business from scratch, influenced every career role she's had since.

- Patty is not one to have regrets, and is extremely positive about her life and work situations. She is well aware that nothing lasts forever.

- Patty doesn't suffer from imposter syndrome. She believes she can eventually figure out a situation.

- Patty's strongest advice for women is to stay the course when things get hard. There are challenges in this world, and everyone needs to help solve them.

CHAPTER 8: SHILPA'S STORY

BIOSKETCH: *Shilpa Lawande is a CEO and co-founder of the artificial intelligence start-up postscript.us in the healthcare space. An engineer and executive for several years, she developed the confidence to go out on her own. After graduating from IIT Bombay and the University of Wisconsin at Madison, both top schools, and while working as an engineer at Oracle, she made the bold decision to work at an early-stage start-up, Vertica Systems, where she went on to become vice president of engineering, running a 200+ person engineering organization. Though her decision was risky, it was also calculated, as she went to work for luminaries in the tech world. What gave her the confidence and experience needed to create her own new venture? Shilpa credits a strong network and her desire to always stretch her limits.*

"Always push your limits. Look for assignments or goals that will take you to the next level; don't be afraid to challenge and stretch yourself. Women often feel like they have to know everything before they take an opportunity, whereas men just jump on it. Raise your hand more often, and if you don't know something, trust that you will learn. Sometimes the only way to learn something is on the job."

— Shilpa Lawande, Founder, postscript.us (AI start-up)

~ ~ ~

Shilpa grew up in what she describes as a typical, highly academic family in India. Her father was a physicist, and her mother a math professor. Their careers inspired her early interest in science and math. An important influence in her life, they always encouraged her to have a career—but one that would allow her to spend time with her own family. They showed her that, while mothers play the central role in a family, fathers can also do their fair share in the kitchen and raising children. She was always encouraged to think for herself and express her opinions, even if different from theirs. Because she grew up with a working mother, and all of her aunts were working professionals as well, she was surrounded by strong female role models from the beginning.

Shilpa wanted to be a physicist like her dad, yet she also felt the urge to pursue a different path by attending one of the top IIT schools in India (Indian Institute of Technology). Admission into these schools is highly competitive, so Shilpa figured that if she didn't make it into an IIT, she would study physics.

The decision was made when she was admitted into IIT Mumbai with a high rank that permitted her to choose her major. Shilpa was deciding between computer science and engineering physics. Her dad encouraged her to major in CS for two practical reasons. "In your generation, everything will be done with computers," he said, "even physics." And a career in software offered a better work–life balance than running experiments in a research lab. Shilpa went with his advice and never regretted her decision (though she continues to read popular books on physics and enjoys astronomy as a hobby).

All students in Indian universities take the same courses in their first year. From the second year on, they specialize in their major. When Shilpa reached the second year of engineering, she was the only female student. I was curious as to why there were so few women in the IITs, given that so many women attend the local engineering colleges. Shilpa said, "My theory is that women have to leave their homes and reside in a boarding school in order to attend IITs, which goes against social norms. I think many parents discourage their daughters from doing that. In local and regional engineering colleges, which students attend from home, the ratio of men and women is closer to fifty-fifty."

The years at IIT were a formative experience for Shilpa. From the age of seventeen, she was the only woman technologist in any given room, which forced her to find her footing and hold her own among a group of brilliant guys. She felt fortunate to have classmates who were highly competitive and yet respectful! Even today, she counts her fellow CS students among her best friends and strongest network.

After completing her bachelor's degree in India, Shilpa came to the United States and earned a CS master's degree from the University of Wisconsin in Madison. Her first job was as an engineer at Oracle, where she became a key member of the Oracle Server Technologies group, co-authored several books, and received credit for a patent. After seven years there, Shilpa decided she was ready for a change.

She came across the small early-stage start-up Vertica Systems, founded by Mike Stonebraker, already a luminary in database systems (and later a Turing Award winner). There were only three people in the company when Shilpa joined Mike's start-up. "It was purely a leap of faith," she recalls. "It was intellectually challenging, that was the only reason I jumped on board. The way Mike pitched it to me was, 'I have no idea if we will succeed or fail, but at least we'll end up building an interesting system. How many people get to build a database from scratch?' Maybe I was young and foolish, but that one risky decision made my career."

Within a year of Shilpa joining Vertica, her boss decided to leave, so Shilpa offered to lead the engineering project until they found a replacement. CEO and co-founder Andy Palmer took a chance on Shilpa and let her do so. She made sure they did not have to hire that replacement! Andy has continued to be a key mentor throughout her career. The amount she learned from the Vertica experience was tremendous.

"I learned how the culture of a start-up comes to be, and how to build teams and rally them behind a mission—all the intangibles they don't teach you in school. Andy had a unique collection of advisors that I interacted with, and I learned a lot outside of my technology domain, about business and about people."

Over a six-year span with Vertica, her career continued to accelerate; she advanced to director and then to vice president of engineering. "Going from a well-established company like Oracle to a Big Data start-up in 2005 was the right decision. I was in the right place at the right time."

When Hewlett Packard (HP) bought Vertica Systems in 2011, Shilpa transferred to HP with her team. During those next four years at HP, Shilpa grew the team to several hundred and expanded her role beyond engineering to also include customer success. She was eventually responsible for the profit and loss (P&L) of the Big Data Platform business within HP.

In 2015, she departed HP to start her own venture, an early-stage artificial intelligence start-up in the healthcare field. Her experience at Vertica and HP built her confidence to move into a venture on her own in a completely new industry vertical.

After her ten years at Vertica/HP and before beginning the new company, Shilpa felt she had the perfect opportunity to do something different. Her older child would be starting kindergarten in eight months, so it was time to tilt her balance toward family for an extended period. She and her husband incorporated travel, learning, and adventure on a five-month tour of five Asian countries: India, Myanmar, Thailand, Indonesia, and Borneo. "It was a tremendous learning experience for my kids, who were ages five and three, and in turn for me to experience the joys and challenges of full-time parenting."

After this break, Shilpa was ready to start a business from scratch. She believes strongly in the importance of trying new things. "Everything is a risk, I have come to realize. Not doing anything different from what you are already doing is a bigger risk. I always like to push my limits a little, and I felt that starting my own company was the right thing for me to do at this time."

While she was growing up, Shilpa viewed success as achieving a particular goal, such as getting into the IIT. But today she views success as a journey. "Success is waking up every day and feeling like you are making an impact in people's lives, personally and professionally. Success is feeling that there's an ongoing purpose and passion to your life, rather than the pursuit of any particular event or accomplishment." Shilpa feels successful, but more importantly, she feels fortunate that she has enjoyed both her work and her home life. Her biggest cheerleader is her husband, who is now supporting her as she goes out on her own to start a company. "It is almost impossible to have a career and a family if both partners are not supporting each other," Shilpa believes. "My husband is also a technologist. We went to IIT together, so it's great to talk work stuff with him."

~ ~ ~

Diversity and inclusion are dear to her heart. While Shilpa herself felt, at the start of our discussion, that she had not experienced overt gender bias, she does believe that both men and women exhibit certain behaviors that can contribute to gender inequality. When she was at HP, she formed a group (following the model of Sheryl Sandberg's Lean In movement[21]) for women to discuss their experiences as professional women and other issues related to gender in the workplace.

She described two moments arising out of this group that cemented her views on why such networking groups are a critical resource for women. After their first gathering, where they discussed Sandberg's views on leaning in, one woman approached her afterward. "That position that we just opened, why wasn't I considered?" Shilpa was surprised to hear that this woman was interested in the position. "It was an indirect sort of exclusion, because it never occurred to me or to this person's manager that she might be interested in a management role. She had never brought it up before." It turned out that she was a great fit for the position, and she eventually got the job. For Shilpa, this illustrated one common behavior of women that contributes to what holds women back: they often don't speak up for roles they might want because they expect others to know of their interest and to ask them.

The other moment involved a woman who successfully renegotiated her compensation during her promotion process, since she would now have additional responsibilities. Her forthrightness was a direct result of the awareness and mentoring that happened within that networking group. "A lot of gender bias is overt, but not always. Often women assume that if they just do the best job, good things will happen for them. It doesn't work like that in the workplace. That has been a learning experience for me. I now try hard to bring this awareness to my colleagues and the women who work for me."

In connection with this, Shilpa also feels that women—including herself—often don't take sufficient credit for their own work, a

---

[21]   Sheryl Sandberg, in her book *Lean In: Women, Work and the Will to Lead* (New York: Knopf, 2013), explores why women remain underrepresented in the global workforce and how to change this phenomenon.

situation that can go against them. "When someone compliments me, I tend to brush it off and say, 'Oh, it was the team.' I see that behavior often. Sometimes that comment sticks in other people's heads and creates the false impression that you didn't contribute much, and eventually, in a decision-making moment, you might get passed over."

These examples of unconscious bias cause women to work harder so they can prove themselves beyond a shadow of a doubt. Shilpa agreed. "Men are oblivious to or willing to overlook a lot of aggressive behaviors in other men because they are just like each other, predominantly men in high positions. When ambitious women do those same things, they stick out and may be labeled as bossy. As a minority in tech, women are always swimming against the current." Speaking of this reminded Shilpa of a comment she has heard repeatedly from men who attend the Grace Hopper Celebrations. "For these men, it is like an epiphany: 'I'm the only guy here, and there are so many women around me—now I understand what women in tech must feel like all the time!'" Their discomfort gives them a glimpse of how women have felt for years about being minority members in the tech arena.

As our discussion of gender bias deepened, Shilpa recalled more personal examples from her own experience. When negotiating her first job at Oracle, she isn't sure she got the best possible offer. Because she found the work she was offered so compelling, she didn't push hard on the terms. Today, she is more aware that she needs to drive a hard bargain, just as men do.

While Shilpa was running the engineering group, she noted that her team had better diversity overall than most teams, and there was no discrimination regarding salary, yet they struggled to find a sufficient number of female candidates. During performance reviews, she found herself confronting labels of assertiveness or aggressiveness. She determined to take this as constructive feedback.

"I have realized about communication styles that it is not about how you communicate, but about how other people hear you. I have learned that you have to understand communication styles appropriately. In particular settings, I have to be aggressive, or else I won't get a word in. In some situations, I am too aggressive, and no one else gets a word in. You have to balance."

~ ~ ~

Shilpa, like most of the women in this book, was mentored by and large by men, with the exception of one amazing executive coach she had during the early Vertica days. She has, however, formed a strong peer group of female leaders in the Boston area, where she now lives. Shilpa reaches out to them for advice, support, and networking. "I hope the women in the group that I created at HP can also be role models for others," she added. "I hope that by setting up these networks of women, we change the status quo of not having female role models and mentors."

As invaluable as it is for women to build our own networks, other forces come into play in women's struggle to build social capital. Women still tend to play the primary role in nuclear families. Between the responsibilities of work and home, they rarely have time to network and hang out with colleagues outside of the work environment. "The relationships you build in those outside settings are not as strong for women as they are for men who have wives at home taking care of their kids. Men have more free time, which allows them more opportunities to interact socially." Of course, some women are helped by husbands who support their high-level careers. Drawing from her own experience, however, Shilpa remarked that it is still extraordinarily challenging to work full-time when you have young kids, especially in a job that requires travel.

"Working full-time and being a parent for the past couple of years has been incredibly draining. You feel as if you are always running and you experience stress from both sides. As a working mother, you often end up feeling like you are not doing a good job in either role, while in reality you are doing the best job possible. It is important to keep in perspective that we only have our kids at home for twenty years, and we have our career for way longer than that. You need to find a way to harmonize the time and effort spent on both."

The disparity in family obligations based on gender is pervasive. Shilpa pointed to one notable article on this topic, "Why Women Still Can't Have It All," written by Anne-Marie Slaughter, an international lawyer, foreign policy analyst, political scientist, and public commentator.[22] Slaughter believes that instead of asking women to lean in, we have to challenge the social norms that exist today. Instead of trying to fit into a man's world, women must insist on changing social policies and career tracks to accommodate their choices.

And yes, of course there is a glass ceiling, Shilpa maintains. "The problem is that there are not a lot of women in the pipeline, all the way from college to entry level, mid-level, and senior positions, so it feels like women can't move any further. We need to increase the numbers of women at every level. The fact that more women than men drop out or are filtered out of the field at every level is also a problem. I don't know that there is a deliberate glass ceiling, but there is definitely an imbalance."

~ ~ ~

Shilpa proposes a three-part approach to getting more women into the tech field. First, "When children are younger, expose them to opposite gender models, like seeing their father in the kitchen, so they don't automatically associate certain roles with gender. This is equally important for boys to see as for girls. Girls should be raised to be confident that they can be what they want to be, and not be or do something just because society expects them to. For example, I do not wear any makeup or jewelry. I made that decision many years ago, and I am entirely comfortable with that. My husband cooks

22 Anne-Marie Slaughter, "Why Women Still Can't Have It All," *The Atlantic* (July/ August 2012): 84–102.

dinner most nights. This type of reverse modeling will go a long way in changing social norms."

Shilpa's second proposal is to do more to encourage women from high school to graduate levels to take STEM courses and enter STEM fields. In the transition to middle school, gender-specific labels tend to creep in and discourage girls from pursuing STEM fields, for fear of being labeled a "geek" or "not cool." As parents, educators, and tech professionals, we have to be watchful that this doesn't happen with our daughters. Education brings the credibility, knowledge, and rigor that one needs to succeed. Although this book contains one example of a woman who didn't finish college (Christine in chapter 11), for the most part we have seen that education sets a woman up for success.

Third, Shilpa stresses the importance of creating a supportive environment for women, which she's been fortunate to have had throughout her career. She described the goals at both Vertica and HP: "Make sure the interview panel is diverse. That encourages women to take the job. When we interview women, we have one or two women on the panel. Offer mentors and a support framework for women so they can be retained in the workplace. Ensure that women have the right support when they decide to have kids, such as flexible hours and a mother's room. This is the time when women are at risk for dropping out of the workforce." Having women on the interview panel is key, to illustrate that they will have other women as coworkers. And having children should not be a barrier to career growth and development.

Lastly, Shilpa offered this advice to female leaders: Always push your limits. Look for assignments or goals that will take you to the next level. Don't be afraid to challenge and stretch yourself.

"Women often feel like they have to know everything before they take an opportunity, whereas men just jump on it. Raise your hand more often, and if you don't know something, trust that you will learn. Sometimes the only way to learn something is on the job."

When she was first asked to run the engineering team at Vertica Systems, she had no idea how to do so, but she seized the opportunity and learned as she went. That was probably the best decision she ever made, because by the end of her tenure as VP and the experience of running an engineering team, she had the confidence to start her own company. Seizing opportunities that come our way, and most importantly, not allowing feelings of uncertainty and fear of the unknown to deter us from achieving our dreams and aspirations, will open up a whole new world, just as it did for Shilpa.

~ ~ ~

TAKEAWAYS

- Shilpa's parents were her biggest inspiration, as they worked in math and science. They were also her early role models for how both genders can share responsibility for household work.

- She took a risk with a start-up company, which greatly accelerated her career.

- It is crucial that women pay attention to the ways in which our behaviors limit our opportunities for growth and advancement; to change such patterns requires awareness.

- Amazing mentors helped her learn the "intangibles" that you can't learn from a book. That encouraged her to venture out on her own.

- She believes networking groups are a critical resource for women.

- Shilpa believes in stretching beyond your limits and taking on challenges.

GIRLS IN TECH

Women are routinely discouraged from pursuing math and science. We get so many messages that math and science are not the "typical" things for a girl to study. The fact that by 1985 about 37% of the CS graduates in the United States were women[23] becomes an impressive statistic, given the general lack of support for girls in the hard sciences. Women who studied or worked in computer fields in the 1970s recall having numerous women around them in those years.

That was then; this is now. Many more women were getting CS degrees and working in tech companies in the 1970s and 1980s than today. "Now" seems to have begun right after 1985, when the percentage of women working in tech began declining significantly. I was born in the 1970s, and in the current workforce, I often find myself the only woman in a meeting.

Why? I think it's the way the computer culture evolved that sent the wrong message to girls. In chapter 1, Telle Whitney describes the evolution of computer culture in her story. She attributes the cultural shift to the gaming industry, which generated a masculine culture based on the types of games that were being made in the seventies and eighties by male developers and gamers. This discouraged a lot of women from pursuing a CS career. As Telle explained to me: "In the early eighties, the PC came out, along with games, so computers came to be more associated with boys. This created a significant image problem for girls going into CS. So, these days, only about 18% of CS graduates are women."

As we wonder why so few women choose to study CS or work in tech, my own experience tells me that a healthy environment balancing learning and growth opportunities, a push to excel, and respect from co-workers are key for women (or any minority group) to thrive. I started programming in tenth grade, around the late eighties, just

---

23   Taken from http://www.computerscience.org/resources/women-in-computer-science/.

when computers were becoming popular in mainstream culture. This helped me to choose software development as a profession. Another encouragement was the Pac-Man game. With the release of Pac-Man in 1980, which featured an engaging digital creature, more female gamers emerged. This finally got some women interested in becoming developers.

Some would argue that women's brains are wired differently from men's. However, neuroscience is far from concluding that there is a "male brain" and a "female brain."[24] Women's brains seem to be just as capable of doing math and science as men's; what's clear is that there are lower expectations of what women are capable of accomplishing in these fields. Consider all the women who were discouraged in their pursuits or never got the decisive intervention at the right time. Their careers might have been so much more successful and fulfilling if they had gotten the encouragement they needed and deserved.

My home country of India doesn't have the same image problem that the United States has, believing that nerdy guys make the best programmers. However, gender bias does influence the number of Indian women who study CS and the number of female CS graduates who gain employment in the corporate world. The primary motivation for many young Indian women to attend college is to facilitate a good marriage. When they graduate, these women receive job offers from prominent corporations, which helps them attract good marriage proposals. These brides-to-be often decline the job offers.

At top engineering schools in India, such as the Indian Institute of Science or the Birla Institute of Technology and Science Pilani, women make up only 12% of the students. By comparison, between 40% and 50% of CS graduates from regional colleges are women. The likely reason for this is that parents are reluctant to send their young daughters away from home for the entrance exam (I left home when I

---

24   http://neurosciencenews.com/male-female-brain-differences-3617/
      http://rstb.royalsocietypublishing.org/content/371/1688/20150451

was seventeen. It wasn't easy, but it helped me become independent and self-confident).

It's clear to me that we must change the public-school curriculum to include one mandatory programming class. For many students, even a single programming class is not an option. How can that be true in the twenty-first century, in a world that is driven by tech? Today we have several nonprofits that assist several young girls to code like Girls Who Code[25], Women Who Code, and CodeChix[26], but we need girls to learn to code from a young age. It's important for children to learn how to write software or, at least to have a grasp of what it entails. What they do with that skill will be up to them, but early exposure will help them decide whether it is the right career path.

25 https://girlswhocode.com/
26 http://codechix.org/

CHAPTER 9: DAHLIA'S STORY

BIOSKETCH: *Dahlia Malkhi is a principal researcher and co-founder of VMware Research. Leading up to her current role at VMware, her research career intertwines a tenured professor position at the Hebrew University with senior researcher roles at AT&T Labs and Microsoft Research. Her distinguished scientific career features more than 150 publications. She was elected as an ACM fellow in 2011, and has won multiple awards and distinctions, and is a sought-after keynote speaker. Dahlia says her career track was not one she planned, nor did she rush to make it happen. Born and raised in Israel, she felt little pressure from her parents. At several junctures along the way, she paused, trying a variety of alternative paths. More than once, it took someone's advice or intervention to push her to the next academic stage. Consequently, her career interweaves academia and industrial research labs, which she believes gives her strengths from both worlds. She focuses on "obsession, not ambition," always valuing her passion for technical challenges over a ladder of titles in her prominent, if unplanned, career trajectory.*

"To succeed in your tech career, you need to do it all. You need to consistently be at the top of your field, you need to be efficient and productive, and then, you still need more. You must be willing to bring your work to execution and present it broadly."

— Dahlia Malkhi, Principal Engineer, VMware

~ ~ ~

Although Dahlia eventually became an acclaimed researcher, the encouragement to excel didn't come from home. During her childhood and youth in Jerusalem, her parents put no pressure on her to pursue higher education, nor did they expect her to become a particularly high achiever. "I don't think I was encouraged at all, but I was not discouraged," she said. During her early years, she did have a certain level of confidence in her math and science abilities, but it wasn't her core focus. "I knew that I could get good grades if I needed to. It wasn't my obsession or my passion."

Starting in childhood Dahlia was, however, strongly influenced by a neighbor who was two years older than her and somewhat "geeky." He introduced her to math, and they created engineering activities together, such as communicating with each other via Morse code across their building. This friend eventually became a successful high-tech entrepreneur in Israel.

As a teenager, Dahlia was also fortunate to have gotten an unexpected boost from her high school teachers, one that may have determined her life course. As juniors in her high school, students had the choice of three math tracks: basic, medium, and advanced. Dahlia chose the medium track. "I didn't think of myself as one of those genius kids." Then a remarkable thing happened. "On the first day of my junior year, when I entered the medium-track math classroom, the teacher said, 'No, we moved you to the advanced track!' and she kicked me out of her classroom." Thankfully, her high school teachers got it right. This was the first effective push for Dahlia into

STEM. The advanced math track not only enabled Dahlia to later enroll in math and computer science in college. It also challenged her, exposed her to a constructive sense of competition with like-minded kids who had a knack for math, and sparked a curiosity and passion that might not have been exposed otherwise.

Dahlia graduated from high school early, which meant she was too young to perform her two years of compulsory service in the Israeli Defense Forces. Instead, she went straight to university, where most of the students were beyond military age. Not fitting in with the older college crowd, she gravitated toward a group of like-minded, high-school-age kids who had also entered college early ("the geeks," as she called them). They became a group of benevolent hackers who spent their free time finding security holes in the university's early Unix systems and reporting them to the school administration.

"We hacked the university's systems, not in a damaging way, but in a fun way. The university quickly did the right thing, which was to hire us to help administer and guard the systems, instead of trying to discipline us. We became a group of teens essentially in charge of most of the department's early computer systems. We had a ton of learning opportunities as well as fun, fun, fun. Almost all of that early group of teens are now industry leaders around the world. They founded and head some of the most successful start-ups in the Israeli industry, including the BRM Group and Check Point."[27]

Because she enjoyed system administration and kernel work[28] so much, Dahlia was not at all in a rush to pursue graduate studies right after completing her BS degree. Instead, Dahlia did some free-lancing systems work, both in the industry and for university laboratories. "I liked being a Unix guru," she said. After a couple of years of part-time work at the Hebrew University, in the CS department's

---

27   https://www.brm.com/, https://www.checkpoint.com/
28   The Linux Information Project defines the kernel as "a program that consti-
      tutes the central core of a computer operating system. It has complete control
      over everything that occurs in the system." (www.linfo.org)

Operating Systems Research Lab, one of her professors said, "Look, you're spending half of your time at the university, you're sitting in on our research projects and doing all sorts of useful technical work. You're participating in discussions. You're doing all this and contributing, why don't you get a degree out of it?" This was the motivation Dahlia needed to go for a master's degree, and the second effective nudge she received in the direction of an academic track. Handily, the tasks she was being paid to perform as a systems administration consultant aligned closely with her degree requirements.

Later, a similar conversation spurred Dahlia to consider a doctorate degree. While she was working at the IBM Watson Research Center, a professor said, "You've mainly worked on the research track all of your career, even though you didn't choose it. You've been in research environments, whether it's been at the university or the research center. Have you considered doing a PhD?" That's when she said, "Oh, you know, maybe it would be fun to get a PhD, if this is what research is about."

"I enjoyed getting my PhD, but was glad I didn't rush into it. By the time I chose to pursue a PhD, I was more mature. I had a more professional vision of where I wanted to go, and I knew about more interesting problems to work on."

~ ~ ~

Three guiding principles have accompanied Dahlia throughout her career, right from her days with other teenage geeks: Learn, Innovate, and Find a great team to share learning and innovating with.

The first principle is her sheer love of learning independently. "I enjoy the process of learning and finding out solutions by myself, with nobody to call, and no tech support." One example of that joy of learning is the passion she developed for exploring and mastering Unix in the early days of that operating system. During our conversation, Dahlia explained that she was amazed at how her brain would look at a problem or a piece of code and have no clue what it meant. Yet, slowly and steadily, the details would fall into place, and everything would start to make sense. Suddenly, Dahlia would have the solution and have no idea why, just that she enjoyed the process of problem-solving without outside help. "I think that my brain is simply happy to learn. There must be some basic biological satisfaction that learning brings to it."

Dahlia's second principle involves taking an innovative approach to everything. She found her passion for discovering and creating new ideas when doing system administration. Along with her group of hacker friends in college, she felt she did some creative work when inventing software tools and finding security vulnerabilities in the university's computer systems. This pattern of using creativity with technology to innovate is an important part of her day-to-day work as a researcher. "I can say that there's nothing like the state of euphoria that comes from finding something new that nobody else knows," Dahlia said. "For those few moments, it's so satisfying—nothing compares, and it is an experience that I cherish."

The third principle that guided her career could be described as team synergy: working with a team that has technical talent, that enjoys working together, and that competes in a friendly way. Her days with her hacker friends at the university were all about this team synergy. She fondly recalls having fun with this group of friends, engaging in discussions, pushing each other to their limits, and competing in a healthy way. Their motivation arose from enjoying the process of brainstorming and doing things together. It didn't really matter which team member got the reward or the credit.

By contrast—and different from most of the other women profiled in this book—Dahlia doesn't attribute her success to mentors or sponsors. "I wouldn't say my female mentors have had a significant role in my career, but it was nice to have a few senior women to look up to." The team synergy within Dahlia's college group, and how it affected their learning and effectiveness, appears to have had a hugely positive effect on all its members. Today, the former members of this group are all famous industry leaders, both in Israel and elsewhere around the world. Although Dahlia was the only one of that group who took the research track, she too has become successful within her sphere. Here, Dahlia reflects on the magnitude of her published research: "When you work on 150 papers, inevitably many of them turn out to have been "incremental," some even "predictable," but a few made it all worthwhile: 'Wow, this was something nobody else figured out.'"

Even today, Dahlia thrives on team synergy. Going about her day-to-day activities as a tech researcher, she flourishes in team settings; when she makes career choices, she looks to join teams who have a friendly culture of collaboration. "You need to have a team that you enjoy interacting with. It's not about egos; it's about finding solutions together. Throughout my career, I was fortunate to be surrounded by brilliant people. I learned something new every time I talked to them."

~ ~ ~

If you meet Dahlia, you will find her unassuming, but actually, she is highly credentialed and successful in her field. When I asked her about imposter syndrome, I assumed that she probably struggled with it only occasionally. I was surprised when she responded, "I have imposter syndrome every single moment of the day." Dahlia says that she would be infinitely more successful if she could quiet that negative voice in her mind, the one that constantly slows her down when addressing a technical question: "I won't be able to solve it, let's give up," or "So many smart people have already tried, how could I succeed?"

Dahlia went on to explain that she also struggles with something she calls "team syndrome." She notices that when people are surrounded by brilliant people, and drive results as a team, some find it difficult to acknowledge their significance in the group effort. Both male and female scientists struggle with this. Those with "team syndrome" tend to downplay their contributions to the group's effort.

"They tend to say things like 'Oh, they could have done it without me,' or 'My contribution was not that significant.' The truth is that it just takes different talents and skills to get ground-breaking work done, and people tend to undervalue their own component. They think, 'Oh, somebody else did the central part of the work—I only did X.' They don't realize how important the X is."

Despite the inevitable inner doubts and voices, Dahlia has achieved a place where she's happy with her career, and she strives to keep the focus of her career on research. Though she has dabbled in management responsibilities, that isn't what she wants to do.

"So far, I've succeeded in creating for myself the best environment regarding enjoying my work and getting the rewards that I want. Any time that I've taken to roles where I have to influence external teams, I don't enjoy them, and I think that would only hinder my ability to do the scientific work that I like."

Dahlia defines success as the impact her innovation has on the "real world, other researchers, and the computer engineering field. There are different ways to measure success, but overall, for me, the primary parameter is the importance of the work that I produce."

~ ~ ~

I asked Dahlia about her ambitions. To my surprise, she replied that she has an "anti-ambition rule." She has had numerous opportunities for more visibility and higher titles, which she refused. Nobody is stopping her from achieving higher status and titles in the workplace except her. Because her natural inclination is to not be ambitious, Dahlia never asked for a raise or promotion. Instead, she has always been given more than she had expected to receive.

"The only thing I strive for is to excel. It's really for myself, and not for any external pleasure. It may sound righteous, but I'm a very minimalist person. I don't have a use for titles or money or power. I have obsessions, but no ambitions."

Her obsessions are the technical challenges she faces every day. When she solves these technical problems with her team, she feels successful. But being successful is not her ultimate goal; solving technical challenges is her end goal.

Dahlia adds that part of the reason she isn't ambitious is that work–life balance is so important to her. She always pushed back on promotions or opportunities that would take time away from her family.

"I always made sure that I had time for myself and my family. I'm a career woman, and I have an incredible job that exceeded my expectations, but at the same time, I was never willing to sacrifice anything from my personal life—not my values, nor freedom. I have obsessions, which I pursue as long as I have the time to, but no ambitions to something that might hinder my freedom."

Dahlia mentioned that an obvious element in obtaining work–life balance is time management. Somewhat whimsically, she said, "I think there's time for everything. It's just a matter of time *well spent*. For example, just drop TV time from your life and there will be time for everything." And in fact, her family has no TV.

I have noticed that many women struggle most with work–family balance. Dahlia was quick to offer her advice on about striking that difficult work–family balance: "You need to get a good partner." Dahlia's advice to women who are considering marriage and family is to be selective with your choice of a life partner. Pick one who will support you at home and in your career. She believes this is the most important decision of your life.

Dahlia and her husband cooperatively take care of their family life. "Your partner has to be 100% behind you," she said. "In my case, my husband was probably more ambitious about my career than I was. He pushed me and encouraged me."

Dahlia shared two pieces of advice for women who want to be successful in the tech industry. First, seize opportunities as they come your way: "What's important is how you feel about taking those opportunities and balancing some choices, and the compromises you make in your life." Sometimes women seem to want their lives completely aligned before they seize opportunities, but that time never arrives. Also, Dahlia stresses the importance of enjoying what you do. "Think about a workout," she said. "If you choose an exercise you're not going to enjoy, you won't persist, right?" If you want to persist in your career, it helps to pick a career that you enjoy.

~ ~ ~

At the end of our conversation, Dahlia shared with me an experience that offers an interesting perspective on persistence. Recently she downloaded the free version of a mobile device game called "Words with Friends" (essentially internet Scrabble) to play with her six-year-old nephew. "And of course, I would win because he's six years old! But it was a lot of fun. But then I got tired of playing with a six-year-old," she said. At some point, she let the app start matching her with other players at her level. "So, at first, the app matched me with relatively low-level players, because all it knew about me was that I was playing with a six-year-old." Gradually the app started matching her with more challenging players.

"I started losing, and I kept losing. It frustrated me. Plus, it frustrated me that the app would display advertisements all the time. The app kept encouraging me to get the paid version so I wouldn't get advertisements. So finally, one day I gave in, and I bought the paid version. Then I started winning."

I was curious to know why she began winning. "First of all, I stopped getting these annoying advertisements, so I was a little more relaxed," she joked. Then, Dahlia offered a more nuanced explanation. "It's not rigged; it doesn't cheat, doesn't give you the answers. What it *does* do is, when you're about to play a word, it gives you an indication of how close you are to the optimal word." Dahlia realized that the word rating feature gave her the push she needed to work harder to find optimal solutions, which drove her to increase her skills.

"When I got this feedback that said 'Oh, your solution is only half as good as it could be,' I would be my usual obsessed self. Why play a fifteen-point word when there's a thirty-point word? I would keep trying. I rarely put out a word that was less than optimal play, and I started winning. My point is that just knowing that there is a solution, and here's how good it is, made a huge difference in my confidence and my persistence."

Dahlia suggested that her experience is a beautiful metaphor for a phenomenon that plays out in our professional lives. For most of us, we live our lives as if we are playing the limited, free version of Words with Friends. As we solve problems at work, no app regularly pops up with status messages. Is there an optimal solution to the dilemma in front of you? How close are you to the optimal solution? What if there's no solution? Are you confronted with an impossible problem? Are you are hitting your head against the wall for nothing? Maybe you are working on something that will take a year, and you have a chance, but it will take so much effort. Maybe the problem will only take an hour. How do you know when to stop?

But Dahlia explained that we are not wasting our time being persistent on problems, even if we don't find a solution.

"The thing I learned early was that if you try for another hour, maybe you won't find a solution, but you spent that hour learning, so it wasn't wasted time. Maybe you learned why some of the things you tried did not work, maybe you find other uses for your work, or possibly side effects that you didn't even expect to find. The extra effort you spend to solve a problem, even if you never solve the problem, is time well spent."

Dahlia's ability to play Words with Friends increased because the app gave her a gauge of the solutions she was considering. But so far in life, there's no app that I know of that will tell you how close you are to optimal solutions. Even without the magic app that rates our solutions in our work, and without that extra push to come up with better solutions, I think the point is that we have to persist to develop our internal drive to come up with better solutions. We have to push through whatever is clouding our minds. What are you capable of? What goals can you set and achieve in your work? I think we have to assume that we are capable of doing bigger things than we ever dreamed we could.

I have mentioned elsewhere in this book that, although the women featured in this book have done some extraordinary things, meeting them made me realize that at the same time they are ordinary women. One thing they all have in common is that they have the remarkable ability to persist despite whatever hurdles are thrown their way. No app keeps them focused on their goals. It is the power of determination in their minds. In reflecting on how things went when I was young, it would have been great if someone had said things like: 'Hey, there is a solution.' 'It's not that hard.' 'You can do this.' 'You can learn this on your own.' I didn't have that, and at times, I wish I did. But in listening to Dahlia, I realize we can do it for ourselves. There may not be an app to help us do that, but with the power of our persistence, we can achieve wonders.

~ ~ ~

TAKEAWAYS

- Dahlia was lucky to have several external nudges in her life. Her school teachers pushed her to take the most challenging math track, and then several professors coaxed her to go for her MS and PhD degrees. She was open to the advice and took heed of it.

- The three principles that have guided Dahlia's career are self-motivation to learn, innovate, and find a great team to share learning and innovating with.

- Working in the industry between academic degrees can give you valuable professional experience and lead to a better sense of what you want to focus on in academia to achieve your goals.

- Nurturing a team dynamic of camaraderie and friendly competition can boost productivity and morale.

- Dahlia deals with imposter syndrome every day; she thinks it is common among scientists and can even occur within a team dynamic.

- Dahlia measures her success on the technical contributions she is making to the computer engineering field, instead of promotions or raises.

- She believes selecting a supportive partner is the most important step in achieving work–family balance.

- She also advises women to seize opportunities and to have fun.

- Even without a magic app that rates our solutions to make us more determined and persistent, we can push ourselves to aim high.

THE BALANCING ACT

I have long believed that the best thing you can do for your career is to choose a partner who supports you, and I can attest to the importance of doing so. I have three kids, an eight-year-old boy and four-year-old twins, a boy and a girl. I balance my family life and my management career in a fast-paced, globalized business unit at VMware. Some meetings start early in the morning, and others end at midnight or later. The only time I have with my family on weekdays is from 5:00 p.m. to 8:00 p.m. When I decided to write this book, I knew it would mean I had to sacrifice my weekends. However, my husband has fully supported me in this project. He is a stay-at-home dad (he calls it a "work-from-home dad"—though he doesn't pick up a paycheck for his work at home, it is most definitely work).

In addition to the challenge of maintaining a healthy work–life balance, I also have struggled against imposter syndrome while writing this book. I am known for my skills as a technologist and a leader—writing has never been a skill I have felt confident about. But my husband believed in me more than I believed in myself. He knew from the day that I decided to write this book that I would be able to do it—even with my work and family commitments. Indeed, he encouraged me, believing I have important things to say that will help other women on their journeys to becoming technology leaders. He has been my rock because he takes care of so much, and I have space to do this work—work that we both knew was important to me.

For every woman who wants to have a career in technology leadership and raise a family, I guarantee that, no matter whom you marry, balancing the two will be difficult, but it will be more manageable if you select a partner who is supportive and willing do their fair share of child-rearing and household chores.

But what do you do when your partner isn't pulling their weight at home or with the kids? Sometimes a conversation is all it takes. One woman who reported to me was an energetic engineer and had high-growth trajectory. I wanted to get her to the next level, but something kept holding her back. When we had a candid conversation, she mentioned that her career inevitably took a back seat to her husband's career. Surprisingly, it took only one conversation with her husband to shift their dynamics. He realized his lack of attention to things at home was unconscious and his thoughtless behavior was holding back her career. After that discussion, things changed significantly at home, and she was able to demonstrate that she was ready for the next level in her career.

Sometimes a situation remains the status quo only because we haven't protested. If we speak up and advocate for ourselves, things may move in the direction we want. Until you try to make things go your way, you won't know if you can.

~ ~ ~

A hard truth is that many women are now the sole breadwinners in the family. We can do it with a great support system, but the cultural expectation is that we'll simultaneously take care of the household. Although that is an unrealistic expectation, guilt often accompanies us when we are out there changing the world with scant time for our families.

It is less common for fathers to be burdened with the guilt of working too much. They may experience guilt, but society does not blame them for being too dedicated to their careers in the same way that it blames women. In households with two working parents, both parents should be equally responsible for raising children. Blaming or shaming only mothers for being absent is unfair. The more we challenge the status quo, the more we will progress as a society and make the availability of work–life balance feasible for everyone.

Having men support women equally, from the moment *their* child is born, is a challenge we need to face as a society. We lose many highly qualified women once they start having children. This means men should also be given copious time for paternity leave. Mark Zuckerberg made that an example by taking two months off and I hope more men follow suit. Making child-rearing an equal-opportunity responsibility will help women get the support structure they need to come back to work. As a bonus, it provides gender-neutral role models for our children.

CHAPTER 10: ALAINA'S STORY

BIOSKETCH: *Alaina Percival is CEO and board chair for Women Who Code, a nonprofit with global reach that works to help women thrive in technology careers. She has an MBA in brand management from Georgia State University and a master's degree in organizational management from Institut d'Administration des Entreprises. Because she leads a tech-oriented nonprofit that supports women, Alaina has a solid knowledge base from which to share her perspectives on the current status of women working in engineering in the technology sector. She has some amazing success stories to tell about the benefits to women who have immersed themselves in the activities of Women Who Code, the organization she started.*

"Women know when they are paid less than their male counterparts, and it leads to them having less career satisfaction, and to leaving the company and the industry faster. That is a huge hidden cost to companies."

— Alaina Percival, CEO, Women Who Code

~ ~ ~

Alaina's personal story began in Atlanta, Georgia, with academic success along with missed opportunities. "During my childhood, I always scored higher on standardized math tests than I did on language tests." Though she excelled in math, she wasn't encouraged to pursue math or technology. "I think that's something that happens with a lot of women and girls," she observed. By the end of high school, Alaina had received a full academic scholarship to any state institution in Georgia. But although her father had graduated from Georgia Tech—one of the top US research universities in science and technology—she never considered going there; no one suggested that she even apply. STEM didn't play a big role in her academic career and her early professional life.

Girls are often told they can't do well at math. Almost every day, Alaina hears this refrain from the girls she meets in her nonprofit work. This is a common phenomenon called "stereotype threat," which refers to being at risk of confirming, as a self-characteristic, a negative stereotype about one's social group.[29] In effect, members of a group perform in accordance with the stereotypes connected to them. As we've seen throughout this book, two of the stereotypes about women are that we are not good at math or science, and we are not technical in the workplace. Researchers have even found that women who are taking math tests under stereotype threat

---

[29] For an overview, see http://www.apa.org/research/action/stereotype.aspx.

show activity in regions of the brain associated with the processing of negative social information;[30] in short, we become anxious.[31]

Although nobody nudged Alaina in a STEM direction, she credits her mother with influencing her own admiration of women at high levels of authority in business. "My mother is a strong, independent woman," she says. "She will ask for what she wants, and she tries challenging things; she might fix a tile floor, or change a tire. She does not conform to gender expectations."

After graduating from Georgia State University, instead of leaning toward a career in STEM, Alaina accepted a one-year congressional fellowship. When that year concluded, she landed a job with one of Germany's most sought-after companies, Puma, as a product manager. To win that position, she had to prove why she was a better hire than other people in the European Union—at a time of 13% unemployment there. Those four years in Germany proved to be, as she put it, her "first career marathon."

"I was most excited about my first job because I was working under a very senior woman. I was also very ambitious, and when I finished my work for the day, I would walk around to the different departments and ask how I could help. I ended up getting promoted pretty quickly as a result of doing that."

Alaina ended up working for a senior executive woman at Puma. In her role, she regularly interacted with the CEO and CFO. Being a junior employee and working with higher-ups in any capacity was an unusual and exciting opportunity. She spent four years with Puma.

Then she returned to Georgia State University for her MBA, after which she joined Nfinity, a small women's performance footwear company in Atlanta, Georgia. With the launch of the first-ever women's volleyball and basketball shoe, the company started to

---

30 Anne C. Krendl et al., "The Negative Consequences of Threat," *Psychological Science* 19, no. 2 (February 2008): 168-75.

31 Cailin O'Connor, "Are Women Worse at Math? It's Time to Stop Asking," *Huffpost* (February 3, 2015), http://www.huffingtonpost.com/cailin-oconnor/women-math-and-science_b_6573074.html.

compete with Nike and Mizuno. "We were a tiny, tiny company (like $10–15 million in annual revenue), and we had no budget to compete, so we all had to think like a start-up. It was then that I started getting involved in the empowerment of women. Empowerment was a theme all through my life, but that was when it surfaced in my career."

Next, Alaina wanted to give the tech world a try. Coincidentally, she had an opportunity to move to the Bay Area to work at a start-up in San Francisco called Snip.it. Alaina didn't have a computer science background, so to expand her options, she took it upon herself to learn to code on her own. Soon afterwards, she joined Women Who Code (WWCode), a global nonprofit organization dedicated to inspiring women to succeed and excel in technology careers, first as a volunteer.

Concurrently, Alaina took a job at Riviera Partners in San Francisco, a tech recruiting company. Running their charitable arm, she worked directly with founders, CTOs, and vice presidents of engineering. Through this experience, she realized that less than 5% of the people going into great tech jobs were women. As she talked to the founders and CTOs, learning what they were doing to become successful, she began incorporating their ideas into what WWCode was offering.

At that time, issues of diversity and inclusion were coming to the forefront in Silicon Valley. Alaina responded with a full heart and plenty of energy, and quickly stepped up as a WWCode leader. "I started making career choices that helped support WWCode, and two other things happened around that time. First, conversations about teaching girls and women how to code began to pick up in the media; and second, I was spending time with brilliant women who were already saying that one of their pain points was having to prove themselves constantly." Alaina's support for women in technology became her life's focus. She is now the CEO of WWCode. Women like Alaina are precipitating change in gender equality within tech spaces.

~ ~ ~

Alaina has often witnessed how women are hurt by their lack of negotiating skills, which she sees as a gender issue. "It's a twofold problem: women don't tend to negotiate because it's harder for them, and the reaction to women negotiating is more negative than it is for men. Women can come across as demanding instead of as simply asserting their worth and what they should be earning. It is a subtle difference, but even a small cultural shift in how women are perceived would make a big difference."

Women in the workplace also miss promotions over their male counterparts, even if they are better candidates. She pointed out that women ask for raises as much as men do, "but there is some societal pressure involved; women tend to request a pay raise more slowly than their male counterparts. Women will negotiate a little less hard, or sometimes not at all, for their salary. And it impacts the whole pipeline." Thus, women are at a disadvantage with both entry-level salaries and incremental salary increases. Alaina believes this argues for more transparency concerning when is the right time to ask for a pay increase.

Alaina has also heard numerous stories of unconscious bias, specifically on the recruiting front. After an interview, recruiters will say about a woman, "She asked for more, but she is not the perfect candidate." About the equivalent male candidate, they will say, "We are giving him more because he deserves more." These instances suggest that women are judged—often harshly—on their performance while men are judged—often generously—on their potential.

These forms of bias and resulting pay inequities affect not only the individual but also the company. "That is a huge hidden cost to companies, one that they don't often see." Alaina pointed out the direct negative impact to a company on productivity, loyalty, and longevity because of women being paid less than their male counterparts. "Women know when they are paid less than their male counterparts," she said, "and it leads to them having less career satisfaction, and to leaving a company and the industry faster."

Conversely, "when you pay women more, they invest 90% in their community and family. That is a huge trickle-down effect."

Alaina also offered this insight: Maybe society isn't ready to hear about the successes of women in the business world because of the gender roles that have been strictly defined for years. The system has been designed by men, for men, and those in power (most often men) are resistant to changing the hierarchy that so deeply benefits themselves.

Once they are further along in their careers, women encounter other barriers that they did not expect. Alaina explains, "Women begin by believing that there won't be a barrier. They don't see a limit to what they can achieve. They don't think their male counterparts will be more successful than they are. What we then see happen a few years into their career is that they are told, 'You understand the product well. Why not become a PM or a marketing person?' This is instead of, 'You understand the product so well that we should pay you more. We need to promote you.'"

~ ~ ~

Alaina had to tackle some internal work to justify her position of CEO to herself. Two issues lay in the way. Because the organizational structure of WWCode is flat, she felt that everyone automatically knew to ask her questions. Giving herself any sort of job title seemed unnecessary. Also, she was quite sensitive to the fact that, while she was working to encourage women to become software engineers and even CTOs, she did not have the level of technical training that they had. These factors intersected to make her ill at ease at the thought of taking on the title of CEO at WWCode.

But she was in fact running an organization aimed at empowering women in software engineering, so she came to realize that she needed to step up and empower herself to claim the reality that she was the leader. "I knew that by stepping up, I would be bringing more people with me instead of pushing other people down, and I had to justify it to myself," she said. This was her way of combating imposter syndrome.

Although at times she still feels awkward with the CEO title, during speeches she forces herself to say, "I am Alaina Percival, and I am the CEO of WWCode." She is gradually becoming more comfortable with the title. Just saying it aloud has helped her improve her self-perception and standing. "If I am not willing to put my title on my LinkedIn page or my résumé, how can I ask others to do it?"

~ ~ ~

Alaina strongly advises women to negotiate. She points to two factors that she believes are helpful for successful negotiation. "First, you can put yourself in a better place to negotiate if you have multiple offers. Second, being willing to walk away is a critical negotiating skill." Although the situation seemed different in Germany— her boss told her there was no negotiation—she did so anyway, and came away with a higher salary as a result.

She also feels that women need to receive supportive actions every step of the way. She observed that in some cultures, although the number of women studying engineering is in close parity with men at the start, they start dropping out of tech in their thirties and never make it to executive positions. In the US, women drop out of tech even earlier than that—in their teens, in fact.

"In the US, we need to be attracting and training people at elementary school level. This needs to be more than a community approach; it needs to be part of the school curriculum. That is the only way you are going to reach the girls, the low-income students, and the minorities, and give them access to these amazing career opportunities."

For women transitioning into the industry, Alaina concurs with my opinion. She says that having even one coding class before starting their adult life will help them learn coding exponentially faster. She has had personal experience with this. Alaina started coding at age thirty when she entered the tech world. She would have been more comfortable with programming if she had had an opportunity to code early on.

Having role models helps women feel like they are not alone and can achieve their dreams and aspirations. Alaina observes, "Women drop off at mid-career because they feel their careers have stalled out, and are seeing their male counterparts accelerating." I see that occurring too. Alaina pointed out that having more women in the industry and bridging the gender gap will help make a better work environment, and as more of these women succeed, they will become role models. Mid-career women who are mothers and are still successful in the workplace help other women see that path as a possibility for themselves.

Alaina is also a big proponent of paternity leave. I like her thinking here. "I view paternity leave to be as important as maternity leave, because you are both the parents, and you are both developing lifelong habits to support that child," she said. "Currently, the habits that we develop arise from the fact that the woman has six weeks or six months of maternity leave, and the man is allowed two weeks. In that short span, the woman develops habits and patterns of behavior that she will then have to maintain for eighteen years, and that will pull her away from her career."

Alaina has had so many heartening success stories with her organization, WWCode. One member travels around the world speaking on technical topics based on her blog. Another member, from Stanford, learned how to code at her company and attracted a technical co-founder with a degree from MIT. The two started their own company. One woman who stepped up to be a leader at WWCode increased her outside salary by 200% in less than a year. Another woman, who had previously always lived below the poverty line, received WWCode scholarships to attend coding school. Today, she is a software engineer and teaches other low-income individuals how to code. "She is not only a success story for herself and her family, but she is also giving back to the broader community, and that is something really powerful," Alaina said. WWCode also helps women who have become mothers return to the workforce. "One of the women recently had a child and received the support she needed to re-enter the workforce because of the connections she made at WWCode." In summary, Alaina and her team work tirelessly to help women succeed in their careers.

Alaina has one final piece of advice. "Find ways to celebrate your successes, and celebrate the women on your team, as well as other women on other teams. Raise your profile and be willing to step into the role-model position—it is important for you, and the people around you." She is an excellent role model for women and girls. Women like Alaina are precipitating changes in gender equality in tech workspaces. As she advocates for women, she brings us immense hope.

~ ~ ~

TAKEAWAYS

- Alaina wasn't initially encouraged in math and science; she views this as a potential reason for missed opportunities in a career path in STEM.

- She was noticed when she worked at Puma by walking around the departments, helping others and becoming known.

- One of her pivotal moments was when she started thinking like a start-up and doing empowerment work.

- Alaina started making career choices that helped women learn to code, thus supporting women in the industry.

- Negotiation is harder for women, who have a more difficult time talking about the subject than men do. It is also hard for society to accept women talking openly about their business success.

- Alaina believes that not supporting women with the challenges they face due to unconscious bias affects the whole company, because it affects productivity and loyalty.

- Alaina finds it hard to use her title of CEO. But she pushes herself to do so, knowing that by empowering herself she encourages other women to do the same.

- The curriculum in secondary schools and colleges needs to be changed to encourage women to study math and science.

- Alaina believes that extended paternity leave should be the norm. Both parents should have an equal stake in sharing child-rearing responsibilities from the start.

- Alaina encourages women to celebrate their own successes, as well as celebrate and support other women.

CHAPTER 11: CHRISTINE'S STORY

BIOSKETCH: *Christine Martino is chief operating officer of cyber security, legal, compliance, and policy at Intuit. Before Intuit, she had an amazing career at Hewlett Packard, where she rose to vice president and general manager of cloud services. Christine achieved this level of success without a college degree. Her career was self-managed and self-directed, defined by a passion for new technologies and new business models and a strong entrepreneurial focus. As her career progressed, she was perceived as a change agent and a "fixer," which enabled her to move into larger roles. Her mindset of being motivated by the next big challenge rather than titles helped her achieve big success in the tech industry, proving to be more valuable than a college degree.*

"There has to be an education and mindset shift in all leaders, both men and women, around the fact that a more diverse team is a better team. Women think differently, they work differently, they have a different angle when they work a problem, and this difference is good, not bad."

— Christine Martino, COO, CyberSecurity, Legal, Compliance, and Policy, Intuit

~ ~ ~

Christine grew up in New York. She was mostly a happy child, with many friends. However, her father's position at IBM required that her family move often. Every move was difficult for her, but the move from New York to California in her middle-school years was the most traumatic. "It hurt my self-esteem to have that happen," Christine recalled. "I felt alone, and I was devastated. I made my poor parents miserable. I cried often. It was tough for me to integrate into the new school and the new system." The year before high school was the worst for Christine. She survived those lonely years by making the Letter Girl team of the cheerleading squad. It gave her a place to belong and people to hang out with.

Unhappy in California and struggling to fit in, Christine showed a dip in her academic record. Despite all that, she was accepted to Cal Poly San Luis Obispo as an engineering major. Cal Poly is an excellent school with a respected engineering department, but Christine chose not to accept their offer. "I didn't want to leave the Bay Area or my boyfriend." Instead, she chose San Jose State University, which wasn't a comfortable fit.

"I kind of mucked around as an engineering major there. I felt out of place; there was no one like me. During the third semester, I changed my major to journalism, tried it, and then dropped out completely. I still remember the day I called my dad from the shoe store where I worked all through high school and college and told him, 'I'm not going to go to school. But I promise you, I will get a job.'"

Christine identified a few factors that contributed to giving up this opportunity for a great education. "I had low self-confidence. Perhaps if I had more people around to support me and give me confidence it would have been different. Also, my father had achieved high levels at IBM without a college degree. He worked there his whole life. I suppose I thought I could follow that route. Further, my boyfriend at the time was not interested in college, and I did not have any friends going to Cal Poly. I just wasn't mature enough to go off on my own when I should have."

She fulfilled her promise of getting a job, and did indeed follow her father's career path into the computer industry. Her first position at a small company in Silicon Valley was as a magnetic tape librarian. "It was a good job and I learned a lot. There were eight women in that department, a totally diverse group: black, Hispanic."

After a year, she got a job at Control Data Corporation (CDC), where she worked in computer operations. "CDC had a networking organization. At that time, you couldn't learn networking in school, and most of the people who worked in computer networking were men who had come out of the military. We all worked together in a tiny room; we didn't have separate offices and the environment was hostile for me. One my peers was particularly obnoxious and aggressive. He would be in charge when the manager wasn't there. One day he tried to make me kiss him for my paycheck—of course I wouldn't. But it was a horrible environment to work in. I was miserable every day going to work, but I still went. I was determined."

Ironically, two unfortunate events with Christine's cars ended up allowing her to escape this negative work environment. First, a driver ran a red light and hit her vehicle. While she was not seriously injured, her car was totaled, so she purchased a new one. Shortly after that, while on a trip to Lake Tahoe, the cabin she was staying in caught fire and burned her new car. The car had to stay in the shop for nine months, making it difficult to get to her branch of CDC. There was, however, another CDC office close to her apartment. "I asked if I could work there while my car was getting fixed. Remember, I was still working with these horrible men in Sunnyvale. Control Data gave me the okay to work in a different office temporarily."

Thankfully, with that move, things changed for the better. "The networking group in the new location was a whole different world," she said. "Everyone was wonderful and professional." She liked coming to work and was doing a great job; CDC let her stay on at that location. One day, her second-level manager said to her, "I know about all the stuff you put up with in Sunnyvale. I'm leaving the company, but I'll feel guilty if I don't have you report your story before I leave." Christine agreed to share her experience.

The head of HR came out to California from Minneapolis to interview her, and his response to what had happened to her was shocking. "You are not going to believe this, but he asked me, 'What did you do to bring this behavior on? What made him ask you to kiss him for your paycheck?'" This is victim-blaming, which happens all too often, both inside and outside of the workplace. It explains why many victims don't come forward; they fear, often rightly so, being held responsible for what occurred. As a result, abusers often don't suffer any consequences for their poor behavior. Christine held her stance, insisting that such treatment was inappropriate. The employee in Sunnyvale got away with a slap on his wrist; he was only made to do a different job for a while. Christine was just thankful to be away from him. "This toughened me up," she says. "And I understood just how ludicrous that HR manager was."

Christine thrived in the new group and location, moved up in the organization, and started to manage a team. As an added bonus, her female boss was a great leader and became her role model. "I remember her not as a woman leader, but as the first great leader I knew," Christine told me. At Intuit (where she works now), executives are encouraged to create their career journey timeline. On her timeline, where it says, 'inspired by a leader,' she lists her former boss from CDC. "It was the first time I saw what a true leader was like, plus she was a woman, and it made a huge impression on me."

"My boss captured the hearts and minds of her employees because she coached them and cared about them, but not in a motherly or friendly way. She had a great personal compass and high standards. She gave me excellent advice and cared about my career. She also gave me the opportunity to oversee two employees. She was my mentor, and her coaching and guidance stuck with me for the rest of my career."

While Christine was working at CDC, she went back to school for her associate's degree. Amazingly, that is as far as her official schooling ever went.

When CDC started rounds of layoffs, Christine took that as her signal to begin looking for a new job. She was hired at Hewlett Packard (HP) at the peak of its cachet in Silicon Valley. "I had the networking experience—that's what got me the job. But I almost didn't get it because I didn't have a bachelor's degree. After I was hired, the man who was screening candidates told me that the hiring manager had put my resume in the 'No' pile. When he asked her why, given that Christine had the networking background they were looking for in the technical support role she had applied for, she pointed to my lack of a degree. He asked to screen me anyway, promising that he wouldn't waste anyone's time unless I looked great.' So, I interviewed for the job, and I got it." Luckily for Christine, she had someone advocating for her.

The move to HP was a good one for her. Her HP journey was long; she worked there for twenty-four years. "All of a sudden, I decided that I wanted to take charge of my life. I broke up with my boyfriend of eight years. It wasn't a bad or abusive relationship, but it wasn't leading anywhere." That breakup coincided with a positive change in her confidence levels. "I became more career-focused when I left CDC and got to HP, asking myself 'What's the next interesting move?' I was always thinking about moving up. Not to manage more people, not to make more money, but to do more important and meaningful things—that's what was driving me."

Describing her career path at HP, Christine said, "My career was self-managed and self-directed, defined by a passion for new technologies, new business models, and change leadership, including everything from digital video to open-source (before it was mainstream) to cloud. Because of these interests, I was frequently in "niche" areas, from a company perspective, which enabled me to experiment, make independent decisions with my team, and have more autonomy." Christine also tried to stay away from large, established HP businesses. She viewed those roles as being a "cog in a wheel" in contrast to her more entrepreneurial focus. As her career progressed, she was perceived as a change agent and a "fixer," which enabled her to move into larger roles where her skills were truly valued. She was never motivated by title, but by the next challenge. She allowed her interests to chart her career, with a strong focus on product management and new technologies.

Eventually Christine ended up running a profit & loss (P&L) at HP of up to a billion dollars. Because of her entrepreneurial bent, she was given an opportunity to start a cloud business unit. With seed funding from an HP executive vice president, Christine grew the unit to 180 engineers within nine months, working closely with the CEO of HP. However, at that point the CEO was replaced, leading to a series of unpleasant changes for Christine. These culminated in a surprising event. "At a regular one-on-one with my boss, he said, 'I am taking you out of your role. Here's the new guy. Hopefully he will find a good role for you on the team.' Just like that. I had ninety seconds with him." I asked Christine if she ever found out why this sudden change was made, and she attributed it to company politics, but at the same time, she had no feedback loop to learn what she could do differently in her job.

For Christine, this was a startling end to her career at HP. She had thought she would work there forever. "I had a big network there, and I didn't want to leave, actually. I just wanted to do something different, because I always could during my whole career. I never planned what I was going to do next."

As Christine started to look externally, she became a mentor with an organization called Women Unlimited, which provides long-term development programs for high-potential women by integrating these three pillars of leadership: mentoring, education, and networking. She also started to build her network outside of HP. "A woman I had worked with at HP (she had been a senior VP there, and I knew her very well) had gone to Intuit and really enjoyed it. She and I would have lunch every year or so. She called me one day and said, 'I know you are looking and I know of a group where you could be a great asset to the team. Will you come talk to us?' I hadn't been looking at Intuit; I had been looking at companies the size and shape of HP, and at cloud companies."

That woman didn't hire Christine directly, but a vice president under her did. He was looking for specific, deep technical skills, and Christine didn't fit the bill, but the senior vice president told him in no uncertain terms, "You need a business person in your organization to help you better interface with the business groups." Christine was hired.

That first year at Intuit proved challenging. Her friend and senior VP left the company six weeks after she joined. The boss who remained continued to think she wasn't ideal for the role. Christine, as usual, persisted. She now has a role at Intuit where some of her GM skills are being leveraged. "But the first year was a tough time. I didn't feel valuable, like I had before. More recently, I've turned a corner. I kept telling myself, 'Keep pushing to use your skills and find meaningful ways to contribute.'" Christine is currently the chief operating officer across four organizations at Intuit: cyber security, legal, compliance, and policy. Despite Christine's low self-confidence, she pressed on in her career. She never finished college, yet found a path that included running a billion-dollar P&L for HP. What a huge accomplishment, and what an excellent role model for women who drop out of college and feel they are not worthy of jobs they are indeed well qualified for.

~ ~ ~

To navigate her path to GM at HP, "I just followed what looked interesting to me. If something didn't work out, I recognized that right away." For example, from her tech support role she jumped over to technical marketing, because she wanted to try that. When that wasn't motivating any longer, her manager there helped her move along to other things. At one point, she became enamored with new technology. "Then my career choices were driven by new technology areas and new business models. I tried things I found interesting."

"Also, I preferred to be a big fish in a small pond, so sometimes took jobs that were ill-defined. That meant bringing in new technology and finding my way. I would ask myself, "What benefit can this bring to customers? How might we productize this? How might we partner? The choices I made always involved new businesses and acquiring a new technology mindset. I was in smaller groups and organizations, but I was making a recognizable difference, so I moved up."

Successful as she has been, Christine doesn't claim to have good negotiation skills. "I never asked for a raise. Ever." So how was she promoted? "I never asked for a promotion either. The way I got my promotions was applying for different, higher-level jobs and getting them, instead of staying in my job." She aimed to perform her job, but at a higher level than was expected.

I described a sharp distinction that I thought I heard here: women seem to be judged on their performance and men on their potential. "That's interesting," Christine replied. "Yes, and I lived that. Men are open to asking for promotions, while women tend to take their time asking for a promotion. I still don't ask for this. Men seem to more easily assume they are adding value."

Another aspect of Christine's career that I wanted to know about was how Christine balanced work and family. When her kids were young, she told me, she and her husband both had full-time jobs. She raised her kids while traveling around the world for work. "Work–life balance has always been a struggle," she admits. "I really try to be present with my kids when I am with them." Christine would travel to Paris, get her job done, then fly back home within twenty-four hours to be with her family. At times, she had to combat the guilt of not being a "good-enough mom" that was placed on her both by herself and by her children's teachers.

It is less common for fathers to be burdened with the guilt of working too much. They may experience guilt, but society does not blame them for being too dedicated to their careers the way it blames women. In households with two working parents, both parents should be equally responsible for raising children. Blaming or shaming only mothers for being absent is unfair. The more we challenge the status quo, the more we will progress as a society and make the availability of work–life balance feasible for everyone.

Juggling the inevitable stresses of managing her intensive career and her family, eventually Christine found ways to strike a workable balance. "When my husband started his business and had flexible hours, that helped. It seemed so much more normal after that—silly things like that there was toilet paper at home all the time." Today, a large piece of her strategy for finding balance is trying to unplug for a good chunk of time on the weekends.

~ ~ ~

I asked Christine if she ever encountered gender bias while working at HP. She acknowledged that she's not good at recognizing gender bias. Perhaps that's because she says she does not think about herself as a woman while she is at work. Rather, she identifies with whatever position she is holding and what she is trying to do. "I remember a male leader I once worked for at HP while I was managing the Linux team. He had a big impact on me. I couldn't get what I needed from a key stakeholder, and I was frustrated. He said, 'Has it ever occurred to you that maybe they are not listening to you because you are a woman?' I was appalled. No, that hadn't occurred to me."

Years later, when Christine found herself pushed out of her role and, ultimately, forced to leave HP, she again didn't initially recognize that the circumstance may have been related to her being a woman. Christine went on to declare to me, "It's really weird: the gender bias of that situation never occurred to me until *right now*. I thought it was just him trying to save himself politically. It absolutely could have been gender bias. I should have thought of that!"

"I work for a woman now," Christine continued. "She's all about outcome and results—I love that about her, because I am that way too. If you were to say to me, 'You are a woman, you should get this promotion,' I would say, 'No. It's all about results. Like a meritocracy.' I do believe that life should be a meritocracy."

The stories in this book illustrate, over and over, the reason I don't believe in meritocracy: because of the unconscious bias that exists. Women hold biases against women too, but possibly Christine is better off because she has a female boss—especially one who shares her work values.

Technical bias, a type of stereotype threat[32] in which women are viewed as naturally less technical than men, touched Christine, and was exacerbated by the fact that she didn't have a college degree. "I originally perceived myself as non-technical, because I didn't have a degree." The technical work she did at Control Data and HP eventually increased her confidence, although she must still guard against this side effect of the tech bias that surrounds her.

---

[32] Negative stereotypes raise inhibiting doubts and high-pressure anxieties in a people's mind, resulting in the phenomenon of "stereotype threat." http://www.apa.org/research/action/stereotype.aspx

Later in their careers, people encounter another bias—age. Christine finds this bias to be at least as prevalent as gender bias. People are often discriminated against based on how young or old they are. Young people are regularly discriminated against due to their limited experience. Older people meet with discrimination for nearly the opposite reason: they are so experienced and effective at their jobs that they have become quite expensive to consider hiring, promoting, and even retaining. "If you are a highly paid woman in your fifties, finding another good job is hard. You aren't in a category that companies want to hire. And it's also hard for men. A male friend told me he interviewed for a position and felt it went well. But he was told he wasn't a good fit. He was pretty sure they rejected him because he was too old." Layoffs often target proportionally more older employees than younger ones, despite the Age Discrimination in Employment Act.[33]

Regarding her own experience with age bias, Christine had this to say. "I think about the end of my career at HP and it makes me sad. I remember my dad telling me, 'You will have the best career growth and your highest earning years in your forties.' For me, that was more than true. My career was still growing into my early fifties. "I feel like I have had a successful career. I accomplished a lot at HP, but I feel like I didn't need to stop moving up when I left. I miss managing a business a lot. I was good at that, and I loved it. I always felt like I was doing something important, regardless of the team size or my title."

~ ~ ~

Christine wants to see the glass ceiling broken by having more role models for younger women. "When women see other women

---

[33] Elizabeth Olson, "Shown the Door, Older Workers Find Bias Hard to Prove," *New York Times*, August 7, 2017, https://www.nytimes.com/2017/08/07/business/dealbook/shown-the-door-older-workers-find-bias-hard-to-prove.html.

succeed, that makes a huge difference. I was a good role model for my daughter because she grew up seeing that her mother was a successful businesswoman. My mom worked her whole life, and I saw that."

She reported that Intuit supports Girls Who Code and other technical programs for colleges. "It's a huge focus here, which is awesome. But now we need a sea change." In Christine's experience, this "sea change" involves networking and mentoring. Christine is a mentor with Women Unlimited, and has had mentors of her own. Her own mentors were people who advocated for her based on her work—she refers to them as her "personal board of directors. People supported me because of my accomplishments."

"But there is a lot more about gender inequality that is societal. There has to be an intervention: changing long standing patterns." One example Christine cited is the acknowledgement and support of stay-at-home dads, both corporate and governmental. "As a society, we are not set up for role reversal. Even though there is more of that now, it is still not the norm."

Perhaps most importantly, Christine advocates that managers at all levels should be trained to expand their perspectives on hiring. "There has to be an education and mindset shift in all leaders, both men and women, around the fact that a more *diverse* team is a *better* team. Women think differently, they work differently, they have a different angle when they work a problem, and this differ-ence is good, not bad. It's just like ethnic diversity, style diversity, and diverse scores on Myers-Briggs personality tests[34]—that's what makes the best teams."

"If you have a team that is all men, you are missing some-thing." Christine looks forward to the day we have a work culture where diversity is embraced as the force it is: a best practice for

---

34   http://www.myersbriggs.org/my-mbti-personality-type/mbti-basics/home.
       htm?bhcp=1

business excellence and empowering for the people who work in those businesses.

~ ~ ~

TAKEAWAYS

- Christine's family moved around a lot when she was a child; growing up, she struggled to find her balance.

- She struggled with self-confidence. This began to change after she found a work position that suited her well. Her focus returned and she was ready to grow.

- She blossomed under the mentorship of a female leader who acknowledged her in a professional way and provided management advice.

- She had an affinity for bringing in new technology. That, and her ability to take on ill-defined charters and make something of them, helped her become GM at HP.

- Christine has experienced bias, especially in the form of "technical bias," which, for her, meant being perceived as "non-technical" both because she didn't have a degree and because she is a woman. The latter is a pervasive stereotype threat in our society.

- She doesn't focus much on promotions. Her motivation comes from taking on new challenges, doing important work, and getting results.

IMPOSTER SYNDROME

Before I started to write this book, I was under the impression that only a few women suffer from imposter syndrome. As I interviewed women I admired, I was surprised to discover that a large majority of them experience it. Recently I chanced upon a quote widely attributed to the Nobel laureate and civil rights activist Maya Angelou (She is my heroine; whenever I need inspiration, I return to her famous poem "Phenomenal Woman"). Here is a cleverly articulated feeling of being an imposter: "I have written eleven books, but each time I think, 'Uh-oh, they're going to find me out now.'" Whenever Angelou spoke publicly, she exuded such confidence; you would never think she suffered from imposter syndrome, but she did.

Several other women in these chapters have pointed out that imposter syndrome is not an exclusively female problem. Indeed, for many years, imposter syndrome was thought to affect only women. Now we know that high-achieving individuals of either gender can experience imposter syndrome, also called fraud syndrome, when they cannot internalize their accomplishments and fear being exposed as a fraud. I have first-hand experience with this misunderstanding about who is affected. One time, when I was out to dinner with my team, a man mentioned that he experiences imposter syndrome. Another man on the team was quick to ask, "But isn't that a syndrome only women have?" Up to that point, I too had believed that only women were affected.

It's a strange paradox that many super-confident women leaders are simultaneously filled with feelings of doubt as they lead. You will find this to be a common thread with the majority of the women in this book.

I can't speak to why these women lack self-confidence, but when I look at myself, I also *appear* confident, but I lack self-confidence because I set a high bar for myself that I can never reach. In short, I am never satisfied; I feel I have big gaps in my knowledge because I just can't keep up. Most times, I am my own worst enemy, critical and hard on myself. My parents were never critical of me. They never liked my direct communication because I challenged them a lot, but I think deep down, they appreciated that in me.

Looking back, I think my confidence took a hit when I was in school. I was extremely confident in my abilities—to the point where I was cocky. I had too many teachers, until high school, who disliked my attitude and constantly suppressed me, especially when it came to sports. That may possibly have hurt my self-assurance. And of course, I have had some bosses in the workforce who also chipped away at my confidence. The majority of them were great, but the few bad bosses had a deep impact on me. It is important to have a good boss. If you don't, you should leave.

Imposter syndrome can be seen as good for you because it indicates that you are getting out of your comfort zone, growing personally and professionally. Yes, sometimes that might be scary. People feel imposter syndrome when they are thrust into new responsibility, or have to walk through uncharted territory. Each time I start a new role at VMware, I go through an "imposter period" because I have to learn about new people, new processes, and a new product—and that all feels daunting.

I think it is important to discuss this topic. Women who are working with technology or moving into leadership should understand that these sorts of feelings are natural as we take on big challenges. But we shouldn't let these feelings get in our way of setting big goals for ourselves.

How do we overcome this? By tackling it head on, becoming disciplined, and learning more about the area we are insecure about. Little by little, that uncomfortable feeling melts away—until another new challenge crops up. Imposter syndrome is a way of life. Every time you feel it, tell yourself it's there for a reason, pushing your limits and hinting that there's something new to conquer. Isn't that exciting? So, embrace that feeling of being a fraud, because when you do, that means that greatness is just around the corner.

CHAPTER 12: MARIANNA'S STORY

BIOSKETCH: *Marianna Tessel's first job experience in the US and in Silicon Valley was a "magical" start-up experience that gave her a great blend of awesome mentors, a gender bias-free environment, and opportunities to hone her leadership skills. After her experience at this start-up, her career accelerated and she developed a well-deserved reputation as a breakthrough technical leader and a tough negotiator. There are so many things I appreciate about Marianna's brand of leadership. If I had to name just a few, I would say that I appreciate how quickly she can learn new things, how she can thrive and lead in the midst of organizations that are experiencing huge growth and change, and her "empathy for what others might be going through."*

"There's something really nice about the fact that people have started to talk about gender bias, because it helps you to realize, 'I'm not the only one. That's not just me.' Otherwise, you take it personally. There's a bit of freedom in saying 'I'm not the only one.'"

— Marianna Tessel, SVP, Docker

~ ~ ~

Marianna was born in Eastern Europe, grew up in Israel, and came to the United States as an adult. Marianna's family is Jewish and originally from Eastern Europe, from which her parents had fled the Nazis during World War II. Marianna says a survivor mentality was instilled in her from early on, and she describes it as a sense that "We will fight. We will survive. We will find a way."

For Marianna, engineering and math came naturally. Both her parents are engineers—in fact, almost everyone in her family is an engineer. "It was just something you did," she said. As a fourth grader, Marianna was offered extra enrichment classes. Much of the curriculum was in technical areas, such as basic computer engineering—advanced topics for a fourth-grade student. She loved the early exposure to technology, and she believes that it gave her a bit of an edge.

Growing up in Israel, Marianna never saw gender bias in the workforce. In Israel, both parents tend to work: the culture supports women in their careers, even after they get married and become mothers.

Military service is compulsory for most Israelis, and Marianna was no exception. She was in a program that allowed her to finish her CS degree before serving. Her work as an engineer for the military was her first real job as an adult. There, Marianna had to produce work reflecting a high level of excellence, since quality is a serious concern in defense applications. That experience taught her a lot, including solid work habits that have assisted her throughout her career. "In the army, you always have a mission to accomplish," she said. "You don't have anyone to complain to or to ask for a budget. You just find ways to get it done."

The Israeli military was relatively free of gender bias—at the time Marianna served, over 30% of its CS engineers were female. Although fewer women take combat roles, in non-combat teams people of both genders are intermixed and collaborate well. "You just get assigned to groups with men and women that all work together. Bias never even crossed my mind."

After her military service, Marianna and her husband took some time off before coming to the US. Like many Israelis, they back-packed through India, Nepal, and Thailand for a few months. "I don't know if it shaped my career," she said, "but traveling shapes who you are as a person." The trip broadened her worldview, introduced her to new cultures, and helped her figure out "how to be independent in life and get by."

Marianna landed her first job in the US as a junior engineer at General Magic. "We were trying to do smartphones before there were smartphones—we called them PDAs (personal digital assistants). The team was just insanely talented, and smart, and nice. It was unbelievable," Marianna said. Founded in 1990, General Magic included true innovators in the industry: Andy Rubin (who went on to invent the Android phone), Megan Smith (who would serve as the chief technology officer of the United States during the Obama administration), Tony Fadell (who later designed the iPhone, iPod, and Nest), Andy Hertzfeld (part of the original Apple Macintosh Development Team), Susan Kare (who designed much of the graphic user interface of the original Macintosh computer), and Kevin Lynch (currently vice president of Technology at Apple), to name just a few. Plus, there was "a guy in the cubicle across from me who was working on this website," Marianna said. That man was Pierre Omidyar, and his website became the online auction site eBay, which revolutionized online shopping.

General Magic's main product was a personal intelligent communicator. Marianna's first project was to write a web browser for the device. She later worked on the operating system (OS) that powered the device. She then transitioned to leadership, and led the OS team. Marianna didn't realize at the time just how unique and bias free General Magic was. The people around her believed she could do anything—just as it had been during her work experience in Israel.

Shortly after being promoted to manager, Marianna was asked to lead a larger team on a project that was much grander in scale. Things began moving quickly and she was promoted before she felt she was ready. Sometimes she even thought to herself, "Wait, wait! What are you guys doing?" However, Marianna was always confident she could learn. When part of General Magic spun off into a new company, she went with that team to help create it. Marianna soon returned to General Magic, at which time the CEO asked her to run all of engineering—her first vice president position. During that period, Marianna says the most meaningful engineering project she led was the OnStar Virtual Advisor, a voice-recognition advisor for cars. General Motors had partnered with General Magic to bring OnStar to life.

Unfortunately, in 2002, General Magic went bankrupt after twelve years. Most people wouldn't remember with fondness a company that failed, but Marianna is still excited about her time there. Her eyes lit up as she spoke about it. Today, General Magic's engineering team is still well remembered; it is described by Forbes Magazine as "the most important dead company in Silicon Valley."[35] General Magic is credited with helping to lay the technological groundwork for the smartphone revolution of the 2010s. No wonder Marianna remembers it so fondly.

---

[35] Michael Kanellos, "General Magic: The Most Important Dead Company in Silicon Valley?" *Forbes*, September 18, 2011, https://www.forbes.com/sites/michaelkanellos/2011/09/18/general-magic-the-most-important-dead-company-in-silicon-valley/#547f3e444d8c

In April 2001, after seven years with General Magic, Marianna followed a group of friends to Ariba.[36] This company was founded in 1996 to streamline the procurement process for businesses. Prior to Marianna joining, the company had become an overnight success. In retrospect, Ariba was something of a missed opportunity for Marianna. She could have joined earlier, and if she had, her career growth there probably would have been tremendous. By the time she joined, she was exhausted from her vice president role at General Magic and desired a smaller management role at Ariba. She joined as a senior director leading the backend server team. Dot-com companies were just starting to go bust all over Silicon Valley, and a smaller role seemed more manageable with family life. Eventually, her team grew to encompass several engineering teams, followed by a promotion to vice president level.

After seven years at Ariba, Marianna's next move was a brief stint at a start-up. Very soon after, a former colleague connected her with VMware, where she was offered a position. Marianna took a six-week break before starting the new position.

During her hiatus, the landscape at VMware changed significantly—Diane Greene, VMware's CEO, departed the company and Paul Maritz was named the new CEO.[37] On Marianna's first day, her new manager told her that he "needed help with partners" and would elaborate in their one-on-one meeting in a few days. That meeting never happened; her manager resigned two days later. "So here I am in a new company where no-one is reporting to me, I joined to help someone who left, and we have a new CEO. My entry at VMware was the first time I had to find my own way in a much more proactive way than I ever had before," Marianna said.

Despite the challenging start, Marianna found her footing and thrived as a leader at VMware. "I wanted to have a position that had

---

36   https://www.ariba.com/, accessed August 12, 2017.
37   https://www.vmware.com/company/news/releases/2008/executive_leadership.html

a little more of a business aspect to it, and that allowed me to see the industry more broadly." Of her many achievements, she is best known for establishing VMware's Technology Partner Ecosystem. When she joined in 2008, VMware had few partners and was struggling to collaborate with them. Marianna helped the company form new partnerships and reshaped how they worked with existing partners, including the hardware ecosystem. "With collaboration across the company, we grew our ecosystem," she explained. "We took a programmatic approach to it that allowed us to scale and do all sorts of interesting integrations." Marianna's negotiating skills were critical again; to grow the ecosystem, she had to negotiate deals with partners on a regular basis. Under Marianna's leadership, the ecosystem flourished. VMware was transformed into a company that other companies wanted to collaborate with, and there were now clear ways to do so.

At VMware, Marianna had a profound impact at the business level, instituting changes she had not been able to effect in her previous roles. Her networking skills were exponentially strengthened, and she learned to identify industry trends early on. "When talking to companies, what I heard was interesting," she told me. "When you work with the ecosystem, you also tend to keep in touch with what's going on technology-wise, and multiple times I was able to say, 'This is a big trend,' when it took others a little longer to spot it."

After many successes at VMware over the course of six years, Marianna once again got that "seven-year itch" and began looking for her next adventure. Because she now had a strong sense of industry trends, she saw that Docker's software containerizing technology had huge potential. She landed a coveted senior vice president role at Docker, where she managed their global engineering team and worked to support and expand Docker's partner ecosystem. Within eighteen months, Marianna rose to executive vice president of strategic development, responsible for scaling current Docker technologies and evaluating new ones.

~ ~ ~

There's no denying that Marianna's career path helped shape her into a successful leader. However, another aspect of her life that shaped her leadership skills was becoming a mother. "Being part of a family really helped me understand other people, and that really shaped me as a leader as well," she said. One of her four children was born early—a micro-preemie. "It was very, very tough. It changed me. It changed how I saw people, and gave me a new level of empathy for what others might be going through. I don't know if it's spiritual or not, but I now have a good understanding of my place in the world. The world is a big place, and we need to give space for each other," Marianna said.

Marianna acknowledged that being a mother of four and being a busy technical leader isn't easy. "I'm not going to be the perfect mom, and I'm not going to be a perfect whatever at work—sometimes something has to give, right? There have been periods when I had to say, 'It's not the right time for my next promotion, I have to focus on my family now.' And there have been periods where I'm missing some things at home, or I'm not the perfect mom and didn't bake the cake for the birthday, or whatever—and that's fine."

~ ~ ~

One of Marianna's duties at Ariba was to negotiate with vendors of products that the team used. Marianna has earned a reputation as a strong negotiator, and she credits this skill, in part, to her Israeli heritage. She explained, "In Israel, it's not uncommon to have to negotiate." This earlier experience gave her a good foundation for negotiating with industry partners and vendors.

Not that negotiating was always easy. Marianna recalls one tough negotiation at Ariba when it took a lot to get both sides to agree, and the deal structure changed greatly in the process. After a huge effort, and when both sides of the table were finally in agreement,

Marianna went to her management for final approval. Her CFO asked her to get a larger discount for Ariba. "That was a tough experience. I had to go back and start the negotiations again," she said. Interestingly, Marianna later became good friends with the executive who was negotiating for the other side, and they have kept in touch ever since. What did Marianna learn from this experience, and what does it say about her negotiation style? "It taught me that you can negotiate hard, and at the same time maintain a relationship. Both sides felt it was a tough deal, but we got to a win-win and all sides were pleased. So, I always look for something that is fair for both sides."

When Marianna looks back on the professional support network that helped her to succeed in her career, she can point to her professional "rocks"—managers, peers, her personal coach, and even team members who reported to her—who have made a big impact on her growth. Marianna's philosophy is to learn from everyone. "At the end of the day, we're all people, and we're all equal," she believes. "I don't look at people at the top with awe, but I also don't look down at people who are in more junior places in their careers, or in other roles, and dismiss them." As for her main pillar of support, professionally and otherwise, Marianna credits her husband, who has been a big supporter of her career—especially since they are the parents of four children. And of course, Marianna is her own rock: "I trust myself to find a solution or come up with new thinking. I feel like an entrepreneur at heart, and I am driven, so I always look to how to evolve things."

~ ~ ~

Marianna knows that experiences of gender bias can slowly erode women's confidence. "There are always these things that chip away at one's belief in oneself. Maybe it's an opportunity for a promotion that you weren't offered, or maybe it's a little thing that somebody said, or maybe an incident that makes you feel you are not taken as seriously as you think you should be."

Marianna was fortunate that her earliest experiences as a junior engineer in Israel and the US were relatively bias free. When she began experiencing bias in the workforce, it came as somewhat of a shock. It wasn't until she moved into more senior roles at various companies that she began to notice that bias was affecting her career. The bias was usually subtle, but it was there nonetheless. She feels that she wasn't taken seriously at times. "Sometimes, I'd be sitting in a room with men from my team, and I'd be the most senior person in the room, yet it would be clear that some of the guys preferred talking to the other men and not to me," she explained. "And I'd think, 'I'm more senior, and I'm right here.'"

Marianna also noticed that men's comments often received more attention. She gave a typical example of a team meeting with a male leader: "We'd all be talking, and my comments for some reason would not pique the lead's interest. But later, a man will say the same thing, and *then* the lead says, 'That's a great idea.' I would think to myself, 'I said the same thing ten minutes ago! Why wasn't that a great idea then?'" Marianna has reached out to other women in the field and asked if they've faced the same type of issues. Universally, the answer has been yes.

It can be difficult not to take experiences like these personally. They can have a big impact on us, even if the biased behavior is unconscious. In instances like these, Marianna believes, "It's kind of freeing to say, 'Maybe they have a bit of a bias, and it's not about me,'" although she agrees that this doesn't solve the problem. *I like the way Marianna thinks about bias. Even if one doesn't call the person out on their bias, one can mentally rise above it. Once you realize it isn't personal, then you don't have to let it mess with your confidence.*

Learning and professional development are two interrelated areas that women struggle with because we also confront a subtle, silent pressure that men are unaware of: stereotype threat. Women must stay abreast of new technologies and changes in the field so we don't run up against the stereotype threat of being perceived as not technical. From my experience, it seems that the more senior your role, the less hands-on and detailed you become, so it's an increasing danger as women climb the executive ladder.

Marianna's approach to learning is refreshingly simple: "When I get into a new area, I'm not freaked out. I say, 'Let's get this figured out.'" Marianna enjoys getting out of her comfort zone. She's also not shy about asking for help from other people, because she believes there's a big distinction between saying, "I don't know this" and saying, "I don't know this *now*, but I will be able to figure it out." This confidence helps her to learn new things, while "understanding that everybody struggles through stuff because we're all human."

Marianna has witnessed more blatant examples of bias too. "They say that women get promoted on performance and men on potential, and I've seen this for myself," she told me. "Sometimes, when my team would interview a woman who didn't meet every single criterion, the attitude would be 'Why should we hire her?' Whereas with a man, if he didn't have all the relevant experience requested for the job, the general attitude was, 'Oh, but he can learn.' Well, she can learn too, you know!"

When it comes to her own promotions, Marianna's experiences later in her career were markedly different from those earlier on. For women, as compared to our male colleagues, the interval of time between promotions tends to get longer, and benchmarks to achieve promotions are higher; many women never make it to the most senior executive roles. "I don't know that there's a glass ceiling per se," Marianna says, "but I feel like our path is longer, and then as a result we don't go as far."

Marianna offered a metaphor to describe how she visualizes the effect of bias. Imagine the moving sidewalks in airports. Although men and women both start at the same point, the female leaders have to walk the whole distance, while the male leaders get to use the moving sidewalks. "It's slower and harder for women," Marianna says.

~ ~ ~

Marianna is demonstrably an excellent negotiator when it comes to her company's needs or the needs of her team; however, when it comes to self-advocacy, she feels her negotiation skills aren't as strong. This is because she feels negotiating for herself is different from negotiating on behalf of the company, so she tends to not champion her own interests aggressively. She says this may be because she wants to be a collaborator, but in doing so, she ends up setting her own interests aside.

I was curious about any decisions Marianna made that may have hindered her career—after all, most of us make a misstep or two along the way. For Marianna, she can't point to one huge mistake, but she says, "There were a lot of mistakes sprinkled along the way—different things that I've done or choices I've made that in retrospect weren't exactly bullseyes." Not joining Ariba earlier was a misstep for her because had she joined earlier she would have been there during a period of incredible growth. Not advocating for herself consistently is another area she works to improve. There were times she was told, "Just do this project and we'll give you a bigger role," but Marianna now realizes she should have insisted on being given a bigger role *before* taking on more responsibility because sometime such promises didn't pan out.

~ ~ ~

As we talked together, Marianna contributed a number of valuable views and observations toward advancing women in technical careers.

Think back to the walkway metaphor that Marianna offered. One way for women to get their careers onto the moving walkways is to network. Not every woman in this book says she is good at networking, but a surprising number of them seem to excel at building relationships within the professional domain. For Marianna, networking and social capital played a role in her success.

You should be networking and building relationships because you care, she pointed out. "In order to have a good network, you need to be genuine and give; you can't just take away. You have to really want to help others. You can't think, 'Oh, I'm doing this just to get something in return.'" When someone asks her to connect them with another person in her network, her attitude is, "Why not help?" If someone asks her for advice, her attitude is, "Why not talk to them?" She thinks that helping others is a good investment to make, but the motivation should come from a place of genuinely wanting to assist people. She went on to say, "And it's a rewarding investment, because at the end of the day, it stays with you no matter what else you do."

Nearly every woman whom I've interviewed for this book has admitted to experiencing some degree of imposter syndrome. Marianna has: "There are moments when I think, 'Is everyone going to find out that I have no clue what I'm doing?'" Actor, writer, and comedian Tina Fey once quipped, "Seriously, I've just realized that almost everyone is a fraud, so I try not to feel too bad about it."[38] Like Fey, Mariana has her own way of handling imposter syndrome: she's not too hard on herself (or others), and she understands and respects that everyone has a low moment or a time when they're unsure of themselves. "If I'm facing something new, I'll say, 'I can do this, let me go and read, and ask, and learn about it—I'll figure it out.'" There's an almost spiritual component to this perspective. Marianna reminds herself, "If I am low, I know that this too shall pass. And that's fine."

Marianna spent six years at General Magic, seven years at Ariba, and another six years at VMware. For some, the strategy of changing

---

[38] Gill Pringle, "Tina Fey - From spoofer to movie stardom," *The Independent*, March 3, 2010, http://www.independent.co.uk/arts-entertainment/films/features/tina-fey-from-spoofer-to-movie-stardom-1923552.html, accessed August 3, 2017

companies frequently is a good way to move up, but Marianna believes that staying with companies for longer amounts of time has been a good approach for her. "It's funny," she said, "sometimes when you stay in one place you develop depth, both in knowledge about the company, and in the opportunities, that present themselves. Sometimes there will be a difficult time, and you will just want to run away. But there's an opportunity there that will present itself if you stay."

This advice happened to be particularly helpful to me right at the point when we were talking together. I was going through a rough patch in my own career, and I had to decide whether to stay in my position or leave. In listening to Marianna, I realized this was a learning opportunity for me: if I left my job, I was never going to learn to navigate the problems I was facing.

Finally, I asked Marianna what her advice was for women who want to succeed in this male-dominated industry. "It's confidence," she promptly replied. "Just allow yourself to fail sometimes and accept it as normal. Sometimes when you look at other people, it seems like their story or their career is just amazing, but it's not like that. They have a lot of ups and downs and turns and twists. Give yourself that space to fail occasionally and have that confidence. If you can't do something today, that doesn't mean you won't be able to do it tomorrow. It's not about what you don't know, or about what you have or don't have—it's that you can learn, you can develop, you can acquire a skill. Have the stubbornness to continue if it's something you want to do. Don't give up."

That's sound advice coming from a leader who practices what she preaches.

~ ~ ~

TAKEAWAYS

- Being mentored at the beginning of your career is extremely valuable. I strive to offer mentoring to junior members of my team. As a leader, if you can actively seek mentors for your team—men or women—that can make a big difference.

- Although some of the basic ingredients for a successful startup are having a great team and building a product that serves a need in the marketplace, so many factors can affect the ultimate success of a startup. Although Marianna found her experience at General Magic to be valuable, the company ultimately failed (partially because the technology they were working on was too immature at the time to be successful). Nevertheless, her startup experience was valuable because of the great team she was working with, the learning opportunities she had at the company, and the inclination of her bosses to promote her into leadership. One takeaway is that even if the start-up you join ultimately fails, there are likely to be other aspects of your experience there that will set you up for future successes.

- Embrace the fact that you must always keep learning, and don't be afraid to ask for help. Technical leaders often find the demands on their time for leadership tasks can take the focus away from maintaining their technical skills. Look for opportunities to keep your technical skills sharp and up to date.

- Just because gender bias exists doesn't mean we have to let it get us down. When someone acts in a biased way, it can be helpful to realize it is not personal.

- Marianna's advice on getting over imposter syndrome is having the confidence that you can learn what you don't know.

- Taking care of your own needs when negotiating for salary and benefits is laudable, not selfish placing you in a better position to help others.

- Because women tend to be promoted on performance and men on potential, take care to judge both genders equally on both performance and potential, and work to put policies into place so that the criteria for awarding promotions are implemented through an objective process.

CHAPTER 13: MALINA'S STORY

BIOSKETCH: *Dr. Malina M. Hills is the senior vice president of the Space Systems Group at The Aerospace Corporation. Though she was interested in science from an early age, she dreamed about majoring in history and becoming a lawyer like the actors she saw on television. Instead, several crucial moments set her up for her career in science. One was validation from a grade-school teacher, and a second was encouragement to study chemistry in college from a woman work-study employer. With a PhD in chemical engineering from the California Institute of Technology, she went to work for The Aerospace Corporation, attaining the ranks of senior VP. As part of her learning, she believes in not shying away from asking questions. She was president of the Aerospace Women's Committee for one year; as part of her many years on this committee, she has supported women and worked hard to hire women at all experience levels.*

"I think we have to be supportive of other women. We have to talk to them about what we did right, what we did wrong, and how we dealt with challenges. I find that younger women engineers learn more when I talk about the mistakes I made in my career, rather than about my successes... Knowing that you can recover from your mistakes is incredibly significant to women."

— Malina Hills, Senior VP Space Systems
Group, The Aerospace Corporation

~ ~ ~

Malina grew up in the 1960s in Walnut Creek, California. She attributes her early success to the deep work ethic of both her parents. Her mother—who was half-Chinese, and one-quarter each Malay and Scottish—had an especially firm sense that education is critical. Malina's father died when she was thirteen, leaving her mother struggling to raise three daughters with that perspective. "It was expected that all three of us would work hard and do very well in school," Malina observed. "As long as I did well in school, I had a lot of freedom. I was raised to work hard, to focus on what I was doing, and to get a good education."

The public education system at that time offered many opportunities for Malina. She could attend summer school, science education was well funded, and her elementary school traveled on many field trips. "When I was growing up, there was a movement in Walnut Creek to save some of the open space areas around Mount Diablo. We would go on school hikes and field trips. I even remember going out on a boat for an oceanography field trip."

Although Malina had a longstanding interest in science, one special moment during a school field trip showed her she had the clarity of thought to solve scientific problems. In many ways, this brief event was the start of her career. As she related it, "We were hiking in Las Trampas, which is near Mount Diablo. We came across the skeletons of a deer and a fawn. My teacher Mrs. Nimitz asked, 'How do you think they died?' One boy answered, 'She could have died giving birth to a baby.' I raised my hand and said, 'That doesn't make any sense because it's in the wrong position, and the fawn's head is too big to come out of the doe.' Mrs. Nimitz replied, 'Yes, Malina, that's correct. Probably they were killed by a coyote.'" This was significant for Malina, because she felt that her ability to think through mysteries had been publicly validated by her teacher.

Growing up, Malina didn't have many role models in engineering or science, either male or female. She also remembers watching far too much TV and thought "Perry Mason" and "Ironside" were cool. "I always identified with males," she said. "I wanted to be like them when I grew up. I certainly didn't want to be the scientist on Gilligan's Island, as there wasn't anything attractive about being a scientist. I wanted to be an outstanding person who could make a difference in the world."

However, at that time she didn't think science or engineering would help her achieve her dreams, even though she took science classes throughout high school and in her first year of college. When she began college at Yale University, she planned to major in history and become a lawyer.

Two factors intervened to change her mind. First, she realized that she hated arguing; thus, the lawyer path was not going to work. Second, as she described it, was "serendipity: a woman who ran the chemistry stockroom asked me to take a part-time job, encouraging me to go into chemistry. I discovered that I liked the way you could describe the world in a macro sense. For example, you turn on a tap, and you examine the way the water flows and the way it hits the bottom of the sink. Sometimes, there is a rise in the water level when it flows out. You can describe this phenomenon as a chemical engineer, and I thought that was cool. I then moved to chemical engineering in college."

In chemical engineering, her classmates were mainly men. Malina did not have a problem with that, but her first brush with gender inequality came as she noticed some discomfort among the faculty. "When I was a junior, that was the tenth anniversary of women being allowed to attend Yale. This was an era in which it was awkward for the professors, who were just getting used to having women in their classes. So, the number of women attending science classes was not that great."

Indeed, Malina had mixed interactions with her professors. One professor was supportive of her. Another gave her a B, even though she had the highest grade in his class; she always suspected that he simply didn't want to give any girl an A. He even ranked her in the bottom of the list for the engineering honors society.

After Yale, she went directly to the California Institute of Technology (Caltech) to pursue doctoral research in chemical engineering—surface chemistry, to be precise. "I studied the interaction of gases with metal surfaces. The application was catalysis. In your car, there's a catalytic converter that speeds the conversion of carbon monoxide into carbon dioxide so that the exhaust is not poisonous. I worked on reactions that were similar to that."

Because her thesis advisor did not have much time for Malina, she performed much of her work independently. The numerous experiments she conducted while there gave her confidence in both her performance and analytical abilities. "The work I did at Caltech was kind of the opposite extreme of chemical engineering, in that normally when you study chemical engineering early in your career, you are focused on macro things like water flow. I was studying atoms on pristine surfaces. So, I went from macro to micro, in nanometers instead of centimeters. These are very different scales, and it was fascinating work."

With her PhD in hand, at age twenty-seven, Malina went to work for The Aerospace Corporation in El Segundo, California. She started as a member of Laboratory Operations. "I worked in the labs for about nine years, and I didn't see an opportunity for promotion," she said. "I started to tire of the kind of work I was doing. I wanted to take the research in one direction, and my boss wanted me to take it in another direction. I felt like I wasn't learning as much as when I'd started." Remaining in a single group of one company for nearly a decade may not be a good strategic plan.

Malina needed a change from the labs, so she took a big risk within the company. "I went to another organization with an entirely different focus, doing intelligence work with foreign space systems in Project West Wing." This was a field she didn't understand; she admitted that her decision was not well thought-out. If she had to do it over again, she would have taken classes to understand the satellite systems better before she took such an enormous leap of faith, because she felt she wasn't sufficiently skilled in the work she was hired for.

In this group, though, she was lucky to have a boss who sponsored her. He shifted her into delving more deeply into foreign space technology, an area in which she could excel. He also promoted her to manager as she proved herself. Although they didn't always agree, this boss was supportive of her.

Around this time, she also got involved in the Aerospace Women's Committee, a network of professional women who supported leadership training for other women. This group held an annual event to honor both female suffrage and women at Aerospace. This event included a Women of the Year ceremony to highlight a few women for what they had achieved at Aerospace and within the larger community.

Men at Aerospace were involved in this event too. For the Women of the Year award, men from Aerospace were included on the selection committee. After seeing the potential of these honored women, the men would want to hire them for their teams; that process changed their attitude toward women. In short, the Aerospace Women's Committee was an organization geared toward both changing people's minds about skilled technical women and fostering diversity within the company. Clearly, it was also an excellent platform for networking. The events organized by the Aerospace Women's Committee were open to anybody. The committee worked with other diversity groups, such as the Aerospace Black Caucus and the Aerospace Asian Pacific American Association, and conducted workshops that men could attend.

Malina served as the president of the Aerospace Women's Committee for one year. Her involvement with this committee led directly to her next opportunity: through this network, she was promoted to run the R&D program at Aerospace. "That was a two-year job, and at the end of the two years, my then-boss, who was a woman, was promoted out of that job. My new boss didn't know me as well, so I had to find my next job through the contacts I had made." Networking was essential to her in that process.

She progressed in her career, moving among organizations within Aerospace. From her position as a general manager (GM) in the systems engineering division of the engineering group, she was offered another GM position where she was responsible for helping the Air Force build military communication satellites. She was somewhat amazed by that opportunity: "I never thought I would have that job at Aerospace, never thought it was achievable, so never dreamed of it." After the GM position, she competed for the position of VP of Space Program Operations and won the selection process. Subsequently she was promoted to senior vice president of the Space Systems Group.

~ ~ ~

The first challenge women encounter in the tech workforce is simply getting there. Malina persevered and got a PhD in chemical engineering in 1987. She gives partial credit to her extended network of women friends. "I am fortunate in that at Caltech, I was in the first year in which there was more than one woman in the chemical engineering grad school group. The support I got from my friends Carol and Julia was critical for me in continuing at Caltech."

Both at Yale and at Caltech, Malina and her women friends conducted informal comparisons of the backstories of women in science. "What we found was that either your father was dead or divorced from your mother, or you were the firstborn child in the family. The firstborn daughters were treated by their engineer dads as if they were boys and were raised to be engineers. It's quite weird: at that time, if your dad is gone, you are free from the stereotypes of what a male should do versus what a female should do; the mothers are expected to handle everything. *Or* you have a dad who expects you to become an engineer because he is an engineer."

It's troubling that the number of women in engineering and CS occupations has declined over the years, from 34% in the 1970s, to 27% in 2011, to 18% in 2017. Malina remarked, "It used to be that in the aerospace industry women dominated software, and now they don't. In my area over the past ten to fifteen years, it's been pretty constant. Over the last eight years, the technical staff has consistently been about 20% women. It's tough to bring women in. So now, we are focusing on the STEM pipeline, and on internships to bring women into our company. You have to get them young, right out of school. You want to keep working with them when they are in school to keep on this path."

Malina reported that The Aerospace Corporation is taking several actions on this front. First, the women in senior positions advocate for women. When I interviewed Malina in 2016, the Aerospace CEO was Wanda Austin. Its board of trustees included four women. One member, Ambassador Barbara Barrett, is a former ambassador to Finland and an astronaut. Both Wanda and Ambassador Barrett are strong proponents of diversity and inclusion. "Ambassador Barrett will call us to check how things are going. One year, we had all white male nominations for AIAA[39] fellowships, and she said, 'Where is the diversity? Why didn't you look for other candidates?'"

In addition, diversity efforts are pushed from the top down at Aerospace. "I am trying to work with HR to understand how to bring diversity into our company more effectively. Yes, it is a problem, and

---

[39] American Institute of Aeronautics and Astronautics

all of the VPs are looking at how we can improve things. The solution involves bringing in diversity and inclusion and creating an environment in which women feel comfortable."

~ ~ ~

I asked Malina if she felt she'd made any missteps or mistakes over the course of her career. She returned to her move from the Aerospace labs to its Project West Wing. "I went into a job where I didn't have the credentials to do the job well. I should have matched my skills against the job requirements, and then talked to the manager and asked what I could do to gain the skills I needed." When she decided to leave Laboratory Operations, her management advised her not to leave. Rather than talking to people outside the labs to get alternative perspectives on the move, she made a leap of faith. "I tended to make decisions on my own, instead of gathering data and asking other people for their advice."

"I have taken sideways moves, as well as promotions; sometimes I got assignments that were really hard. I could have looked at them as negative experiences, but decided not to. For example, I got two six-month assignments on the East Coast in which I managed not only my current job on the West Coast but also the second job. It was hard, but taking those duties and being successful at them showed the more senior people in the company that I was agile, and that I could complete hard, poorly defined tasks."

Malina also suspects that she may have been asked to take on these assignments because she was a single female. "I went ahead and did it, and I got it done. In the end that did contribute to my being promoted. Promotions at Aerospace are done by consensus at the VP level and up—I would never have become a GM or VP if I hadn't demonstrated my ability to do tough things."

Referring to the full arc of her career track, Malina remarked, "I did good work, and I hoped people would notice it," she said, referring to her career track. "However, I didn't get to be GM until

I started letting my hair go gray. Perhaps some people assume that women who look younger are not ready to be promoted."

"Discrimination never entirely goes away, whether it's assumptions based on youth or something else. For instance, sometimes I will be the senior person in a meeting, and the male engineer will not look me in the eye during a technical discussion, even though he's there to brief me. He'll look at the man sitting next to me." She added, "You have to deal with it all the time. I don't think it will go away for a while. There is far less overt gender bias in my company now, but you have to remind people to be conscious of how they are behaving and not allow their subconscious mind to control their brain."

~ ~ ~

One of the frequent criticisms women face in the tech world is being viewed as not technical enough. Yet women are also criticized for exactly the opposite problem as well: if they seem too technical, or too forceful in their technical drive or opinions, they are often called "aggressive." Women are judged heavily in the tech field, no matter what.

Insofar as possible, Malina met that challenge with her educational background; a BS degree from Yale and her PhD from Caltech spoke volumes. "The credentials are important," she stresses. "In my era, it was important to go to a good school."

Another critique women face in the workplace is being emotional. Emotions are considered a negative in professional spheres. Behaviors such as being passionate, standing up for yourself, or being assertive are deemed "emotional." Malina feels she's usually transparent in that regard. "Except when I try to have a poker face. Others can read my face in a meeting. So even if I don't say anything, they can tell when I am upset or mad. But generally, people don't think of me being as emotional in a negative way. I try to be supportive, and I probably smile more than I should.

Successful as she is, Malina is nevertheless not immune to imposter syndrome. "I continue to have self-doubt, but because I recognize it, I can control it somewhat. Sometimes I feel like, 'Wow, I am in over my head, and people are going to notice.' Then I tell myself, 'Nah, it's that stupid voice inside of you that's always there.' I then think about the things I am doing pretty well, even if this one didn't go so well. This is what I need to do differently next time." When she heeds her own advice, she improves her standing. "I am good at standing up for myself if I have an opinion; I will think through what I want to say, and will state my opinion. That is how I get respect from my colleagues: by speaking out."

In Malina's experience, after becoming a vice president, one doesn't get a lot of feedback, either positive or negative. "You just have to do your best, try to assess where you are personally, and do not let yourself get bogged down in self-doubt."

"Another thing about imposter syndrome," Malina added. "I used to avoid asking a lot of questions, because I didn't want to look dumb. "Then I realized that people love to talk about their work. It's good to ask a lot of questions, because people want to share what they know—and I get to learn it." Businesswomen often shy away from asking a lot of questions for the same reason Malina mentioned. This raises a serious danger: that you'll sacrifice a deeper understanding of the area you are responsible for; and that's when self-doubt and low confidence kick in. Never be afraid to request more knowledge.

~ ~ ~

As with each of the women I spoke with, I asked Malina about her mentors and support framework. "I never had formal mentors. But that doesn't mean I didn't have people helping me," she explained. "Aerospace is one place where people like to talk about their work. I got technical mentoring from everybody around me. I made a couple of moves where I didn't know much technically; for instance, when I first went over to systems engineering, I was not a systems engineer. I had to learn quickly. I would walk around and talk to people about their work, and they would just love to explain it to me."

Wanda Austin was Malina's boss when she ran the R&D program. Although Wanda was not technically a mentor, Malina learned a tremendous amount from observing her. Wanda set the bar high, believing that people should demonstrate total ownership of the areas they are responsible for and ensure that everything is running smoothly. She emphasized that leaders ought to gain consensus on decisions, not make unilateral decisions. Wanda helped Malina accomplish several career moves.

How she was able to obtain such quality mentorship, without formal mentoring relationships? Malina said, "My way of getting mentored is to ask many people different things to get different perspectives. One friend is our chief velocity officer, and his brain is wired differently than mine; I go to him when I need advice from a very different perspective. One person is not going to give you the full perspective that you need. Having a network, you can reach out to is incredibly important. Whether you call specific individuals mentors or colleagues, it's the dialogue that matters, and the diversity of thought and opinion."

~ ~ ~

Malina is a strong believer in the power and efficiency of teamwork in solving problems. "If you are solving a complex problem and there are multiple ways of trying to address it, you are more likely to get to an optimal solution if several people take different routes. Computer simulations have validated that. Scott Paige talks about that in his book *The Difference*."[40]

---

[40]   Scott Paige, *The Difference: How the Power of Diversity Creates Better Groups, Firms, Schools, and Societies* (Princeton University Press, 2007).

Scott Paige, political scientist and economist, looked into mathematical models of different groups trying to solve problems. He found that groups that were formed to attract particularly smart members did barely as well as—and sometimes worse than—groups who had moderately intelligent members. This suggests that the diversity of team members might be as important to a team's problem-solving capabilities as the IQ or ability of individual group members.

Malina appreciates Wanda Austin's commitment to consensus building. "Wanda is very much a person who believes in teamwork and making sure her employees have shared destinies so that they work well together," she reflected. I think Wanda has all the VPs trained, so hopefully, we don't drift away from what she taught us."

"Women like to work collectively. They like teamwork. I think we have to look at our culture and make sure we are including opportunities to collaborate and to work in teams to create an inclusive environment for both genders."

~ ~ ~

What advice does Malina have for women? "I think we have to be supportive of other women. We have to talk to them about what we did right, what we did wrong, and how we dealt with challenges. When I talk to younger engineers, I find that they learn more when I talk about the mistakes I made in my career, rather than my successes. I think we have to talk to that—especially because of imposter syndrome—because knowing that you can recover from your mistakes is incredibly significant to women. Maybe our shared wisdom will allow women to take more risks, and I do believe you need to take some risks in your career to move to the next level. We need to make them feel supported, we need to have an inclusive environment, and we also need to give them some opportunities to take some risks—calculated risks."

She also stressed the importance of groups such as the Aerospace Women's Committee. These organizations "provide opportunities for women to get together, to network, and to demonstrate leadership in their companies," said Malina, which are all "excellent things to help bring women up the ranks." She also emphasized the benefits of succession planning, to "make sure there are women in positions that are getting the training they need."

What about the hope we have for women who have demonstrated great potential? Malina's answer was optimistic. "We are in a transition period. We've got proof that women can hold a CEO job in a technical area, and that women can do well in technical fields, but we don't have critical mass. To get to critical mass, we also need to keep hiring not just outstanding women, but also good women. Their presence will make the environment more accepting of *all* women. We want to reach a place where an average female in a tech workplace is treated the same as an average male, and women don't need to be superbly qualified to get a job or promotion."

What would happen to our tech workplaces if the average woman were treated the same as an average man? Three things: Contribute to leveling the playing field for women, so they'd be judged and treated fairly. Help us not lose women at every stage of their career. Create an ideal environment where every person will be able to thrive based on where they are in their growth trajectory. This is only fair. Wouldn't you want that fairness for yourself and for the generations to come? I do.

~ ~ ~

TAKEAWAYS

- Malina always had an interest in science and believes in the importance of a good teacher.

- Malina has always wanted to learn as much as possible.

- She appreciates that her family of origin taught her to work hard and focus on getting a good education.

- Because she believes in the importance of diversity in the office, Malina works hard to hire women at different experience levels.

- It's important to have a strong network of support and to ask plenty of questions.

- Of course, Malina believes firmly in the importance of supporting women, and has put in time and energy toward that end.

THAT GLASS CEILING

"There is always going to be something hanging over a woman making it harder for her, which is just her gender. Even when you achieve success, there is still something holding you down. It doesn't matter where you are in your career—you are still going to hit that ceiling."

— Pam Kostka

When I first set out to write this book, I thought of using the title *There's No Glass Ceiling*, because I believed women were shattering it. But the more I talked to these women, the more I realized that the glass ceiling does exist, with both conscious and unconscious bias, both external and internalized, working to construct it.

There are plenty of reasons why we have a glass ceiling today. One of them—internalized by men—is the strong "old boys club," or better said, the "ultimate boys club." These are groups of men who are at their own private tables making decisions; women are not factored into those decisions.

I remember a story I was told at the Grace Hopper 2016 conference by a woman who was a bank executive. One day she was in a meeting with a bunch of men, and that meeting did not culminate in a decision. After the meeting, the men went into the bathroom, discussed the matter further, and walked out with a decision made. Because they made the decision in the men's bathroom, she was left out of the decision-making process. Next time, she was in another meeting with them which resulted in a similar outcome—no decision. This time when the men went into the bathroom, she used a novel strategy. She followed them into the bathroom and announced that she was there to discuss the matter further.

At first blush, this sounds like a funny story, but how unfortunate that women have to constantly think of creative ways to get around this problem of the old boys' network.

As another subtle form of bias, some women face a glass cliff, where women in leadership roles are given an opportunity during a crisis in a company, when the chances of failure are high. Glass cliff positions tend to have an outsize impact on women's reputations and career prospects because, when the company performs poorly, those women are blamed for it without having the crisis factors taken into account. Research has found that women tend not to get second chances when they fail in such circumstances, because they don't have access to a support structure of mentors, sponsors, and the "good old boys' network."

~ ~ ~

When women hit a glass ceiling, experiencing that stereotyping can have an enormous impact on women's confidence. It erodes their sense of competence, fuels their doubts about their leadership abilities, and makes them anxious. Self-doubt is the essence of imposter syndrome, which can be an enormous barrier to taking the necessary bold steps to have a successful career.

I believe that feelings of self-doubt can affect women's careers. One of the areas in which self-doubt can come into play is in not negotiating well enough for ourselves. Negotiating well for oneself requires rejecting the imposter syndrome. To negotiate well, you must believe that you deserve the compensation, title, or benefits you are asking for.

Opportunities rarely come knocking at our doors. But when they do, don't let that little voice in your head talk you out of it. Distilling facts from the false narrative we tell ourselves because of our lack of confidence will help us make better decisions. Then, once you make a decision, make peace with it so you can avoid regrets later.

~ ~ ~

The book *Through the Labyrinth,* written by Alice H. Eagly and Linda L. Carli,[41] echoes what Yanbing discovered in chapter 3. The authors argue that the metaphor of the glass ceiling to describe the barrier that keeps women from entering top leadership roles is inaccurate and outdated. More women of this generation are being offered CEO and C-suite roles, so in a sense, one could say that the glass ceiling has been shattered. However, significant barriers still keep most women from entering those high-power jobs.

Eagly and Carli propose a new metaphor to characterize how a woman's path toward career advancement is in fact winding and filled with barriers along the route. The book compares the new corporate landscape to a metaphorical labyrinth for women—a maze with elaborate, confusing twists and turns. Navigating this maze requires persistence, awareness of one's progress, and a careful analysis of the obstacles that lie ahead. The authors make their case through hundreds of empirical studies, surveys, polls, small group studies, case studies, and behavioral experiments (as well as some apropos anecdotes). They conclude that "advancing in a male-dominated hierarchy requires an exceptionally strong, skillful, and persistent woman."

While I do recommend *Through the Labyrinth,* based on the interviews I conducted for this book I see the glass ceiling metaphor as still relevant. As this book reveals, many high-potential women leaders get to points in their careers where it isn't just a maze they have to navigate to get to the next level in their career. They will encounter a substantial but invisible organizational barrier in their way, blocking their advancement. To get past such a barrier requires more than navigation; it requires breaking through. And many women encounter not just one such glass ceiling, but quite a few, each one requiring different skills to breach.

~ ~ ~

---

41 Alice H. Eagly and Linda L. Carli, *Through the Labyrinth: The Truth About How Women Become Leaders* (Boston, MA: Harvard Business School Press, 2007), p 191.

There are many breakthrough stories I have enjoyed learning about while writing this book. Some involve changing companies or working for a new team within the same company. Others include challenging conversations with people in one's management chain. Still others have required executive coaching, including honest reality checks of the unproductive aspects of one's leadership. Some career breakthroughs can require intercession, and it was heartening to hear from these women how many of the thoughtful course corrections came from a man who had the inclination to lend a hand. Similarly, getting a strong sponsor can take one's career to the next level, and again, most sponsors for these women were men. While it has been encouraging for me to hear the breakthrough stories, I must conclude that there are still many glass ceilings to be shattered by high-performing female leaders in tech.

The women shattering the glass ceilings are not as visible as their male counterparts. I want to use women's voices as role models, revealing that they have broken their own glass ceilings, even when their successes are not widely recognized. Until the movie *Hidden Figures* came out, most people did not know there were three brilliant women at NASA—*Katherine Johnson, Dorothy Vaughan, and Mary Jackson*—who were "human computers," calculating complex equations that allowed space heroes like Neil Armstrong to travel safely to space. Let's speak their names proudly and loudly for all women who have persisted and done incredible work in male-dominated industries.

CHAPTER 14: SARAH'S STORY

BIOSKETCH: *Sarah Clatterbuck's parents instilled in her the importance of helping people. Today she uses her influence as a leader in tech to do just that. As part of her role as senior director at LinkedIn, Sarah leads the Presentation Infrastructure team and serves on the Women in Tech exec team driving the high school trainee program. Earlier in her tenure at LinkedIn, she started the accessibility task force. Sarah also serves as a board member of Girl Scouts of Northern California, where she works on strategic STEM initiatives to expose many thousands of girls to computer science. Though Sarah was talented in math as a child, math and computers were never her passion growing up. It wasn't until an on-the-job experience showed her how computer technology could help people—that event enabled her to see herself having a career in tech.*

"If people outside of you perceive confidence, even if you don't feel it, you will get that runway of opportunity to arrive at that positive place. In a way, you're buying yourself some time to become confident by acting confident."

— Sarah Clatterbuck, Senior Director, LinkedIn

~ ~ ~

"It's been a wild ride. I've loved it. I love what I do," says Sarah Clatterbuck about her career in tech. Sarah's parents were supportive of her and consistently emphasized the importance of having a meaningful impact on society. Her upbringing gave her the confidence that she could do anything she put her mind to. She grew up loving math, and during the summer after second grade, she amused herself by memorizing multiplication tables. She began learning algebra in early fifth grade. She was part of the gifted student program at her school, in which she attended accelerated classes one afternoon a week.

In junior high, she had her first exposure to computer science. "Mr. Riley taught us the binary system," Sarah recalled, "and we wrote a program on a Tandy 80. The program was to generate random numbers. The computer was so slow that we had to set up our program and come back the next morning to verify that it worked as intended and didn't have any bugs. I really enjoyed learning the binary system. In terms of the program, it was interesting in an academic way, but I wasn't really inspired to pursue CS at that point. I didn't find it all that interesting."

Sarah did well throughout high school, played basketball, ran track, and was the valedictorian of her class. In college, she was torn between studying math or applied design. She chose applied design, with the goal of becoming an art director in advertising.

The balance shifted during her senior year. An internship at a software start-up called Softpress Systems was what prompted her to focus her professional life on technology. The start-up was building a program for designers to do WYSIWYG web page creation: what the web designer would see on the computer screen would closely match how the web page would be displayed when a user referenced the page in the internet browser. To have her gain a better understanding of their product, Softpress began sending Sarah to programming classes.

"They wanted me to understand how the software worked under the hood so that I could do a better job of debugging problems that our customers were having. That's when I fell in love with programming. That's where I understood that software could actually impact how people solved problems in the real world. It wasn't just an academic exercise but had a practical application. That's where it got me excited about the field."

After Sarah's experience at Softpress, a true passion for technology grew. "I started to write programs on the side, just to learn. I started building web pages as a freelancer, initially for family and friends, and then it expanded from there." To round off her career credentials, Sarah earned a master's degree in information science from San Jose State University, with an emphasis on information architecture and systems design.

"I took a whole series of algorithm and data structure classes, and that's the path I continued on: solving problems and impacting the world with software. I've always been a natural leader, even growing up when we had class projects in school. I always was the de facto leader of the group. I gravitated toward leadership roles, once I got into software engineering. That's taken the form of being both a tech lead at times and a manager. A few years ago, I put myself fully on the managerial path. That's what I have been doing ever since."

In 1999, Sarah took a full-time job with Resonate, a late stage start-up, as a full-stack web developer and systems administrator. The company eventually went public and then collapsed in the dot-com bust. Following a short stint at Apple doing web application development, she was recruited by her former director at

Resonate to work at a small public company called Packeteer. She was there for just over four years, initially working as a tech lead and then as the manager of the web team, her first leadership role. She moved to Yahoo! in 2007, where she held roles as both a tech lead and manager during her tenure. Sarah valued the opportunity to learn about so many technical areas of security, performance, and accessibility. Being at Yahoo! also broadened her network via her collaborations with several engineering teams there. With her wider network, she can reach out to many more individuals for advice, expertise, and introductions (and the return of favors).

After four years of holding various roles at Yahoo!, Sarah knew she was ready for something new. As she pondered what kind of change she wanted, she realized that she had always been solving interesting technical problems. This time she sought a company where she could feel the impact of her problem-solving skills on society. LinkedIn was on the top of her list, as it was making an impact in creating economic opportunity. This could be the world-changing job that her parents had dreamt of for her. Hired as an engineer there in 2012, she quickly shifted into management. Over time, she started taking on significant responsibilities and was quickly promoted to senior manager, then director, and most recently, senior director.

~ ~ ~

Sarah's path underscores the value of communicating with one's bosses. "Generally speaking, it's been important to talk to my managers about my career goals along the way—then there are no surprises. If we can periodically align growth interests within the company, that is a good thing. Typically, after each acceptance of additional responsibility, there is a period of mastery leading to a promotion. It's nice to have another set of conversations then around how I can provide additional value to the company and department while growing my capabilities."

Apart from having regular conversations with the bosses in her command chain, taking significant responsibility, and displaying mastery, Sarah has also surrounded herself with mentors—and, more importantly, sponsors—who have played a significant role in career progression. When she was working as an individual contributor at Packeteer, she had a female manager who tapped her to be a leader. The manager saw that Sarah was on a promising growth trajectory and sent Sarah to management training. Even today, Sarah appreciates how this woman coached and mentored her at key decision points. Her mentor asks the right questions, yet avoids telling Sarah what to do.

Sarah was also fortunate to find a sponsor who played an active role in advancing her career at LinkedIn. One of the vice presidents noticed her work and said, "You are doing amazing work. Let's find you more responsibility." In a series of conversations, he charted out what more responsibility looked like and orchestrated an environment that would make that happen for her. Not only did he provide more responsibility, he also advocated for her with his peers and helped build her reputation within the company. This is a positive example of sponsorship.

What Sarah said next was interesting. "One sponsor begets more sponsors. The VP at LinkedIn was initially my sponsor, but other sponsors have since taken up that mantle. I now have three or four sponsors invested in my career, which is pretty amazing." It would be great if more women on a rapid growth trajectory had sponsors, as Sarah does.

So how do you go about getting a sponsor? Sarah offered her thoughts: "I think it would be awkward just to say, 'Will you be my sponsor?' I don't even know if those people at senior levels of the company actually know they are sponsors." Sarah's approach has been more organic. First, she developed a sense of trust with her prospective sponsor. From there she was able to go to him and say she wanted to do more, and she asked his advice. "That could be the conversation: 'Show me the way to do more. Help me think through that.'" One of her sponsors was also part of an underrepresented group at the company, and had empathy in raising up other under-represented groups.

While seeking sponsors, Sarah believes that it's important to still communicate regularly with your direct manager. Transparency with additional bosses throughout the sponsor process helps ensure no feelings are hurt or relationships damaged.

~ ~ ~

Sarah presents a steadfast confidence. Surely, she doesn't suffer from imposter syndrome? "Everyone does. If anyone told you they don't have imposter syndrome, I would be shocked. Even the men that I talk to—in quiet moments of trust—will admit that they do, all the time. It's part of the human condition. Women may express it more readily than men, but everyone feels they are in over their head at times."

Sarah's strategy for dealing with imposter's syndrome is to "fake confidence," because perceptions matter. She believes that experiencing imposter syndrome is part of the growth process. You usually feel like an imposter when you are trying to do something big, or taking on a new challenge, or getting outside your comfort zone. When you get past that and achieve what you set out to do, then you have grown. "If people outside of you perceive confidence, even if you don't feel it, you will get that runway of opportunity to arrive at that positive place. In a way, you're buying yourself some time to become confident by acting confident."

One decision that may have hindered her career provides a great example of why one should avoid letting self-doubt get in the way of opportunities that present themselves. Initially, Sarah joined Yahoo! as a manager, but transitioned into being a staff engineer on a different project to get a chance to return to hands-on development. At one point, her team at Yahoo! was looking for a senior manager, and she was asked if she would be interested in applying. She decided against that option. She loved her responsibilities as staff engineer, and more significantly, she doubted her ability to perform well in the senior manager role because it involved managing engineers outside her area of expertise. But the fact that the team had asked her to assume that role was a strong indication that she would perform well in that job. Fortunately, she got a second chance to take that role. When the senior manager left, Sarah stepped into the manager role and thus ended up in the role she was afraid of getting into—but without the title.

In hindsight, she feels she would have been further along in her career if she had grabbed the opportunity in the first place. Her advice is, "Fake it 'til you make it. That is the world we live in. People trust people who are confident." However, Sarah also cautions that there is a delicate balance between displaying confidence and over-promising. You have to set the right expectations while showing that confidence.

~ ~ ~

Like most of the women interviewed in this book, Sarah believes that, within the tech industry at least, promotions, raises, and opportunities are not offered purely based on skills and perfor-mance. Sarah has some salient opinions on this topic. "It's wrong for men to say the tech industry is a meritocracy, and it's wrong for me as a relatively privileged person, a Caucasian middle-class person raised in the US, to say it is a meritocracy. That would be just foolish," Sarah said emphatically.

She explained that a person who grew up in lower-middle-class poverty, worked their way through state school, and then ended up in tech has done a lot more work than an individual who was raised in an upper-middle-class family. Sarah continued, "I think America has this reputation that anyone can come here and make a name for themselves, no matter where you come from or who you are: a really nice, feel-good story. But if that's what you tell yourself, then you're turning a blind eye to the inequities and injustice that exist in society." Because promotions and opportunities are not in fact handed out equitably, it is necessary to look at all forms of institutionalized bias, including gender bias, and try to correct them. Sarah added that it is also important to look at unconscious bias—because it's so subtle that it's hard to detect. We have to be hyper-vigilant to see it.

Sarah is emphatic about one example: women need to negotiate better for their compensation in the first job of their career. "Women leave millions of dollars on the table when they don't negotiate on their first job. That's the money you could start a company with," Sarah said. She feels proud that she managed to negotiate for a higher salary in her first job. She says that women can do more to maximize their earning potential by being more assertive about compensation. Another strategy that can work is to ask for more responsibility and often compensation will follow. She believes compensation follows when you love what you do *and combine that with speaking up for yourself.* In her experience, she has noticed that men are much more direct about their compensation requirements, and they will be assertive about their needs for raises.

Sarah also cites another example of unconscious bias: the interview process. More often than not, women are judged on their confidence rather than on their skills. Once, Sarah's team was interviewing a woman candidate. One of the interviewers told her, "She got the right answer, but she wasn't confident, and took a long time checking her answer, so we shouldn't hire her." Sarah challenged the interviewer. "I told the interviewer 'We are not judging based on confidence. We are judging based on the person's problem-solving skills.' I went back and argued for another interview," Sarah said. Sarah countered a form of bias that values the appearance of confidence over skills. By doing so, she enabled the interview panel to make a fair assessment of the candidate.

Another way gender bias manifests itself is that women have to prove themselves far more than men. Sarah says, "I do often feel that I have to prove myself doubly. I have to be approximately 50 to 100% more accomplished than a man to earn that next step." I asked her whether she sees gender bias as creating the fabled glass ceiling. "I don't believe there is an absolute ceiling," was her reply, "but I do believe that you have to prove yourself beyond a shadow of a doubt." Sarah remarked that the burden women shoulder to prove themselves often causes them to drop out of the workforce. So, fewer women are left to continue on that arduous climb to senior roles. The number of women who have to prove themselves "beyond a shadow of a doubt" becomes consistently smaller as they move up the leadership ladder. This creates a natural culling effect, whereby women tend to hold themselves back as the path to higher levels gets more challenging.

~ ~ ~

As in all my interviews, I asked Sarah for her thoughts on how to help attract and retain women in the tech fields, despite the unfair force of gender bias. On a personal level, Sarah permits herself to prioritize work–life balance. She makes sure she has everything in place to make her days successful. For example, like the majority of the interviewees in this book, she has the support of her husband, who does more than his share of work around the house. She outsources cleaning and yard work, and she makes sure she gets enough sleep. "I have three non-negotiables: sleep, spiritual life, and exercise. I know that if I am exhausted, I am not effective. You can do short bursts of long working hours, but you can't sustain that long term."

Sarah further recommends two things we can each do to get more women into the pipeline and leadership positions. First, as individuals, "Women must develop grit, or mental toughness, or resilience. That's the number one thing that is going to make a difference. If you get demoralized with every change, with every setback, with every micro-aggression, you are just not going to be in a good place." She recommends sports to develop this mental toughness. "Being resilient can make a huge difference," she urges. "You can stand out from your colleagues when you have that sort of peace in your emotional toolkit. I hike and enjoy cycling. I even did competitive cycling for a few years. I do longer bike rides to push myself, or I climb hills."

Second, women can do more to support each other in the workplace. "There is a significant aspect of helping each other collectively: being aware of what other women want and verbalizing that for each other." As an example, Sarah described the clever strategy of "amplification" that female staffers developed during the first term of the Obama administration, when there were only a few women in his cabinet.

"The women there realized they would raise ideas that would get talked over. A man would raise the same idea ten minutes later, and the other men would say, 'Oh, that's such a great idea.' The women took action. Any time a woman would say something, another woman at the table would say, 'Hey, what so-and-so just said was a great idea.' They kept repeating what each other said until they started getting recognized and gained more influence in that room."

This amplification strategy forced the men to recognize the female source of the contribution. As the female staffers continued to use this technique, more awareness grew about the ways unconscious gender bias played out. A deliberate process was put in place to counter that bias, which led to Obama's second term having an equal split of men and women.

It's amazing how a critical mass of women can change the age-old behaviors of society. The next time you have a woman on your team who makes an important point in a meeting, speak up and give her credit. I have taken this advice to heart, and I now actively support other women, and men, on my team. Yes, there are men who also have a hard time speaking up and getting their voices heard. Regardless of gender, being supportive of your coworkers and making sure their voices are heard is a good thing to do. Sarah's advice is easy to implement because every day we have opportunities to amplify our voices. All we have to do is look around, listen, and be aware.

~ ~ ~

TAKEAWAYS

- Sarah is a natural leader who has gravitated toward leadership roles in software engineering.

- She realized programming could be used to help people and impact society, and when she discovered the practical applications of software, she fell in love with programming.

- Her parents wanted her to impact society by helping people; this drive stayed with her into adulthood.

- Experiencing a real-world application made software meaningful to Sarah. She keeps this in mind when she tries to inspire the next generation of girls by making them aware that software solves real-world human problems, and it's not just an academic exercise.

- She believes that everyone has imposter syndrome (both men and women). We can combat this with fake confidence. Sometimes perception is all that matters.

- Concerning negotiation, Sarah cares more about career growth than compensation.

- Meritocracy doesn't exist, because "we don't all enter the workforce on an even playing field."

- Women should support each other by helping to verbalize our desires and goals.

CHAPTER 15: ANA'S STORY

BIOSKETCH: *Ana Pinczuk says that she thrives on taking on big jobs that "aren't for the faint of heart." Her experiences when she was young gave her the confidence that she could succeed even in the face of challenging situations. She admits to becoming easily bored and likes to try new things. As a result, she has had an amazing career spanning different technologies and diverse businesses. Currently she is president of PointNext Services at Hewlett Packard Enterprise, responsible for a multibillion-dollar profit and loss (P&L) organization.*

"I'm very ambivalent about the glass ceiling, because I don't like to dwell on obstacles and I always think I can do anything—yet we can't ignore data. As I consider what's helped me nudge that glass ceiling, three things stand out: striving to be really good at what I do, truly listening to feedback, and having people that are willing to stake their reputation on me."

— Ana Pinczuk, President of PointNext
Services, Hewlett Packard Enterprise

~ ~ ~

Ana was born in Argentina, where her parents worked as scientists and professors. Her mother fled for the United States with Ana and her younger brother in 1976 as a result of political unrest caused by a military coup d'état when she was a young teen. After the coup, about 30,000 Argentinians disappeared or were murdered—scientists included. Fortunately, Ana's father was out of the country at that time, and her mother managed to reunite with him in New York.

This was a pivotal moment in Ana's life, as her family rebuilt their lives in the United States. They had no money, and her parents started with temporary research jobs. "My parents weren't in a great frame of mind—imagine going through that," Ana said. She coped with the strain of the next two years by harboring the illusion that her family would go back to Argentina. It wasn't until her junior year of high school that she finally accepted the new reality that she would be staying in the US.

Ana's forced relocation made her self-reliant and, most importantly, resilient. "I had to learn what it took to really advance in the US," she told me. Her parents didn't know about things like preparing for college applications, so Ana had to be her own guide through many aspects of her life here. "I always think back to that: that if I can survive what I survived at the age of thirteen, I can do anything," says Ana.

A bright student in high school, Ana was awarded a scholarship to Cornell University. Initially, she double-majored in French and math. However, one of her friends had decided to switch to engineering, and her boyfriend was an engineer. She wanted to study with her friends, so embarked on the journey of switching her major from arts and sciences to engineering. At Cornell, this involved reapplying to the university and filling in missing coursework over the summer. The process was an empowering experience. "There's a kind of power in going for something and then doing it." She recalls doing a bit of a celebration dance in front of the engineering school when she and her friend both made it into the program. Ana stayed one extra year, graduating with a master's degree in mechanical engineering with a focus on robotics and control systems.

Ana's first job fresh out of school in 1985 was working for Bell Labs, the research and development arm of AT&T. Professionalism didn't come easily for Ana. "I was a ball of energy, and had not quite transitioned out of college mode," Ana recalled. She said that one of the important lessons she learned during her early years at Bell Labs was how to build a more professional brand.

There weren't many women at Bell Labs at the time, although she formed a close friendship with Patty Hatter (who is featured in chapter 7), a fellow mechanical engineer who arrived shortly after Ana. "Patty and I stood out," Ana noted, in a building with five thousand engineers—most of them men. "It didn't dawn on me at first that I had to transition from college student to professional, and that it would be important to establish a brand as a more serious person." Ana added that she didn't really pick up a corporate style of professionalism from her parents. "I was a daughter of scientists. My mom had this view that they don't take you seriously at work if you look too professional. At Bell Labs, I was twenty-four years old, and I moved to this new group where I interacted more with customers, so I really had to become more professional," she said.

The attention that Ana then put into establishing her brand and taking on a bit of gravitas paid off when her boss chose to sponsor her in moving up the ladder. When he moved out of the core engineering group at AT&T into a technical marketing role, she followed him. He was promoted soon after and trained her as his successor. "Now here I was, twenty-six years old and I was managing a group of twenty-eight people. I remember I was managing a guy who was sixty-four years old, and he told me I was younger than his daughter. I give my first team a lot of credit for teaching me how to be a good manager and a leader." Though she was a young manager, she felt supported by her team. They respected her in part because she had started out as the technical expert in the domain.

In 1994, an opportunity arose in South America doing wireless business development. "I had never done wireless. I didn't know the market or the products, but I had enough confidence to know 'Hey, I can do this.' At the same time, I should have thought about it more." Ana became regional director of business development for Alcatel-Lucent for the Southern Cone of South America. The position ended up being more challenging than she'd expected. On the positive side, it exposed her to new markets and customers, and it was a great opportunity to gain global expertise. On the challenging side, there were many variables to learn: new market, products, customers. She came away from that experience understanding that some risks require careful consideration and that working from a position of strength is important.

"Every time I think of that role, I think of myself jumping off a roof and seeing if I can land. It was that feeling of being a cat and launching yourself—'I hope I don't break any bones.' I was just traveling everywhere in South America. I had to learn the products. I had to gain respect from customers. We won a big deal, and by the end of that, I learned to flourish and how to study. I mean I had to really, *actually* study. This idea of constant learning in your career, it was important," she said.

While in South America, Ana got a call from one of her mentors, encouraging her to investigate a similar business development role in New York running AT&T's global sales account for JP Morgan. She got the job and thrived in that role, being selected as #1 Global Sales Professional out of a sales force of two thousand people.

Ana had certainly made some interesting career moves in that first decade of her career. She went from engineering to technical marketing to sales, when many others start as engineers, move into management, and remain in engineering. Ana attributes her deviation from the norm to her curiosity. She enjoys delving into the unknown and trying out new things. This has served her well, as she gained breadth with numerous functional roles.

While in New York, she was asked by her mentor (who was by then the CTO of AT&T Bell Labs) to run managed services at Bell Labs. Thus, she jumped from sales back to her core area of expertise, technology, leading their research, development, and engineering organizations. She was next promoted to the vice president level to run the IP backbone for AT&T, just when the growth of the commercial internet was taking off, the dot-com boom was in full swing, and AT&T was the second biggest internet service provider (ISP) in the US. While running the AT&T backbone, she worked closely with Cisco, drawing on her experience in both engineering and sales.

As Ana worked more closely with Cisco to resolve product issues, Cisco executives approached Ana for her AT&T expertise in their own IP platform. They knew she could add tremendous value to the company, working on problems for all ISPs.

Moving from AT&T to Cisco was a major transition for her. She would be moving from the East Coast to the West Coast, but more importantly, it was also a step-down transition, from vice president to one of several senior directors. Furthermore, Ana was seven and half months pregnant at the time. Cisco was a smaller company than AT&T, and Ana appreciated having an opportunity to start in a new environment. She made several wise decisions. First, she made sure her compensation and growth potential would be strong at Cisco, to compensate for losing the vice president title. Next, she negotiated the ability to start working for Cisco in New Jersey and then move to Silicon Valley after the birth of her baby. Also, she researched the

California offices, and was pleased to discover that Cisco had just opened up their on-site day care, which would allow her to better manage work and family. She made the jump.

At Cisco, she shifted management positions every few years, taking on increasing responsibilities for a variety of groups including the service provider group, iOS software, product management, and engineering. About ten years into her Cisco experience, all of the Cisco technical support services worldwide were consolidated under Ana. After three years in this role, Ana was promoted to senior vice president and COO for services. Her exposure to opportunities and career growth at Cisco was tremendous. In her new role, she worked with Cisco's CFO and COO, and helped to drive the creation and growth of Cisco's security, analytics, cloud, and professional services businesses. From there, she became senior vice president of sales, further consolidating her global knowledge.

Despite her already impressive career growth by that point, Ana still had significant career goals. Her next objective was to run a P&L center; however, at Cisco there weren't any such roles available at that time. A choice possibility came up at Veritas for a P&L position as well as further growth as successor to the executive vice president and chief product officer. "I took that job because it would expand my personal portfolio and had growth potential," she said. "I had the opportunity to not just run my business, but also to help the company figure out what path to take." When a private equity firm acquired Veritas and her boss departed, Veritas came through on their commitment to Ana, promoting Ana to CPO and executive vice president.

Shortly after my interview with Ana, she accepted a role at Hewlett Packard Enterprise, as senior vice president and general manager at HPE Pointnext, a merger of IT consulting and support groups into a single global services organization. She also serves on several boards: the Anita Borg Institute for Women and Technology, Carnegie Mellon's engineering school, Cornell's school of Computer and Information Sciences, and Delphi Automotive. It is generally hard for women to get on boards. Ana attributes her success to having a strong reputation, a good technical background, and having built a strong network that can vouch for her capabilities and character.

~ ~ ~

In Ana's journey from Cisco to Veritas, she had to negotiate, be skillful in her leadership, and stick to her position. Her vision was to eventually run a P&L and become an executive vice president, and she attained that goal. Early on, when she moved back from vice president to senior director at Cisco, she learned that when you step back and don't have a plan for how to move up, the return journey can be a long road. "I did take a step back in my career. Part of this experience was learning that when you take a risk to go somewhere new, it's important to learn to navigate the new organization and have the backing to accelerate one's career."

Ana's experience in moving to Cisco is not uncommon. As we see for other women in these chapters, changing companies is often coupled with the requirement to retreat a step or two down on the career ladder. What happens, however, is that you have to prove yourself all over again. What happens when unfamiliar challenges crop up in the new company? One might have a steep learning curve to gain the necessary skills to overcome those challenges. Remember the labyrinth discussed in *The Glass Ceiling* essay. Women often end up navigating a maze again when they take a step back in their career. It can be exhausting and depleting, both physically and mentally.

"Looking back, I am glad that I took a step down to pursue a new career opportunity, as it was very worthwhile in the long term. That said, I saw several guys negotiate much more strongly to get their promotions," she said. "It took me about four years to get back to VP." Ana also had a few political setbacks while navigating this maze to her first Cisco vice president position, but she was able to survive them because she had a great network and a strong reputation.

Perhaps her decision to move backward at that juncture gives a hint that Ana isn't immune to imposter syndrome. Actually, this is not surprising since she loves to take on new and unfamiliar challenges head on. Remembering a time, she interviewed for a new role, Ana said, "When you go after something new, there can be an initial tinge of doubt. Am I ready for that?"

~ ~ ~

It always helps to have someone out there who is willing to advocate for you. People who are willing to do this from a higher position can become one's sponsors. Ana had an enlightening perspective to offer about sponsorship. At AT&T, Ana gained a sponsor at the C-suite level: a brilliant visionary, inclusive persona, and somewhat quirky leader. Ana hadn't asked to be sponsored. That relationship emerged because she was able to deliver on a project that this executive really cared about. Because AT&T was trying to move toward a data-driven sales force at the time, this man needed a small team to define the sales strategy. He asked Ana to be part of the team. This project gave Ana a huge opportunity, because it required her to connect with all the sales leaders, to talk to consultants, to help define the strategy, and finally to present the strategy to the head of sales.

The project was successful, and the executive was impressed with Ana's ability to deliver. This led to him handing her more projects. That's why Ana says, "Sponsorship is earned. It's earned through a mutual activity that both people care about, and that showcases what you can do."

In Ana's opinion, directly asking someone to sponsor you may not work unless there is an established relationship. More often than not, a potential sponsor has to know you well and have a good sense of your work. Ana herself is reluctant to sponsor someone unless she has already seen potential in them. "Many people have asked me, 'Can you be my sponsor?' And I say, 'I'm not going to sponsor you if I don't really know what you can do.'" However, she does sponsor people, first ensuring that she has the type of relationship where she can both give and get feedback.

She mentioned an instance where she promoted a leader to director and then later recommended him for a promotion to senior director. Apart from sponsoring him, he also received some negative input from her. Ana recalled, "I gave him some really tough feedback. I told him, 'If you don't change some of these things, you're never going to make the senior executive ranks.' The guy called me later and said, 'I so appreciate that you were so relentless on me.' I replied that I did it because I cared." He's a successful vice president now.

~ ~ ~

From an external perspective, anyone would agree that Ana has attained success in her field. For Ana herself, success is multifaceted, encompassing much more than simply adding titles to her résumé. During our conversation, she highlighted various experiences along her journey that she considers elements of her success, and from which she distilled useful insights.

As she was in the midst of a job search when we met for the interview, I was interested to hear about Ana's decision process for selecting her next step. She was interviewing with a couple of CEOs from Fortune 500 companies for some highly coveted jobs. I asked her to explain her general approach to decision making. "I am an intuitive person; I start with my gut. That has served me well," Ana said.

Her strategy for picking her next company and role was to build a decision matrix and fill in answers to the following questions: "Where do I want to go in my career? How can I best contribute? Can I build my own team? What is the growth potential of the company, or is it a turnaround that I can influence?" Based on her matrix and her gut, she eliminated seven companies. "I start with a feeling, saying, 'Ahh, I don't know if I like that company.' Then my husband asks, "Why don't you like it?' and I reply, 'I don't know, I just have this feeling.' Her husband's advice to her is always to parse her feelings into data and then use the data to make the decision. She agrees that making data-driven decisions about a job is important, but that too involves both art and science.

On developing one's career in general, Ana's advice is to "think two jobs ahead" and be conscious of your journey and your brand. "One of the fundamental things you need to do is to know where you are and where you are perceived to be in your career—and then the journey is the difference. Understand your priorities, so that you know how much you're willing to sacrifice, and understand where your brand is relative to the job that you want, and bridge that gap."

When negotiating, Ana's initial advice here is simple: "Do your homework and see what others command, and then ask for what you think is fair." But she is quick to add that you must also have the courage to walk away if it doesn't suit you. "You've got to figure out what's important to you, as well. Is it compensation? Benefits? Flexibility?" She recommends asking oneself, "Which are important to you: the title, pay, charter, team, or all of the above?"

Ana learned early on that if you don't ask, you don't get—though it wasn't easy for her to ask for a raise either. In one job, she found out she was making $30,000 less than her male peer. She chose not to bring that up to her boss. Instead, she used this information to negotiate a higher salary when she was promoted to a new role, asking about average salaries and making it known that she cared about making more money—as her male peers had probably done earlier.

She further suggests leveraging the interview process, whether for promotion or in seeking a new position, as a way to benchmark yourself. "Testing out your street value on the job market every once in a while, is a way to check if your role and compensation is appropriate." I would also caution women to remember that our "street value" can be skewed by gender pay inequity, and to consider that factor when conducting your research.

One emerging theme in Ana's journey is prioritizing. Health, originally something of an afterthought for Ana, proved to be a significant example. As her career unfolded, she encountered several medical difficulties, which has led her to a passion for wellness. "I've had a couple of incidents in my career where I did not take care of myself. Once I ended up in the hospital with heart palpitations. In the process, I actually discovered that I had premature ventricular contractions." She wisely took this incident as a wake-up call to reprioritize. Her order of priorities is now "family, health, work, and school."

Ana combats stress in a three-fold manner. First, she does regimented exercise, particularly a vigorous form of yoga. "I don't do restorative yoga. I like to do power yoga. I also do high-intensity cardio, because when I do power yoga or boot camp, my mind can't think about anything else." Second, she participates in Friday night weekly gatherings with close friends. The third element of her relaxation plan is the consistent support of her husband, who helps her to balance her work and family life.

Women are likely to encounter gender bias at multiple points throughout their careers. Ana has a strategy for combating gender bias. "One of the things I've had to do was to really think about how I could be successful in the face of bias. Gravitas helps." Gravitas is an ancient Roman virtue that was considered essential to leaders. In Latin, it translates to "seriousness, dignity, importance, and depth of personality." Ana mentioned that early in her career she made a deliberate effort to make gravitas part of her professional brand. "I can walk into a room, and people will know that I'm the boss—or that I've got the title—not because I came in on a horse, but because of my confidence and how I behave."

For some women, the word "gravitas" connotes male authority; thus, some have an aversion to the word. Another of the women I interviewed thinks the word implies that women have be "like a man" in order to be confident and successful. Ana, however, begs to differ. "I don't think that way about it," she told me. "Gravitas means having seriousness of purpose and confidence in your abilities, as well as the ability to project those attitudes in a way so that other people can take you seriously."

Building one's gravitas is about developing an executive presence, I agree. This is something both women and men can do to give credibility to their leadership skills. Because we have fewer women leaders as role models, we also have fewer examples of women with gravitas. So perhaps that's where the misconception arises about gravitas being reserved as a male quality.

~ ~ ~

Now that Ana is at the C-suite level, does she bump into the infamous glass ceiling? Rather, does she think she has a glass ceiling? "I'm ambivalent about the glass ceiling," was her first response, "because I don't like to dwell on obstacles, and I always think I can do anything."

"Yet we can't ignore data," she continued. "As I consider what's helped me nudge that glass ceiling, three things stand out: striving to be really good at what I do, truly listening to feedback, and having people that are willing to stake their reputation on me."

Most of the women in this book have figured out their own ways to deal with the glass ceiling. For Ana, "One other thing that breaks the glass ceiling to me has been the network." Ana revealed that she is not a natural networker. When she was at AT&T, she had sponsors and mentors who were watching out for her and helping her to get strategic responsibilities, which significantly contributed to helping her career grow and flourish. Later in her career, she was at a company where she didn't have nearly that level of support. There, Ana realized the importance of building a network and a strong reputation, both within and outside of the company.

"You have to start to build a credible reputation. As a manager, your brand matters inside the organization. It's like, when you're a first grader, what matters to you encompasses your neighborhood, your street, the corner store, and your friends. When you go to high school, one new thing that might matter to you is the fact that you can drive. Your world expands as you grow up."

In the same manner, the scope of your network should expand as your career progresses. Ana went on to say that as you rise through the different levels in your career, you start to realize that the scope of your network should start to reach beyond the confines of the cubicles and walls of your organization. Her advice is to make your network expand by making it a priority. Allocate time to build relationships with people in your network.

Ana cautions that success is not just about building your network, it's also about nurturing those connections. This requires conscious effort, and significant time. Ana has prioritized building and nurturing her network, which has made her well known in the tech industry. She has a strong brand and reputation. Ana has numerous examples where relationships with people in her network have been helpful for her to break glass ceilings that she has encountered.

~ ~ ~

When I think about the essence of Ana's career success, I think it is her ability to make leaps. Ana says she makes bold career leaps partly because she gets bored easily, but in part, the strategy also works well for her.

Early in her life, she had to leave Argentina and jump into the life of being teenager in the United States. This unfortunate set of circumstances seems like the proverbial cloud with a silver lining, in that it gave Ana an innate sense of confidence to aid her when jumping into new situations. In her career, she made all kinds of leaps. She has also leapt in and out of technical knowledge domains, both in school and in the field, as she identified industry trends that would make promising career avenues.

She attributes some of her success as a leader of technology organizations to the fact that she has developed two areas of core technical expertise as well as significant breadth in business skills. She says that it is important to have your core, an area in which you have deep expertise. Once you have that unshakable expertise, it is great to add on other functional roles that expand your business skills. Ana calls it a "π," to symbolize your two cores of expertise (the two vertical lines) and your breadth (the horizontal line). Ana has come to believe that to be better positioned for success in technology, you have to spot emerging trends in technology and pick ones that would be promising areas to gain additional core expertise. For Ana, hardware networking was her core before the growth of technology moved networking into the software realm. She made an effective decision to add core expertise in software and the cloud.

Anna ended our conversation with this piece of wisdom. "I don't think there is just one core," she believes. "I think you need to look at your core but then figure out how you make sure you don't rely on old expertise. That is really important."

~ ~ ~

TAKEAWAYS

- Ana's childhood experiences with the Argentinian coup d'état shaped her career. She grew up as a survivor, and learned decision-making skills that allowed her to become a leader.

- Ana loves to learn. She detests relying on old knowledge and constantly wants to keep herself up to date.

- Her main advice: Know your priorities, maintain them, and structure your life based on them. Also, know your brand.

- Ana believes one's core is structured like a pi symbol (π). It's crucial to have to have two core areas of deep expertise like the two legs of the π, and then to reach out for breadth across those areas.

- She says trust your intuition, but also make data-driven decisions.

- Ana believes in looking two jobs ahead of where you are, understanding how you are perceived today at work (recognizing your brand), and managing your brand relative to that gap so that you can eventually get there.

- One way that Ana counteracts gender bias is by deeply knowing what makes her successful as a woman. For her, that meant becoming the best leader she can be and building gravitas early in her career.

- Ana also consciously built and nurtures her network not just within her company, but also within the larger tech community.

SPONSORS: THE STRONGEST LINK

Gaining the support of a sponsor will have a pivotal effect on your professional trajectory. It makes all the difference to have someone who either is in your command chain or has authority who recognizes your potential and actively works on taking you to the next level.

While a mentor can teach and advise from any level of greater experience when you request guidance, a sponsor can improve your job options throughout your career. From an influential management level, your sponsor has made an active investment in you with some expectation of results (i.e., your efforts make your sponsor look good), is willing to advocate for you, and has the power to recommend you for particular companies and positions, putting her or his reputation behind you. Sponsors are often the decisive factor in getting a strategic project, visibility, the next promotion, or a raise.

When a leader sponsors someone, the leader's reputation is on the line, so it is prudent for them to perform their due diligence in getting to know the abilities and potential of the person they are considering sponsoring. Preparing a person to be sponsored can involve giving her special projects and—at times—direct feedback on areas that need to be improved to get to the next level.

Deciding whom to sponsor is currently a subjective decision. All too often, male senior leaders direct the benefits of sponsorship to people who are similar to themselves. That may help to explain why men get more promotions than women. Data from McKinsey & Company indicates that for every hundred women promoted to manager, 130 men are promoted.[42] More work needs to be done to encourage senior male leaders to be more objective in choosing whom to sponsor.

One of my friends once said, "Lift while you climb." One role of senior leaders in a company is to identify individuals in the company who are capable of taking on larger leadership responsibilities and giving those

---

[42]   Taken from https://qz.com/793109/a-mckinsey-and-lean-in-report-on-women-in-the-workplace-study-shows-women-are-still-trailing-men-in-opportunities/.

individuals the opportunities both to increase their leadership skills and to have opportunities to gain visibility within the company. This is what sponsorship is all about. It's wise for anyone in a leadership position to advocate for and "raise others up," just as they advocate for and promote themselves. Helping each other reach their potential helps the company and fosters a better world.

~ ~ ~

Apart from sponsorship, mentors and role models are vital. Although there are far more men than women in most workplaces, it's useful for both men and women to have a mix of male and female mentors. Having diverse mentors helps us learn different perspectives and different ways to handle situations we find ourselves in. We need women to start mentoring both men and women in the workplace.

Role models can work in a similar way to mentors. Many of the people who have the leadership qualities that we would want to emulate may not have the time or inclination to sit down with us and be our personal mentors. But that doesn't mean we can't view them from afar and learn from them by example.

The best way to the bridge the gap between male and female leadership is to sponsor high potential women. According to a report[43] by Judith Warner, Senior Fellow at the Center for American Progress, it's been estimated that with the current rate of change, it will take until 2085 for women to reach parity with men in leadership roles. But that doesn't deter me from dreaming of the day when we have diversity of thought and opinion in leadership and we talk about sponsoring a high potential *individual* rather someone than based on their gender or race. In essence, diversity becomes a way of life.

---

43   Judith Warner, Senior Fellow at the Center for American Progress
      https://www.americanprogress.org/issues/women/reports/2014/03/07/85467/
      womens-leadership/

CHAPTER 16: ERICA'S STORY

BIOSKETCH: *Erica Lockheimer is a senior director at LinkedIn, heading the growth engineering team since 2010. A vocal advocate for women's careers in technology, she is also the head of Women in Tech at LinkedIn and a board member for the Anita Borg Institute of Women in Technology (the nonprofit that organizes the annual Grace Hopper Celebration of Women in Computing). Her story demonstrates how developing a strong network of relationships can lead to extraordinary career opportunities.*

"Early in my career, technology was a boys' club. It wasn't inclusive. I just didn't feel like I belonged. Not that the men were doing it on purpose; they were comfortable working with men, and I didn't fit into that. I definitely felt gender bias plenty of times. I didn't say anything, didn't talk about it. Now I'm totally talking about it. I have nothing to lose. I am older now. I simply want to pay it forward to help others, and do the right thing!"

— Erica (Ewing) Lockheimer, Senior Director, LinkedIn

~ ~ ~

From her youngest days, Erica's father was a major influence in her life. He offered Erica and her two sisters a consistent source of encouragement. Although nobody in his family had gone to college, he impressed upon his three daughters the importance of education, encouraging them all to be highly proficient at math. Erica recalls, "My writing skills were horrible, my geography skills were horrible, but I was really good at math." He recently died of cancer, but the lessons he imparted live on. "All my sisters are independent, and we are all super close."

Erica's dad did not have an easy life. Not only did his dad leave when he was young, but his dad split up the family by taking two of the three brothers, leaving Erica's dad to take care of his mom. Erica's dad worked at a meat company in San Jose, California, which through hard work and persistence, he later owned. The meat business wasn't his passion; his dream was to become an engineer. To that end, he took several college-level electronics courses, but family responsibilities and life took over, and he never fulfilled that dream. Yet he gave Erica the confidence that she could be an engineer, if that's what she wanted. He took time to show her his electronics books and teach her circuitry. "I was the one who followed in his footsteps," Erica said.

When Erica entered San Jose State University (SJSU), her father also worked hard to provide the means for her education. "He paid for college and books in cash," she recalled. Erica continued to make progress in her education and developed a good foundation to become an engineer. Throughout, her father remained her champion. "Anytime I was doubtful, we would talk about it, and he would tell me, 'Go, go, go!'"

Although she knew that math would be her focus, it took Erica some time to figure out specifically what she wanted to major in at college. While walking down a hall of the engineering building at SJSU, she noticed a glass case that said, "Society of Women Engineers." It was inspirational to her to learn that there was a professional engineering society for women, and that motivated her to explore a major in engineering. Within the broad field of engineering, she first chose civil engineering.

"I thought, that's cool. It's outdoors, I will work on buildings. But I had no clue what it meant. I soon realized civil engineering wasn't right for me, and I switched to computer engineering, which proved to be a fit. And since I couldn't decide between hardware or software, I did both."

College didn't come easily for Erica. She found the classes extremely challenging, perhaps because she was simultaneously working more than twenty hours per week to contribute toward college expenses. She also found the lack of women colleagues disheartening. "Not having many women in the classroom was frustrating, and I remember failing just miserably," she said. Luckily for her, one of her classmates—a guy named Aaron—reached out to see if she wanted some help. He told her about a study group that would last until one or two in the morning.

That study group was key to her successful completion of her computer engineering degree. "I practically lived in that study room. There was no way I would have passed those classes if those people didn't bring me along. We got through the classes, we learned a lot, and we challenged each other. It was fantastic." She graduated from

SJSU in 2000—a big achievement for her. Erica was the first person in her family to graduate college.

She began her career with a start-up company called Critical Path.[44] A man named Frank became her mentor, teaching her how to program and write beautifully optimized code. "I was lucky that someone wanted to invest in me, lift me up, and guide me along the way," Erica said.

Many software engineers who are fresh out of college trip up due to their lack of experience. At Critical Path, Erica made such a mistake, which could have seriously tarnished her reputation. "I really wanted to work on a project by myself. My boss said I could work on a calendaring system," she recalled. "It was a big deal to have a calendar online at that time. We needed some numbers to present to the board, statistics to show how our back-end services were performing and so on." But things didn't go exactly as planned. "I was such an amateur! I was clearing my disk space all the time, because we didn't have enough disk space back then. And I wasn't checking in my code into our version control system, where all the files were stored. I accidentally deleted all my code—all of it." She said she felt like an "utter failure."

Erica panicked. When she told her colleagues what she had done, they scrambled to help her. They tried to recover the files from the hard drive but were unable to do so. Dejected, Erica went to her boss and told him what happened. His disappointment was obvious, and she started to cry. She promised to rewrite all her code in two days, even though she had no idea how to pull that off in such a short time. "It was an amazing feat. I stayed up all night," she said. "Code stays in your memory—you can actually write it better the second time around. I did it. My peers were stunned. It was awesome." Right from the beginning of her career, Erica proved that she could be persistent and effective when facing a huge challenge.

44　The company she joined was RemarQ, which was purchased by Critical Path soon thereafter.

By rewriting a couple weeks of code in two days, Erica not only redeemed herself in the eyes of her boss, but she established herself as the kind of person to invite to the early stage of a start-up company. Her boss, along with a few other engineers, decided to create a new company called Good Technology and asked Erica to join. She stayed there for nine years, working with Microsoft Exchange Server, RIM BlackBerry 950 and 957, and Palm Treo devices. With the help of her mentor, Frank, she and the team delivered the first server that could wirelessly send email and data to a mobile phone.

Erica met her husband at Good Technology. "I got married and had babies," she said. "I remember being worried about that. I thought, 'Gosh, I don't want to take too much time off or I will lose my job.' It wasn't common to see pregnant women walking through the hallways of the company. I felt uncomfortable. I took maternity leave, but I also had an itch to get back to work."

Her management journey began with a jolt. While home on maternity leave, she received a phone call from work. She thought she was being laid off. Instead, they told her they were doing a reorganization of the company and asked her if she wanted to manage a team—the beginning of her management journey. At Good Technology, her career in the management track advanced considerably. She went from being a junior engineer to becoming a director. "I organically got into management by just doing it and working with our customers."

Erica eventually became the director of the Server Engineering group at Good Technology, with a team of seventeen senior engineers reporting to her. She established herself in that role and she felt settled in her job. "I was there for nine years. I was good and happy, had two kids, and had everything under control." Then an opportunity to transition to a different company came along.

"Our CEO knew the VP of product engineering at LinkedIn. They were looking for someone that knew Microsoft Exchange Server." Since Erica had spent nearly a decade integrating with Microsoft Exchange Server, she knew she could help. However, she was not interested in leaving Good Technology. Despite her reservations, she met with the people at LinkedIn and discussed ideas. Those discussions turned into an interview. "When I met the team, it was tough! I met the heads of engineering, product, operations, and the rest of the team. The team was brilliant, and I was intrigued. But I loved the folks at Good. Not only do I attach myself to the mission of the company, but I attach myself to people. I am a people person." After several panel interviews, she moved to LinkedIn.

"That was scary. I was well established at Good Technology. I was good at my job and happy there. I had my reputation, my brand, and I had everything under control. I didn't want to go to a company where nobody knew me at all." Erica had doubts that she could be successful elsewhere, but she also knew that LinkedIn was doing interesting work combining business objectives with social media. She accepted the internal challenge to prove herself in a new environment. "I felt I could do this again. I decided to take a leap of faith, but I cried when I left Good," she told me.

The one downside to the job offer at LinkedIn was that they were not willing to hire Erica as a director. Instead, they brought her in as a senior manager. Though the transition was one step down in the corporate ladder, she felt it was an opportunity to prove herself in a new environment. It took her just over three years to be promoted back to director level and another two years to reach senior director level, but she did it. "I basically worked really hard and got the opportunities," she said.

~ ~ ~

Many people (women *and* men) feel nervous when they move from an individual contributor role to a manager role. "I do remember feeling insecure at times, especially during my transition from engineer to manager. I felt my worth when I checked in code. In my management role, I am not checking in the code, so what is my value? You can get confused in that state." The insecurity can even get worse when one starts managing managers.

In Erica's opinion, the antidote to that insecurity is trust. She says that managers should be trusting and trusted partners with the people that report to them. The manager's role is to build people's leadership skills to the point that the manager doesn't have to do much to keep the team functioning well. "I should be totally replaceable," she says. "My value now is leading the team, pointing people in the right direction, orchestrating, and being strategic. I need as many leaders around me as possible, for me to scale. If I do that, then I get other opportunities to do even greater things and have laser focus," she says.

Another way that insecurity can hit people is in the form of imposter syndrome. It has become apparent to me that most people suffer from imposter syndrome in some sphere of their lives. Naturally, I was curious to know, with all of Erica's achievements and responsibilities, if she sometimes feels inadequate too. "I experience it all the time," she responded. "I still do." Erica knows that imposter syndrome is normal, and that a lot of the feeling is "in your head. It's just stories you tell yourself."

Erica shared a few of her strategies for dealing with imposter syndrome. "You talk about it, but not to everybody," she explained. "There are some people you confide in: 'This is how I am feeling. What do you think?' I have men and women I confide in. Sometimes you have to play it out and work through the emotions. The more you talk to other people, the more you realize that they feel that way, too. But you don't need to dump it out for everyone else to see," she advises.

Another suggestion she had for dealing with imposter syndrome is simply not allowing yourself to give in to it. "You hear that voice and say, 'No, no, no.'" She accepts the positive side of imposter syndrome: it can push you to be humble and examine the flaws that get in your way. "When you are on that edge of self-doubt, you stretch, you grow, and you have the opportunity to improve in that moment. It is not the total disaster you may think it is."

~ ~ ~

As I reflected on Erica's career journey, it was obvious that human connections were important to her success. At SJSU, the relationships that she had with the members of her study group were instrumental in her getting through her coursework and graduating. The mentoring she got from Frank at RemarkQ helped her learn to write quality production code right from the beginning of her career. The relationships and reputation she built both at Critical Path led to her being asked to join Good Technology. The relationships built at Good Technology led to her opportunity at LinkedIn. She says, "All of those foundational relationships—some formed ten to fifteen years ago—are so important, even to this day."

The role mentoring and sponsorship have played in her career has spurred Erica to pay it forward to others. "What I learned is that I have to do the same for other women and men in my team," she said. "I have stories where I have helped grow people, even when they didn't even believe in themselves."

Erica shared with me a story of one high-potential woman in her team for whom she went to bat. "I was having a reorg and I had an opening in my team. I thought, 'Who am I going to give this opportunity to?' There was one woman I had been mentoring. I knew it was a stretch for her, but I told her about it. And she said, 'Are you sure I can do it?' How come she wasn't excited? I knew it was because she was scared. I knew it was a stretch.

"The woman said she would think about it. She came back the next day and said she would do it. I told her I would be her partner all the way—because that's how you grow. That's what I told her: 'You are not going to be totally ready for it. That's the whole point of growing.'"

Sponsoring the woman for her promotion was a leap of faith, and it paid off. The woman's leadership blossomed, and she is now one of Erica's best managers. Erica eventually promoted her to director. When it comes to sponsoring high-potential women, this is one place where many companies drop the ball. Erica wonders whether anyone else would have sponsored that woman as she did.

As we see throughout the stories in this book, sponsors are important for getting you the opportunities. However, obtaining sponsorship can be hard; you can't just walk into someone's office and say, "Hey, sponsor me." Erica says women have to look toward the men. "Most of the sponsors are men. Last time I checked, men still have most of the power (for now at least). That's the way you can get to the next level. Only one person who has the authority needs to believe in you."

Erica attributes her success and career progression to the senior director role to the sponsors she had. She says people can be stuck in their careers for various reasons. Sometimes they might not be in the right place, or they are not the right fit for the company, or perhaps they have a bad manager. Her advice is that if a company is not right for you, or if someone isn't willing to take you to the next level, then leave the company.

I have a dear friend who has amazing potential, but unfortunately, she worked for a manager who had a lot of challenges. He was unable to trust his team, his peers, or his own boss. He was insecure and would resist giving opportunities for his team members to shine. He had a hard time giving up control and providing constructive feedback. This boss was her glass ceiling. It took serious courage to leave, but she went to work for a boss who is now both her mentor and her sponsor. I am so excited for her, because she is set up for success. I am certain she is going to succeed.

Many managers out there are not suited to be leaders, like the one my friend had. To avoid micromanaging her own managers, Erica emphasizes autonomy and giving people complete ownership of a charter or a project. "I am not going to be all into your stuff," she said. "I will let you do it your way, but if I see something that's not right, then I will tell you."

When you are a manager, part of the job is getting and giving feedback—and not all of it is positive. "I think receiving feedback is just a matter of being okay with failure." Erica points out that part of being a leader is stretching, and failures will happen, but leaders grow when they thoughtfully reflect on their failures and learn from them. Early in her career, she didn't want to hear the negative feedback. "I used to take it so personally when getting feedback," she said. But now, Erica has come to the realization that if your boss isn't giving you feedback, they are doing you a disservice.

Some managers have a hard time with handing out negative feedback to people who report to them, but Erica sees it as a gift. She says, "When I give negative feedback to people, I'm really providing opportunities. I have had people come back and say, 'Thank you, no one else ever told me.' Even if they choose to leave the company. I am a bad manager if I don't tell you what's not working. It's up to you—you take the feedback and change." As she learned from one of her amazing mentors, "Feedback is a gift; you can take it or leave it. You can decide what you want to do with it."

It's been found that managers, both men and women, have a hard time giving tough feedback, especially to women. One reason they don't want to give feedback to women is that they think women are too emotional and that they can't handle tough feedback. I discuss this more in the *Emotion in the Workplace* essay.

Our conversation turned to how Erica handled negotiations. She told me that when she was a student without a lot of money, she received two simultaneous job offers. One job paid more than the other. She ended up taking the lower-paying job that she preferred— but she failed to negotiate her pay, even with that second offer as leverage. Looking back, she had this to say: "I think negotiating is important to do, and knowing better now, I would have been more aggressive about it." She added, "I also don't want to make decisions solely on money, because I do believe that you should enjoy what you do, and the money will come. I don't believe that the right thing will always necessarily happen naturally, and I do think you need to enjoy your job. But you should definitely negotiate." In her current position, she sees employment offers coming in, and she notices a difference in pay whenever women do not negotiate. "It happens—it's the truth."

~ ~ ~

There were times in her career when the meritocracy narrative—succeeding purely based on one's abilities—worked well for Erica. However, other times it took more than hard work for her to advance. Erica shared with me one experience that demonstrates how it can pay off to be vocal and strategic regarding promotional aspirations.

"At one point, I saw people getting promoted around me," she said. "I wondered, 'What's up with that?' My boss ended up leaving, and my peer wound up becoming my boss." She liked the man who was promoted, but her situation just felt wrong. She voiced her concerns to one person in the company, and before she knew it, she was talking to several company leaders. "I walked into one of the executive offices, where they asked me, 'What's going on? How do you feel?' They were having this serious conversation with me."

This was a powerful moment for Erica. "I remember being overwhelmed by the response," she recalls, "and not being ready for it. I cried in front of all of them. I didn't even understand how to deal with the emotions."

What an awkward situation for Erica. First, she had her peer promoted to become her boss, then there she was crying about her promotional aspirations in front of a whole group of executives. I wondered aloud why she hadn't been considered for the promotion. Was this an example of gender bias? All too often, when a man and a woman are equally qualified candidates and are vying for an opportunity to advance, the promotion is handed to the man. Erica replied that that wasn't the case here. Time and experience have given her more perspective about the circumstances that led to her peer's promotion. He had two things going for him. First, he had more seniority. Secondly, he asked for the promotion, presenting an effective story for why he deserved it. Erica ended up seeing that he was the logical choice.

As a direct result of this situation, one of the vice presidents gave her great advice, advice that turned out to be key. He suggested to Erica that she get executive coaching. He told her, "I do it every week. I offer it to my leadership team. If you are up for it, you will love it."

Erica agreed to try it. When she started to work with executive coaches, one of the areas they focused on was promotions. They asked her if she had ever asked for a promotion. Erica told them, "No, I worked hard and got rewarded, and that's what has always happened." They coached her on how to go about asking for a promotion.

Ironically, her request led to a bit of awkwardness. Erica's boss—the same one who had been her peer—was also being coached by the same group of executive coaches. "It forced us to have a few hard but good conversations," Erica said. But her boss responded positively to her request for the promotion. "He said, 'Let's work on your packet.' He wrote an amazing packet for me." And when the promotion went through, it meant that Erica and her boss became peers again. Erica later heard from the executive coaches that her boss fought for her and sponsored her.

~ ~ ~

The way promotions work at some companies is that managers and senior engineers have to pitch a justification as to why they want to promote someone in their team. At LinkedIn, Erica says that their typical pitch is a story about leadership, execution, and craftsmanship. Erica stresses the importance of being convincing. If

Erica can't create that story for a person on her team, then she can't promote them.

"You have to have a clear message. When you are thinking about promoting someone, you need to tell a story to your higher-ups as to why this person needs to be promoted. I have to convince myself, and I have to convince other people. It's my job to make that story happen to you. I give you the opportunity for the story, and then it is up to you to deliver on that opportunity."

Deciding whether a person deserves a promotion is just one of many decisions that leaders need to make. Leaders make decisions every day, and they often have to make tough calls. A leader's reputation is built on making decisions that have positive outcomes. Erica says, "From a decision-making point of view, I think early on, I realized that when I started taking management positions or having more authority, I felt like I am the person who needs to be making the decision. It's up to me. I need to do it." She believes in getting a lot of input before making decisions. She does her homework and gathers all the data by talking to various people. "I recognized early on—thank God—that if I were to make the decision by myself, I would most likely be making the wrong decision."

Erica strives to make data-driven decisions. She admitted to me that she wasn't always good at them at first. Sometimes the decision means taking a risk and calling her intuition into play as well. "At the end of the day, your gut tells you what you should do, and I have learned that. Even our executive leadership talk about that a lot—how they make some of their decisions that way." She went on to caution against making a decision you're unsure of. "Just make sure you understand *why* you are doing it, and then you can fight for that decision. That's the difference," she said.

~ ~ ~

A major aspect of Erica's job at LinkedIn is leading a project that fosters the success of women in technology, both inside and outside the company. She is the head of the Women in Tech (WIT) Initiative at LinkedIn, having helped to found the effort. She described the organic formation of this initiative to advance the careers of women in technology at LinkedIn. It grew out of conversations that some of the women at LinkedIn were having about the bias they were experiencing in their careers. In 2010, a group of women from LinkedIn decided to go the Grace Hooper Celebration (GHC). LinkedIn didn't have a booth or anything, the group simply wanted to see what GHC was about. That group had an amazing experience, and the next year they decided to bring a larger team of people from the company.

Erica says that one the most effective tactics in WIT's quest to generate awareness at LinkedIn was making sure that male executives from LinkedIn would attend GHC. As she describes it: "The biggest thing at GHC, between our engineering and HR initiatives, is that we wanted all of our male executives to be there. Guess what? They are the ones with majority power; they are the ones who are going to need to think differently. That's how you scale it." Over the years, the group from LinkedIn that goes to GHC has gotten larger and larger. In 2016, not only did they have a booth, but 120 people from LinkedIn attended, including seven male executives. Erica says her male executives enjoy going to GHC and attend year after year. "They are repeaters. Isn't that awesome?"

To scale an initiative toward helping advance the careers of women at a large company like LinkedIn, it helped that the top leaders of the company understood the importance of the project. Having those men attend GHC has led to them providing significant funding and resources for WIT. Erica and the other leaders of WIT were granted 20% of their work time to work on the Initiative. "It is funded just like any other major engineering project at LinkedIn," Erica reported.

The initiative is focused on making things happen both inside and outside the company. One of the WIT projects inside the company is Invest @ LinkedIn which focuses on investing in women leaders and potential leaders at LinkedIn. One of the strategies is allocating resources for executive coaching for key women leaders. These leaders have found it helpful to get the executive coaching, and it makes them want to mentor other women and see to it that they also get access to executive coaching.

Another WIT project, this one focused outside the company, is a LinkedIn program that gives teenage girls the opportunity to understand what it is like to be a software engineer. Some girls have the misconception that software programmers are always sitting in front of their computers, but the program helps them see that developing software is an interactive discipline that requires communication and collaboration. During the program, the girls come to LinkedIn to build a web app, doing everything a software engineer does. In its first year, the program had a Net Promoter[45] score (NPS) of one hundred and was successful in getting young women to declare computer-related majors.

Erica has been vocal about backing women's careers at LinkedIn for years. With the establishment of WIT, there is significant momentum toward advancing women's careers in technology at LinkedIn. How wonderful that she gets to spend 20% or her time working on advancing the careers of women in technology, both inside and outside the company! With Erica leading the initiative, I wondered how that affected people's perception of her. I struggle with people's perception of me at work. My own experience has been that odd things can happen when you become a champion of women's careers in the workplace. There is something of a backlash, and people slap the feminist label on you, which for many can have negative connotations. Earlier in my career, I would avoid any of the "up with women" programs at work, partially because I was raised to be undiscerning about gender. I considered myself an engineer, not a female engineer; a leader, not a female leader. My beliefs on this changed in 2016. I started to attend tech conferences designed for women, and then I began work on this book. As I became more vocal

---

45   For more information, see https://www.netpromoter.com/know/.

about women in technology, I worried about how people's perception of me would change.

I asked Erica how she handled this. "I know a ton of people who
think I am an idiot, a ton of people who think it doesn't matter, and
a ton of people who think I am doing it wrong," she asserted. "I need
to get a thicker skin, because most people know I am doing something right. They appreciate that I am doing something, and they're
aware of the fact that I have male executive support. I got people
who have my back. When you know someone has your back, it feels
different. And maybe you're putting yourself out there and it's a risk,
but how boring is it to sit on the sidelines and watch someone else
do it when you feel just as passionately about it?"

Concerning my own situation, Erica offered this advice: "You are
doing what you need to do. You will be talked about. You will have
negative things said about you. Get used to it." Good advice. Since
my conversation with Erica, I have become more at peace with what
has been thrown my way, and I have been more active and vocal.
With the support of the management chain in my business unit,
I started an initiative with some of my women coworkers called
Dialogue Circles. We now gather small groups of women to share
aspirations and challenges. This initiative has become a catalyst for
some serious cultural changes in the business unit.

Toward the end of our conversation, Erica mentioned a talk by
Michael Kimmel, Distinguished Professor of Sociology at Stony
Brook University in New York, who specializes in gender studies.
Michael is a longtime feminist. He spoke about how men should
"walk the talk." Erica said, "Men support women—after all, some have
daughters—but they don't publicly admit it. You have to actually
walk the talk." What she means by that is that men have to actively
stand up for women. "Next time, when a man is deciding who is
going to get the next project, he needs to actually come out and
say it: 'A qualified woman deserves to get this chance.' Making these
kinds of fundamental decisions aloud in front of other people will
encourage them to think differently. That's one stage of awareness."

Like most women who strive for diversity in the workplace, Erica is not advocating quotas for women. She wants a system in which we make a concerted effort to look at all people who are qualified for a job and open up a funnel to create diverse leadership.

~ ~ ~

In her already impressive career, Erica has achieved so much. I wondered, where does Erica go from here? Does she believe she has a glass ceiling? Her answer to this question was, "No. I still have belief that I will break it. I believe in change. I see change. I get invitations asking if I want to run for VP of engineering at a start-up. It's some validation that people are thinking differently. They are thinking about me as a viable candidate. Women are viewed as credible leaders."

Erica says that her boss pesters her with questions about what the future holds for her career. He asks her things like, "What do you want to do one day? Do you want to be CEO of a company? You will get to VP. What do want to do next?" Erica wonders if becoming a vice president or a CEO means everything to her. She says that even if she reaches her own glass ceiling, she will probably get bored and will want to try out a new challenge. That's because Erica has so much energy and is always iterating like software; she has so much passion when it comes to women in tech. She strongly believes that the younger generation is thinking differently and that significant change for women in technology is possible. When you are around Erica, you can't help but feel the same way.

~ ~ ~

TAKEAWAYS

- Erica's father was the biggest influence in her life, and he paved the path for her career.

- Erica got the support she needed to handle the challenges of her engineering classes by participating in an effective and tight-knit study group.

- In her career, she was fortunate to have both great mentors and sponsors.

- Step-down transitions can be a big risk, but they can also reap big rewards once you prove yourself and re-attain your earlier position.

- She builds leaders around her so she can scale and grow.

- Going the extra mile when your reputation is on the line can help one to be sponsored.

- She stresses the importance of accepting failure, and of being receptive to hearing negative feedback, as that's where the growth lies.

- As you build your career, you need people to confide in along the way—and you need people (and all the data) to help you make decisions.

- Women's careers in companies can thrive when both men and women voice the need for equity.

EMOTION IN THE WORKPLACE

In order to create environments that support strong female leaders, the way in which women's emotions are viewed in the workplace needs to change.

My experience has shown that if you want to be respected in the world of tech, you have to conform to the prevailing social norms and leave your emotions at the door. Executive presence is practically synonymous with emotional self-control,[46] but it seems there is a double standard that allows men to display strong emotions at work, whereas women are judged harshly when they behave similarly.

Should women just conform to the social norms and keep any display of emotion in check, or should we expect the norms around emotions to change? There isn't much consensus on this.

Take crying for example. A survey done by Anne Kreamer for her book, *It's Always Personal: Navigating Emotion in the New Workplace*, found that 41% of the women said they had cried at work, whereas only 9% of the men admitted to crying. However, Kreamer notes that most women feel bad afterward. "In spite of the cathartic physiological benefits, women who cry at work feel rotten afterward, as if they've failed a feminism test."[47]

Women leaders offer differing advice on showing tears in the workplace. On one side there is Sheryl Sandberg, Facebook COO and founder of Lean In Foundation, who says, "I've cried at work. I try to be myself." On the other side, there is Frances Hesselbein, former CEO of Girl Scouts of the USA, who says, "I believe that tears should be private and no matter what issue, or what situation, we should have a dignified demeanor."[48]

---

46   "Emotional Discipline, Presence, and Leadership," Carolina Perez Sanz, Retrieved: Jan 27, 2018 http://templaradvisors.com/blog/emotional-discipline-presence-leadership
47   "What 15 Female Leaders Really Think About Crying at Work", Catherine Pearson, Huffington Post, 2014 Retrieved: Jan 27, 2018 https://www.huffingtonpost.com/2014/05/28/crying-at-work-women_n_5365872.html
48   Ibid

In my opinion, based on my discussions with women, you need to be selective about whom you trust with your tears. Some people might judge you harshly, while others know that crying can help people think through tough situations more clearly. I heard a story about a woman manager who cried in the office of one of her male executives, many levels superior to her. At the end of the conversation, when she was apologetic for crying, the exec said, "Don't worry about it. A lot of people come in my office and cry."

When it comes to showing anger at work, there is a big double standard. For instance, there is a popular story about how Steve Ballmer, when he was CEO of Microsoft, allegedly threw a chair across the room at Mark Lukovsky, one of his valued engineers, when Lukovsky was in Ballmer's office to announce he was resigning to work at Google.[49] Though Ballmer disputes the allegation that he threw the chair, he doesn't dispute the rage he displayed, not to mention the epithets and off-color things he said at the time about Google.[50] Everyone talks about this incident as though it were funny, but imagine if a woman behaved in a similar fashion in the workplace? In all likelihood, her reputation would never recover.

In addition, the underlying assumption that women are too emotional affects their growth in the workplace. It affects the kinds of reality-check feedback women receive, which undermines their growth as leaders. It's been found that both male and female managers, have a hard time giving tough feedback to women.[51] One reason they avoid it is that they think women can't handle it. What happens when women are not given honest feedback? They can't improve.

Those that think that women are too emotional to handle tough feedback could learn a thing or two from the legendary Geno Auriemma,

---

49   Cade Metz, "Man Survives Steve Ballmer's Flying Chair to Build 21st Century Linux,'" *Wired* (November 18, 2011), https://www.wired.com/2011/11/cloud-foundry/.

50   http://www.businessinsider.com/steve-ballmer-i-didnt-throw-the-chair-at-th-google-engineer-2017-7

51   Kim Scott, *Radical Candor: Be a Kick-Ass Boss Without Losing Your Humanity* (New York: St. Martin's Press, 2017).

who has been the head coach of the University of Connecticut Huskies women's basketball team for over three decades, in which time they have won a record eleven national titles. His secret to success has been delivering tough-love feedback to his team. He says leaders should stop treating women as if they were fragile, but rather work with them as they would any other player on the team.[52]

Yes, we should treat women at work like any other player on the team. The fact is, both men and women feel emotions at work and, when they show their emotions, we shouldn't be quick to judge. In the long term, in order to foster workplace cultures that allow women leaders to thrive, the double standard for emotions needs to be addressed. In the meantime, in the words of one well-respected female tech leader whom I talked to, "You need people you can confide in, and you don't show your emotions to everyone."

---

[52] https://finance.yahoo.com/video/coach-auriemma-feedback-stop-treat-ing-080707657.html

CHAPTER 17: ORNA BERRY'S STORY

BIOSKETCH: *Orna Berry appreciates women who are leaders in technology because she feels there is something sincere and capable about women who reach these positions. To use the words sincere and capable to describe Orna is a major understatement. She is currently a vice president for Dell EMC and general manager of the Israel Center of Excellence. She was appointed Chief Scientist of Israel in 1997, and to date she is the only woman to have held this post. She was an officer in the Israeli Air Force, an entrepreneur, a businesswoman, and a government administrator. As a volunteer, she has offered her time and expertise to numerous prestigious projects, including volunteering for the Women in Industrial Research Organization of the European Commission. Now, in her current role with Dell EMC, she is involved in helping companies access technical resources in Israel to build successful technologies. The core of Orna's success has always been to let go of what she calls "gendered expectations."*

"I've always had an affinity for equality but came to recognize it as a necessity when I served as chief scientist. I realized we need more people with expertise in a particular area in order to retain a constant pool of human capital in times of economic growth. Consequently, I started viewing diversity from an economic perspective, rather than just from a justice and equality perspective. I found that teams were much stronger when they had a good percentage of women in them."

— Orna Berry, CVP and GM, Israel
Center of Excellence, Dell EMC

~ ~ ~

Orna was born in Jerusalem and raised in Tel Aviv and France. She says that although her mother was extremely smart and a pillar of the family, the household was not progressive with regard to traditional gender roles. Her father did not encourage or support her education. He tutored her brothers in electronics but left her out. But her father's interest in science and his entrepreneurial bent propelled her to follow in his footsteps. She considered him a role model who was instrumental in her successful career in engineering and entrepreneurship.

Orna's decision to focus on science and technology came during her service in the Israeli Air Force. She was assigned to work on ground programs at the flight academy. Knowledge of math, physics, and aeronautical design was necessary for the kinds of problems she needed to solve—and all of these subjects interested her. She was also intrigued by the interaction between methodologies, people, and technology.

When she left the military, Orna made a conscious decision to choose a career that was independent of language, location, and culture. She also wanted a career that wouldn't be limited by the level of salary generally offered to women. "So, I decided to study sciences," she said.

A decisive moment in Orna's educational career took place when she was completing her undergraduate degree in math from Haifa University. She was driving a professor home and he asked her what she was planning to do after graduation. She told him she was done with schooling and intended to join the workforce. The professor said, "I won't tell you you're smart, but I will tell you that people who are more stupid than you have PhDs." He told her that if she applied to graduate school, he would give her a letter of recommendation. It was a brief five-minute conversation, but it completely altered Orna's career path. She realized she had both the potential to get a PhD and the professor's support. "So, I did apply!"

In Israel, there was no direct path to a PhD with just an undergraduate degree. Therefore, Orna applied to the master's program in statistics at Tel Aviv University. After completing her master's degree, she moved to the United States. She applied to PhD programs in the US and graduated with a PhD in computer science from the University of Southern California in 1986.

With PhD in hand, Orna entered the workforce in 1986, an exciting time to be in data communication. Online communities were just forming, and the US internet protocols (TCP/IP) were starting to beat rival protocols. Many of the technologies that were laying the groundwork for the commercial internet as we know it were being developed.[53] "I was lucky to be interested in data communication, which quickly transitioned from an academic discipline to a flourishing business sector," Orna said.

Much of Orna's work at that time revolved around computer networking, and she made significant technological contributions to the local area network (LAN) industry. She worked at System Development Corporation, which later became Burroughs and

---

53 For an overview, see http://www.computerhistory.org/timeline/networking-the-web/.

Unisys. In 1987, she returned to Israel and worked in IBM's Research Laboratory in Haifa. Then in 1989, at a company called Fibronics, she launched her management journey.

In 1993, Orna co-founded a company called Ornet Data Communication Technologies, which designed and manufactured Ethernet switches. During this time, she had a mentor, Meir Burstin, who became the chair of Ornet. "Meir was my mentor in terms of having me prepare a business plan and talk to investors, allowing me to plunge in and guiding me carefully and thoroughly. I'm always joking that he saved me the fees for an MBA. To me, he was an MBA substitute." Siemens acquired Ornet in 1995. Not only was this a big moment for Orna, but it was also a historic moment for Israel because it was the first time that a European conglomerate acquired an Israeli start-up.

In late 1996, the government of Israel appointed Orna chief scientist for the industrial R&D operations of the Israeli Ministry of Industry and Trade (currently the Ministry of Economy). She served in that position from 1997 to 2000, and was the first woman to hold this title. She was in charge of a considerable budget, operations, national and international issues, and staff.

Following her tenure as chief scientist, she returned to the private sector and became a venture partner at Gemini Israel Funds, recruiting investors and expanding her entrepreneurship involvement in the Israeli scene in areas such as networking, optical communication, machine vision, and networking security. At Gemini, she chaired Riverhead Networks (acquired by Cisco), Lambda Crossing (which sold its semiconductor fabrication plant to ColorChip and its filtering technology to another company), and PrimeSense (sold to Apple). PrimeSense created renowned video gaming technology, which was marketed, beginning in 2010, as Microsoft's Xbox Kinect. The Xbox Kinect allowed gamers' actions to be captured in real time, creating a revolutionary way of interacting with video games. Orna resigned from her chair position at PrimeSense to join EMC, and remained on the board of PrimeSense until it was sold to Apple in 2013 for around $360 million.[54]

Overlapping with her entrepreneurial activities, Orna participated in research in women in the private sector under the auspices of the European Union as part of the Women in Industrial Research Organization of the European Commission. Following that, she was invited to join the EU research advisory board for three years.

To understand Orna's activity and career, it is helpful to understand the key role of innovation in Israel's economy. Israel has been dubbed the "start-up nation"[55] because of the central role that start-up companies play in the Israeli economy and how those companies develop technologies that boost the global economy. As of 2017, Israel is ranked number one globally in venture capital per capita; number two in the number of start-ups (after Silicon Valley); number one in the ratio of scientists and tech professionals per ten thousand people in its overall population; and number three in companies listed on the NASDAQ (after the US and China).[56] [57] Orna quips that in Israeli culture it's easy to start a company on a Thursday and have a working prototype by Monday. For this reason, many investors and corporations look to Israel to get their technologies developed and brought to the marketplace.

Orna's career has been closely entwined with the Israeli technology start-up culture over the last three decades. She worked in Israeli start-ups; was an entrepreneur; chaired Israeli start-ups; served in the role of Chief Scientist of Israel, handling investments that boost Israeli competitiveness and economic growth, policy decisions that affect Israeli start-ups from funding to the ease of doing business

---

54   https://www.forbes.com/sites/shelisrael/2013/11/25/why-would-apple-buy-primesense/#1a878671e690, accessed August 5, 2017.

55   Dan Senor and Saul Singer, *Start-up Nation: The Story of Israel's Economic Miracle* (New York: Hachette, 2011).

56   https://medium.com/@BlueFuture/venture-capital-in-israel-landscape-overview-f9d733fa62f9

57   http://nocamels.com/2017/11/israel-companies-nasdaq-new-york/

through acquisition of knowledge through academic and organic innovation; and was a Venture Partner who assists with building, financing, and managing Israeli start-ups.

In 2008, after the financial meltdown, Orna decided that her next major career move would be to join a multinational corporation with strategic activities in Israel. This opportunity arose when Dell EMC came knocking on her door. Following a week of Skype interviews, she was invited to the United States for face-to-face interviews at both EMC and VMware, a subsidiary of EMC. The EMC people who interviewed her displayed a solid understanding of Israel from a strategy and product perspective, which was very appealing to her. "I decided that EMC was going to be my next home." Today she works for Dell EMC, where she heads the Center of Excellence of Dell EMC Israel. Independent of Dell EMC, she remains deeply involved in the development of the Israeli innovation ecosystem through defense, academia, and industrial advising and collaboration.

~ ~ ~

During her tenure as Israel's chief scientist, Orna got a close view of gender bias in an organizational setting. "I've always had an affinity for equality," she told me, "but I came to recognize it as a necessity when I served as chief scientist. I realized we need more people with expertise in a particular area in order to retain a constant pool of human capital in times of economic growth. Consequently, I started viewing diversity from an economic perspective, rather than just from a justice and equality perspective. I found that teams were much stronger when they had a good percentage of women in them."

She describes glimpsing gender bias during this time. "Early in my career, someone said, 'You're not that good-looking. What did you do in order to reach those achievements?' I didn't stay around people who asked questions that I considered inappropriate," she states.

Orna believes that some of the gender bias she encountered as an individual was because people weren't accustomed to seeing women in positions of high authority in technology. But Orna wasn't the type to be fazed by gender bias; sometimes she would ignore it, and sometimes she would be amused by it.

One incident she shared with me took place during her tenure as Israel's chief scientist. One day, a man came looking for the chief scientist. Orna was standing by the door to her office, and this man was standing in front of her two executive assistants. In Hebrew, there are different words for male and female chief scientists. "His question included the masculine form in Hebrew, so I showed him the door to my room, but did not introduce myself." It was an awkward moment. The man didn't know the chief scientist was a woman and furthermore, he didn't realize he was standing right in front of her. "I waited for him to apologize for actually asking for me, without knowing that I was the chief scientist," Orna said.

Orna managed to pass along the ability to be unruffled by gender-biased attitudes to her youngest daughter. When the girl was nine years old, Orna retrieved her from a university course on space and missiles for gifted children. "As I was picking her up, I heard the advisor for the gifted program—who happened to be a woman—asking my daughter a very odd question. Mind you, I was the chief scientist at the time, but the woman didn't know it. She asked my daughter, 'Don't you feel uncomfortable being the only girl in class?' The question hit me straight in the heart. I was afraid for a second that the woman's thoughtless question might blow my daughter's interest in science. However, my daughter answered, 'I came to this class because I was interested in the topic—not for social reasons.' I was happy that, at the age of nine, my daughter was able to tell the woman to 'bug off.'"

Orna was proud of her daughter's response. She has always strived to encourage her three children to find their personal paths. But Orna herself did not receive much encouragement from her parents. How did she manage to blossom into the person she became? "I didn't overcome the lack of encouragement," she told me, "I just did what I thought was right, and what I thought served me well. As I told you, I wanted to be employed independent of culture and compensated equally with men, so I chose a field where this dream could become real for me."

I was curious to know whether she felt that any of the decisions she made along the way had hindered her career. She responded, "I think what might have hindered my career is that I decided early on to be myself, and beyond a certain point I don't conform," she told me. "If someone tries to tell me what to do regarding innovation, for example, and I think I know better, I will stand my ground." If she finds someone being vindictive or playing politics, she doesn't work with them. "If all that you're trying to do is intimidate me, okay, then go on without me. I'm not afraid of being fired; I'm not glued to any chair. If somebody thinks my services are unnecessary—or that they aren't good enough—that's fine, so be it." There was a sense of freedom in Orna's response.

~ ~ ~

Even though Orna has a confident work persona and many successful ventures under her belt, she says she constantly doubts herself. She feels that self-doubt is part of what keeps her on top of things. "I don't take on easy challenges," she said. "I embrace complex challenges, and I want them to follow a path I think is significant. Consequently, I am in a constant uphill battle my entire life, but that is my choice. It's not like I'm living in a constant state of introspection and stress." Orna's approach here is a conscious decision because the results she wants outweigh any consequences that come with her choices.

I was surprised to hear that even with all the successful ventures that Orna has led, she doubts herself regularly. She also believes she didn't negotiate well enough—not because of lack of confidence, but because material interests are not her core focus. She told me, "I could have negotiated better, but eventually, for most of my career, I ended up in a good place. I could have ended up in an even better place, but I ended up in a good place," she said.

~ ~ ~

It could be argued that Orna is one of the most prominent female technology leaders of her generation in Israel. The volume and level of work she did in industry, government, and the nonprofit sector is astounding. I was naturally curious to learn if her family life suffered because of her functioning at such a high level in the corporate and public domains.

Orna admits that work–life balance was a challenge for her when her children were young. She has discussed family responsibilities with her children. Following the advice of her middle daughter, they decided they would each focus on the things that they were good at, so they shared the chores. Orna feels she did a better job of being available for the family on the weekends than during the week. She told me, "We did our best, and I think everyone turned out well."

Unfortunately, Orna had to face an aggressive type of cancer recently. She dialed back on her work commitments to make her health her primary responsibility. "It is a matter of prioritization—you need to know what is important. If any of my children need special care, that immediately took and takes priority," she said.

~ ~ ~

Orna and I talked about the key point of inquiry in this book: why is there such a struggle to place women in senior leadership positions? "I think that there is confusion about the role of women in the family," she said. "Partially, it's due to childbearing and the fact that women tend to take time off at certain points in their life—even though they can share that responsibility with their husbands or significant others. But somehow—and I noticed this a lot in academia—women tend to take a little longer to get to tenure, for example. When women work part-time for a while or focus on their family life, it removes them from the racetrack."

Orna believes that in striving to break the glass ceiling, women must support other women. More work needs to be done in this area, since some women still tend to be uncomfortable in supporting female colleagues. The reasons for this vary, but some women feel uncomfortable identifying with other women. "There are women who feel that if they identify with other women, they will be relegated to a separate group, for promotions and recognition." I have seen this too. Many women don't want to speak up about women's issues in the workplace or openly voice support for the advancement of the careers of female colleagues for fear that this would be perceived negatively.

Overall, Orna is hopeful. "Equality will come, but right now we're experiencing a lot of fundamentalism, which runs counter to policies that promote equality, so I wouldn't want to be a prophet and say we are headed in a good direction," she told me. She says that we have a long way to go toward equality. She doesn't think the situation for gender diversity in technology is hopeless, just challenging. "I believe we should decide that gender equity is what we want. It's in our hands; it won't just happen on its own."

Orna's advice to women is: "If you want to do something, just do it. Find your personal path, and just do it. It's a matter of decision." Echoing her Haifa University professor, yet from an altogether different perspective, she noted that getting a PhD is not about how smart you are, it's about making the decision and following it through. "You get a PhD if you want to get a PhD. So, if you want something, you go and get it."

Orna's discussion with me was insightful. I enjoyed hearing her stories about how she managed her career in a way that defied typical societal expectations that limit women. Orna says she has achieved a personal level of satisfaction. "At the end of the day, I look at my position, at the respect that I get professionally, and at my family. I feel lucky," she remarked. Orna ended our discussion with a smile. "Other than the fact that I didn't succeed in bringing peace to the Middle East, I think most of what I've done ended up being successful."

~ ~ ~

TAKEAWAYS

- Having done research about women in the private sector, Orna advocates diversity; she believes teams are stronger when there is a good percentage of women in them.

- Big changes in one's career path can occur unexpectedly. A short conversation with a professor in college made a huge difference in Orna's career trajectory.

- Don't be surprised when someone makes an ignorant comment around technology-savvy, accomplished women. Orna opts to stay professional in such awkward moments but also avoids people who say inappropriate things.

- Struggling with imposter syndrome isn't necessarily a negative thing. Possibly, you are taking on a worthwhile challenge where it is natural to experience periodic feelings of self-doubt.

- More work is needed on women supporting other women's careers and changing the corporate culture to encourage such support, rather than viewing it negatively.

- "Go get it!" Orna's primary advice to women is simple. Make the big decisions to do significant things, and then follow through with those decisions. Success is more about the power of making decisions and following through than having some special skill set.

CAREER INTERVENTIONS

Before I started this book, I had never heard of the concept of "career intervention." Career interventions are used to enhance a person's career and to help them make sound decisions about the best next step. There are many types of career interventions, some of which fall under the category of career counseling. They can range from one-on-one sessions with a trained psychologist to assessment tests.

Not surprisingly, there isn't any one agreed upon definition as to just what a career intervention is. But most of the definitions describe it as some type of formal career guidance provided by professionals. Yet all of the stories about career interventions discussed in this book came from informal sources. It was parents, professors, mentors, and sponsors, saying the right words at the right time that made the difference.

While I would have thought that all job growth came from career advice professionals, that was not the case. Unfortunately, most people, both men and women, do not use professional career guidance services. A recent poll indicated that only 24% of randomly chosen respondents reported ever using the services of a trained career counselor.[58]

Fortunately, as shown in the stories shared in this book, informal and sometimes unexpected sources can be very effective sources for career advancement. For instance, in Telle Whitney's case (chapter 1), the decisive impetus came from her stepmom, who recommended that Telle take an inventory test. "Because the suggestion came from my stepmother, it was the last thing on earth I wanted to do, but I had run out of options, so I did it." For Orna Berry (chapter 17), it was a professor telling her, "I won't tell you you're smart, but I will tell you that

---

[58] In 2013, National Career Development Association and the Society for Vocational Psychology co-authored a paper that published a poll on the usage of career counseling service. Astonishingly, of the respondents to the poll, only 24% reported ever using the services of a trained career counselor. Susan C. Whiston and David L. Blustein. *"The Impact of Career Interventions: Preparing our Citizens for 21st Century Jobs."* by Susan C. Whiston & David L. Bluestein https://www.ncda.org/aws/NCDA/asset_manager/get_file/63826?ver=167

people who are more stupid than you have PhDs." That single comment inspired her to work toward her doctorate, which then propelled her into an amazing career.

Perhaps we need another way of looking at what a career intervention can be. From my point of view, an informal career intervention is when someone offers an outside perspective that encourages an individual to see new possibilities for their career. This kind of input implies that you have confidence in the person to whom you are giving advice. When you suggest to someone that they aim high for a promotion or a new degree, you are implicitly letting them know that you believe that they are capable of more than they may realize. Sometimes that outside validation is all it takes.

While I was writing this book, I had an experience that proved to me how simple it can be to offer an intervention and how profound the results can be. One day, I was chatting with a very talented and hard-working woman engineer who had once reported to me and was now working under a different manager. I asked her why she hadn't been promoted yet. She answered, "I don't know." I asked her if she had discussed the possibility of being promoted with her manager. Her reply was, "I didn't know I could. I think he should promote me if he thinks I am good." I suggested to her that she ask for a promotion directly.

A couple of months later, while I was looking through the organization's database, I happened to notice that she had received a promotion. I sent a text congratulating her. She said, "Thanks, Pratima. It's all thanks to you for telling me to push for the promotion." She had already done all the hard work to prove herself, but she hadn't realized she needed to communicate with her manager. I told her what I thought her next best step would be. The reason it worked for her was that she is a great software engineer. She had done the hard work and proven herself, but she had to nudge her manager to do the right thing. Sometimes you need to do that. Offering the advice to her was easy, and it was great to see that it got results.

Jocelyn Goldfein, one of the female tech executives I interviewed, offered some sage advice on interventions and women's careers. She said that at whatever point you choose to intervene, it has the potential to help a woman's career. "You can intervene at any stage and have a positive impact downstream of that stage, and even *upstream* if it inspires younger girls with possibilities."

I offer two takeaways on this concept of career intervention. First, it would appear we need to make more use of the career professionals who can help guide us on our journey. Second, parents, professors, mentors, sponsors, and colleagues have a greater ability than they realize to provide the advice that can make a huge difference in a woman's career. We should all take advantage of that knowledge and help one another make our career aspirations come true.

CHAPTER 18: LILY'S STORY

BIOSKETCH: *Lily Chang was born and raised in Taiwan. After completing her undergraduate degree from the best university in Taiwan, her mother encouraged her to relocate to the United States. She attended the University of Wisconsin at Madison, graduating with a master's degree in computer science. Lily started her career as a compiler/tools software developer. She soon moved into engineering leadership roles and has been vice president of engineering at several companies for various industry sectors (embedded systems/electronic design automation (EDA), semiconductors, cloud computing/virtualization). Lily has a strong commitment to helping women succeed in technology. At VMware, she launched four Women Who Code networks, in India, Bulgaria, and China (Beijing and Shanghai). Lily's confidence and persistence in negotiating and effecting changes have been crucial strengths that contribute to her impressive success as a technology leader.*

"You should never give up your passion because of your gender. You have to be true to yourself. There is no reason to be intimidated in a male-dominated world."

— Lily Chang, VP, Strategic Transformation,
and SVM-JV Project, VMware

~ ~ ~

Lily's upbringing was quite different from that of other Taiwanese women growing up in the fifties and sixties. Most parents of her female friends invested in their daughters' education only to enhance their likelihood for marriage into prominent or wealthy families. "A college degree from a reputable university makes you more presentable at social occasions, such as business banquets," Lily told me. However, she added, "My mom was against that scenario for me; she had an advanced perspective."

Her mother, Michin Hsu Chang, was the most important person in her life growing up. Lily described her as very special and maybe even unusual for her generation. Back then, it was almost unthinkable to get a professional education degree as a woman. Michin was a wife, a full-time mother, and a caregiver to her own parents and younger brother. Yet with a college degree in education, Michin enrolled in evening school to obtain an advanced degree and fulfill her dream of becoming an elementary school teacher. She completed her teaching requirements and became a teacher at a public school, covering a broad curriculum, most notably science courses.

Because Michin wanted Lily to have the best education possible, Michin moved her to a private Catholic school early on. At that time, Catholicism was beginning to gain acceptance in Taiwan. Catholic schools already had a better reputation than the public schools did—and they taught English. Though a Catholic education was expensive, Michin convinced Lily's father, Hsingwu Chang, that the investment was worthwhile. "My mom didn't think the public school system was good for me, so I actually studied kindergarten and first grade twice, first in a public school and then in the Catholic school." From the first grade on, nuns and priests were her teachers, and she learned English from the Bible. "This was a critical and unusual education decision that my mother made, because most people would just let their girls go through the public education system."

Though Hsingwu was a traditional man, he gave Lily a unique opportunity. "For all his life, since age seventeen, he was a businessman. He had his own business. I remember that in my teenage years he started taking me to his business meetings," she said. In many Asian countries, during the time Lily was growing up, business negotiations happened over lunch or dinner, and at parties. "A lot of times, my mom refused to go with my dad, as she wanted to go to evening school or do something that was more important to her. She told my dad, 'Take Lily.'" That's how her father started to mentor her in business skills. Lily remembers soaking it all up. "A lot of the skills he taught me were about negotiation: How do you position things? How do you tell bullshit from reality? How do you read personalities? These kinds of things are difficult to learn. I am pretty grateful for that." He taught her a priceless skill: to be a tough negotiator. This has been a crucial element in her success.

Private schooling gave Lily a good foundation academically, and she ended up graduating from one of the top universities, the National Taiwan University in Taipei. Unfortunately, even though she had a diploma from an excellent school in Taiwan, she had great difficulty getting a job in her chosen field of study. At that time, there were two "attractive" career options for professional women, and Lily did not fit either role.

One was "a secretary who took notes and didn't speak up in meetings," as Lily recalled. This did not work well for Lily, as she had taken her mother's lesson to heart: "If you believe in something, you speak up." Furthermore, as a child, Lily was a tomboy, and "did not accept the status quo." That quality also would not fit into a secretarial job, "because you are supposed to just follow the orders."

The second career option for her was to be a flight attendant. "A group of my classmates and I, we all thought we were pretty intelligent, but we couldn't get any good jobs, so we applied for airline stewardess jobs," Lily recalled. "The interview was intriguing. We had to dress up in traditional Chinese outfits and put on makeup. Then we walked around on a stage, like a fashion show. That was the interview. The judges were a panel of men, and the selection criteria were: tall, skinny, big eyes, and good looking."

Lily became depressed when she failed to get either job. She felt she was unemployable. "It was like the end of the world. I felt bad, because my parents had already invested in me," she said. Lily recalled her parents debating what would now be best for Lily. Michin advocated strongly for Lily to pursue graduate study in the United States. "She did her research and believed the US would be best for me—I could learn new things and establish myself." But this meant even more of an investment from Lily's parents. Her parents finally agreed on having Lily go to a US graduate school, which opened a new chapter of career options and development for Lily. "In retrospect, the number one person I am grateful to is my mom, because in the critical moments she stepped in and made all the right decisions."

Lily came to the US on a student visa and was admitted to the MBA program at the University of Wisconsin (UW) at Madison. There she felt she performed merely adequately. One day, a product marketing professor had a "defining conversation" with her.

"Lily, I would like to better understand your career goals," he said. "You are in an MBA program. What do you want to do after you graduate?"

"I kind of want to manage people and things," Lily answered.

"That's not a very good career goal. What kind of people and things do you want to manage?" 'Lily had no answer. "That's a real problem," he told her. "And that explains some of the answers you are giving me in class."

The professor explained to Lily that an effective manager needs to have domain knowledge or expertise. He advised her to *first* find the field she was interested in and become an expert in it; *then* the MBA program could help her to be a better manager and leader. "He said I was starting off on the wrong end," Lily recalls.

"You need to go back to the basics," he told Lily. "You need to answer this fundamental question: What is your passion?"

"I think I want to do computer science," Lily replied.

With his encouragement, Lily took her first programming class in Pascal, and fell in love with it. Her professor suggested that she shift her graduate-school focus to a CS degree, because knowing computer science well would be key before she could manage software and systems teams. Lily graduated with a master's degree in CS from UW-Madison. The coaching environment at the university was instrumental in helping her find the field she is passionate about, and in setting her career in the right direction.

After obtaining her CS degree, she received several job offers. She selected a position that involved building a new compiler. "I like the stability and predictability of compilers," she said. "You have to make sure that the algorithm is predictable and reliable. That's why I chose that job. It was the beginning of my technical journey."

Lily's expertise with compilers gave her the opportunity to work with leading technologists in C++ and object-oriented programming. Lily led the three-person team that put out the first C++ UNIX release from Sun Microsystems. At that time, Sun was competing to be the best UNIX system provider.

"When I started the project, it was supposed to be ready for market in six months. In reality, it took us close to two years, which I could see early on. To my surprise, Bill Joy, co-founder of Sun Microsystems, publicly announced that Sun would rewrite UNIX in C++ in the middle of our 'short and sweet' project. I don't know how I had the guts, but I went to Bill and told him that we were no longer going to be done in six months. He responded by granting us the time we needed. I was fortunate that the top technologists at Sun coached me to be a 'change agent' contributing to the defining moments of technology history—in retrospect, I am grateful for the opportunity."

"I was surrounded by top-notch talented architects and engineers at Sun. It was like going back to graduate school for two years. And I was trying to finish my project to be promoted to staff engineer. Sun had a simple promotion checklist: You need to see a product from beginning to release. Since C++ was so new, one hundred letters from happy customers would be required. I thought it would be easy, but it was very difficult. I did it, but it was a very tough journey."

However, there was much more to the story. "At that time, the language definition of C++ was considered the biggest risk to finishing our project on time, because Bell Labs people were still creating the underlying C++ language. It's a big problem when the language keeps changing." Sun's primary competitor at that time, Hewlett Packard (HP), was also working on C++ projects at the time. Lily decided that the only way for her to release the project in the specified timeline and get a promotion was to collaborate with HP. "I reached out to HP and suggested that we work together to stabilize the C++ language. It turned out HP was thinking about that as well. It was incredible that Sun and HP agreed to gather a bunch of companies with Bell Labs to establish ANSI[59] standards for the language. In retrospect, that defining conversation did contribute to the first ANSI technical meeting in 1990 in Somerset, New Jersey, to set standards for the C++ language."

Lily subsequently moved to Mentor Graphics (then Microtec Research), an embedded systems development company. There, Lily's mission was to create optimizing embedded C++ for the embedded industry. "I wanted to be a manager, but at Sun Microsystems I learned that I'd need to wait in line for that. So, I decided to bring C++ to the embedded industry. I was successful not only in releasing

---

59   ANSI – American National Standards Institute helps create industry standards in a variety of industries.

the highly competitive optimizing C++, but also I made C++ represent a substantial part of the company's top line and portfolio." Lily grew from a manager of a small team to the Mentor Graphics vice president of engineering.

Her management career trajectory also encompassed eight years at KLA-Tencor and two years as vice president of engineering at Xilinx before she began her tenure at VMware in 2010. Entering as a senior director of the EcoSystem & Solutions Infrastructure/ Tools groups, she rose to become the vice president of Strategic Transformation Office (XMO) while simultaneously being vice president of the Sugon-VMware Joint Venture Project Office and a Sugon-VMware JV board member. She is also a board member of Women Who Code, a nonprofit organization dedicated to inspiring women to excel in tech careers. In my conversation with Lily, she shared several stories about her management journey.

~ ~ ~

Early on, Lily suffered from stage fright in meetings. She was good at one-on-one conversations, but when she had to deal with more than one person in the room, she would freeze. Her boss noticed that about her, and he coached her out of the stage fright. He was a bit harsh in how he phrased it. He told Lily she needed to speak up, because he was not going to do that on her behalf. Lily feels that by twisting her arm, her boss helped her take that leap.

After she got over her stage fright in meetings, she had to overcome other challenges. Over time, she had several experiences that impressed upon her the need to soften what others perceived as an overly assertive style.

While working at one of her first start-up companies, the CEO came to Lily one afternoon and announced, "Congratulations! You were nominated as the scariest person in the company." Earlier that day, in a technical meeting, Lily had insisted that her way was the right way to solve a particular problem. "I argued with everybody, because they didn't want to put in the work, although they agreed that my approach was right, and even revolutionary." She recalled her CEO saying, "You were nominated because you took off your shoe and pounded it on the table and said, 'You will do it this way.' All the people were shocked into agreeing!" He concluded, "It was a very effective negotiation meeting—but it also won you the nomination for the Most Scary Person award."

Though this story is a great example of how Lily can get her way, over the year at that start-up, through trial and error, Lily realized she needed to negotiate less aggressively and smooth her rough edges. As she told me, "It is in my DNA to believe in what I believe in, to drive for what I believe in and not give up. If I'm interested in a particular area at work, and if a boss or anyone tells me that I won't be able to do it, that just adds fuel to my fire and makes me want to prove them wrong. But I realized insistence is not the only means for a successful negotiation."

"I needed to tamp it down and be less of a bull in a china shop, because then you break stuff. I received a lot of coaching on how to smooth the edges, and to listen more, rather than just insist on my own ideas. It is more critical to negotiate the *right way* rather than negotiate the *right thing* persistently."

Further along in her career, she had another experience—a "revelation" as she termed it—that gave her a new perspective on aspects of her brand at work that were working against her. "After days of strategy meetings at the start-up I was in, one of the executives pulled me aside. He said, 'Did you notice that you are the only female in the room?' I said, 'No.' He said, 'Maybe you need to be self-aware. When you go back into the room, take a look.' I did, and it was indeed true. Throughout the week, they brought in different teams, and I continued to notice he was right, I was the only female." Lily's long experience of going to negotiation meetings, all the way back to her teenage years with her dad, had kept her somewhat oblivious as to how people perceived her at work. "I worked in those environments believing I was equal, and I behaved in a certain way on the assumption that basically I was equal."

What Lily learned from this revelation was not that there was anything particularly wrong with her style, but that she needed to add some emotional wisdom to how she interacted with people. Daniel Goleman, author of *Emotional Intelligence*,[60] summarizes the notion of self-awareness as "knowing one's internal states, preferences, resources, and intuitions." I found it interesting that prior to this incident, Lily had been attending all these meetings with men, with no personal awareness of the gender dynamics.

Personally, I would have been offended by her colleague's observation, or by any indication that I needed to back down because I was a woman. Like Lily, I was raised to believe I was equal. I did not receive the message that my behavior should be different based on my gender. My family included many strong-minded women, and I always took it for granted that women could speak their minds and have influence in the world.

What I took from Lily's story about her male colleague's remark that she should become "self-aware" is that it is useful for strong-minded women to be aware of *other people's* gender-based expectations. People do not necessarily expect women to be extremely strong-willed. Gaining the insight that the men she worked with had certain expectations about her based on her gender did help Lily progress to the next managerial level. She didn't need to avoid being persistent; things simply went better for when she smoothed her edges and listened more. Her colleague was trying to help Lily realize that sometimes she drives a hard bargain. Lily told me that, in some situations, "I may want to step back a little bit and allow other aspects of my DNA to come out. It was an interesting way to coach me."

---

60   Daniel Goleman, *Emotional Intelligence: Why It Can Matter More Than IQ* (Bantam Books, 1995).

~ ~ ~ Lily referred to that colleague as a "defining-moment mentor." The defining-moment mentors were mentors who made her aware of "aha moments" as she went along. "For whatever odd reason, they just decided they needed to single me out, pull me aside, and tell me, 'This is important for you to think about.'" She appreciated how these mentors stuck with her on some of the areas she needed to work on.

She also spoke of "lifetime mentors," people who remain in her life today. "They are more like father figures to a large extent." They were bosses, all men, who coached and mentored her.

Lily's story of her family life, her education, and her career exhibits mentoring and advice all along the way; people were looking out for her, and it made a huge difference. I asked Lily what she thought it was that prompted this extra assistance. "They look for people who can do the job for them. They look for people they can trust and depend on. Another key factor is determination—do they have the fire in the belly? They value that. Passion is another one. And the last is the courage to take on different challenges."

Early on in her career, Lily decided that she did not want to be an expert in any particular area; she did not have the patience for that, and she enjoyed being the generalist in the team. "In the early days of my career, before I became a director, I was aiming for a couple of things." She set a goal that whenever she joined a new team, she would be heads-down focused on her job, but she would also look at other areas in her organization for a broader perspective on the company and its products. "I looked at the team and company portfolio. My career goal was to be a generalist and not a specialist—those were my principals. That turned out to be very helpful."

~ ~ ~

Lily loves her job, which is perhaps the single most important ingredient of success. She also defined some other criteria: "I don't leave the job until I am done. The job does not define me; I define it. I must feel I am doing something important. I must have the sense that I am making contributions, and I must believe I can leave a legacy in the company." Based on those criteria, she feels she is successful.

Lily has two children, a boy and a girl. Her experience as a parent helped her to appreciate frustration management. "A big part of parenthood is to be there when your children feel frustrated, to guide and coach them about the why and what of their frustrations," observed Lily. "Through the years, children, as resilient as they are, learn how to handle frustration and roadblocks. There is no particular recipe," Lily told me. "You have to constantly provide an intervention." As we can see from Lily's experience, interventions are not necessarily a bad thing, since Lily had plenty of guidance in her life that has shaped her career and has made her successful in her profession.

Lily offered advice for young women who are trying to enter the tech industry and for any women who are tempted to drop out of the workforce. She said that no matter where you are today and what your upbringing may be, "You should never give up your passion because of your gender. You have to be true to yourself. There is no reason to be intimidated."

~ ~ ~

TAKEAWAYS

- Although many of the decisions that Lily's parents made about her education defied cultural traditions and norms around gender in Taiwanese society, these decisions helped give Lily a strong background to become a successful technical leader.

- Lily was consistently vocal about her likes and dislikes. This helped her get into computer science in graduate school, and it helped her find rewarding work opportunities.

- When a person moves from an individual contributor role to management, leadership flaws may show up. One of Lily's flaws was that she was tough to the point of being "scary."

- She was fortunate to have people who gave her feedback on her leadership flaws so she could work on them to become an even more effective leader.

- Emotional intelligence, which can be learned to a significant degree, is a valuable leadership skill to cultivate.

- Lily tends to approach work as a generalist and not as specialist, which proved to be a successful strategy for her.

- Lily tries to look at the big picture and gain a broader perspective when solving a problem.

THE AGGRESSIVE LABEL

One of my close friends is working with an executive coach who is helping her get to the next level. Her performance reviews generally indicate that she is on track for a promotion. But when one of the male execs on her panel gave her the feedback that she is "aggressive" and recommended that she be "less aggressive," her morale was shaken. What does that mean? Is that feedback specific enough to make improvement actionable? Does less aggressive mean to attack but soften the blow? Or does it mean she should pursue her own interests less forcefully? I think many effective women leaders are justifiably confused when they get vague feedback like this, as well as other nonactionable suggestions for improvement.

Throughout my career, I have been labeled as aggressive. At first, I thought this was a positive description of my performance. I took it to mean that I was a go-getter and that my colleagues and managers appreciated that I had a mind of my own. Born and raised in India, I grew up surrounded by assertive women whom I viewed as role models. However, as time went by, it became clear to me that the term aggressive has a negative connotation, especially in the United States.

When I interviewed women for this book, it was both eye-opening and a relief to hear them share their experiences of being dogged by this same descriptor. Pam Kostka was given the title "dragon lady," but she did not change her management approach. "I never backed down from being aggressive or direct just because somebody was going to criticize me for it. I won't apologize for being a woman. I tend to have a direct communication style, which is also penalized in women. Women are supposed to be more empathetic in their style, but I am more direct and logical. Maybe I am that way because I need to be in order to get my voice heard."

Annabel Liu received similar feedback; she was told she had an aggressive and authoritarian style. Her way of responding to this was to evolve her brand to be less abrasive while still being assertive. Shilpa Lawande also found herself confronting labels of assertiveness or aggressiveness. She chose to take it as constructive feedback and strove toward finding more balance based on each situation.

Let's look at the definition of the word aggressive. Merriam-Webster dictionary defines it as "a forceful action or procedure (such as an unprovoked attack) especially when intended to dominate or master." And further, as "the practice of making attacks or encroachments." When a woman speaks her mind and is assertive, she is likely to be labeled as aggressive. So, are these women confronting and attacking their colleagues, or are they simply being effective leaders?

I find this topic to be profoundly troubling. It is hard to imagine anyone leading effectively *without* being assertive. And it would appear that there is a double standard. An article in the *Harvard Business Review*, which looked at two hundred performance reviews within one company, revealed bias in this type of feedback[61]. The results tallied the number of references to being "too aggressive" in the reviews and, not surprisingly, 76% of the instances were attributed to women, whereas only 24% of men were identified as having such a communication style.

There is a broader implication to this discussion. Because the aggressive label doesn't just come up in informal discussions, but also appears in performance reviews, it can have a major impact on careers. Several studies indicate women are far more likely to be judged on their performance in ways that don't specifically clarify the level of performance or include focused explanations of what can be improved[62]. Being told in a performance review that one is "aggressive" and being advised to be "less aggressive" is one example of how women's performance reviews can exhibit patterns of bias, vague feedback, and nonactionable suggestions for improvement. Though companies are becoming much better about analyzing and correcting for when women's salaries are not commensurate with men's, it seems

---

61 https://hbr.org/2016/04/research-vague-feedback-is-holding-women-back
62 Reference the same HBR article. And see: http://www.slate.com/blogs/
    xx_factor/2016/05/02/stanford_researchers_say_women_get_vague_feed-
    back_in_performance_reviews.html

that performance reviews need to be subjected to the same scrutiny. Those who have the responsibility for reviewing another person's performance must choose their words carefully. There is a world of difference between being aggressive and being professionally assertive. Having ambition and speaking with authority are not aggressive acts. The words we choose when describing someone's performance in the workplace matter—they can have a profound impact on their career.

CHAPTER 19: ORNA BERRYMAN'S STORY

BIOSKETCH: *Life experiences create lasting impressions. For Orna Berryman, the experience of being a civilian in a town turned war zone had a dramatic impact on her perspective as a leader in tech. Israel, Orna's birthplace, has fought more than eight wars since 1948. Part of Orna's infancy was spent in a shelter. Freedom of speech, bravery, and heroism, plus a strong democratic press, were the imprints of her childhood. In her twenties, she was a young mother who had to make a split-second life-or-death decision as a civilian in a war zone. Orna later became a director of operations and program management in a technology-focused Fortune 500 company.*

"Take risks; don't be afraid to speak up your mind. 'Risk with excellence of results' is my recipe. Work really hard to excel, and demonstrate your work. Risk-taking fuels excellence and buries the lazy. I know no other way—there is no pedigree, no particular luck, there is just sweat, long hours, and the superb product of your work."

— Orna Berryman, Director of Business
Operations, Office of the CTO, VMware

~ ~ ~

"War is not a theory, or an idea, or a movie; it is up close and personal," says Orna, speaking of friends lost at war and of her personal experiences. In Israel, it touches one's gut and soul. In August 1990, Iraq invaded Kuwait. An alliance of Israel and other countries, the biggest since World War II, formed a military coalition to remove Iraqi troops from Kuwait, and in response Iraq launched a series of Scud missile attacks toward Israel. Saddam Hussein, the president of Iraq at the time, had also made veiled threats of launching Scuds armed with chemical weapons into Israel.

As the threat of total annihilation and the fear of chemical devastation swept over Israel, the country moved into action. Israel supplied its entire population with gas masks, gas-proof tents, EpiPens, and other protective measures. This was the first time in Israel's history that an attack was aimed deep into the civilian population. Doors and windows were taped in preparation for shattered glass. People prepared sealed rooms in case they needed to be in them while waiting to find out if the attack was chemical in nature.

"Missiles began falling all over Israel," Orna recalls. Her house was in a threatened region, due to its proximity to strategic targets. "The beautiful view from my bedroom window included the tall chimneys that constitute the epicenter of oil processing in Israel." With Haifa's navy base and Israel's only granary also nearby, Orna's city of Haifa made an alluring, strategic target for Saddam Hussein's campaign.

As part of the rushed attempt to defend its citizens, the Israeli security forces distributed sealed plastic tents for babies who were too small for the ominous-looking adult masks. "Only much later did we learn that the tents were truly sealed, inside and out, resulting in several suffocation fatalities."

The routine was carefully prescribed. When you hear the bomb explode, it means you may have missed your opportunity to go to your sealed room. Yet you can still defend yourself from chemical exposure: run to your designated sealed room with your children, seal the door, put the mask on yourself first, and then protect your children by inserting them into the sealed, clear tent. Turn on the radio and listen to the announcer, who will tell you when it is safe to take the mask off. Keep the mask with you at all times. Do not leave without the tent.

"Those were the instructions—and being the defiantly creative Israelis that we are, a fashion statement of carrying gas mask bags sprouted quickly. The instructional videos were almost peaceful, not unlike the smiling mom who puts the air mask on their child in the airplane safety video."

However, reality was extremely different for Orna. One night while her husband was away in the Israeli Defense Forces reserve, Orna and her ten-month-old son Tom were woken to the sound of an explosion some miles away. The blast shattered the glass window of her bedroom and she knew a Scud missile had landed close to her house.

Flashes of her beloved dead boyfriend came to her mind—her friend from high school who died at eighteen during the war. She thought, "Am I next? Is my newly born son going to die? I ran in a mad dash to my son's crib, which was in the sealed room. He was crying unrelentingly, reflecting what I was feeling with the honesty of a ten-month-old who had been awakened by the explosion."

"I wanted to grab him and hold him, but I knew the routine—shut the sealed room door; seal the door cracks with soda-soaked rag; cover the side of the door with tape; put your gas mask on—and so I did. Quickly after, I grabbed Tom and opened the tent on the floor. Tom refused to get in. He was kicking and screaming, scared not only from the strange-looking mask-covered alien that snatched him in the middle of the night from his crib, but also from the sterile smell of the tiny opening of his new plastic cage. Never have I felt worse than forcing my son into that tent; he almost knew it was dangerous, better than all of the experts. But danger was high, fear took over, and it was the right thing to do—so said the experts. Every breath of air seemed to be poisonous, and I was protected with the gas mask, while he could be suffocated at any time from toxic gas carried from Iraq. I was able with much force to shove him in and closed the zipper tight over his tiny begging hands."

Orna turned on the radio, which the general population was instructed to listen to for the "all clear" message. People had to wait for the armed forces to reach the scene and examine the air to determine whether the region was "all clear."

"Those seconds, minutes, took forever, and that night, the announcement just didn't come. Tom's crying was relentless, but putting my face close to the plastic sheet made it worse. I realized I looked like a black-skull monster, as all these masks did. Even movie directors realized the scary look of a gas mask and put Hannibal Lecter in a similar-looking mouthpiece. I was torn. I knew I had to be strong; the air could be poisoned. I looked at the tent. Humidity started to settle on the cover, and I could see it was becoming fogged in while his cry was getting fainter. Is he calmed down? How can that be? Why can't I see him clearly? And then I realized my son is running out of oxygen and is weakened by the lack of air. What can I do? Is it more dangerous in the tent or out? Should I take him out and kill him with a phantom chemical gas, or leave him in the tent, where he will be killed from suffocation?

When Orna saw that her son was suffocating in the anti-chemical weapon tent, she decided to test the air on herself. She ripped the gas mask off her face and took a deep breath. The air was clean and Orna was fine, so she grabbed Tom out of the tent and held him tightly in her arms. Orna was flooded with anger, frustration, and the knowledge that the very tent that was meant to save lives turned out to be deadly.

"My perception of the authority's recommendations, or what 'odds' truly means and what consequences are, changed in a second. What I thought was a saving device was deadly, and thus the need to question norms and apply judgment—even if the recommendation is different—calcified into me that night. And most of all, the gut feeling of what the right decision is guides me until today. It has yet to fail me."

Lev HaMifratz Mall, located in Haifa, Israel, was severely bombed that night, while still under construction. It was clear that the target was Israel's oil refineries, located only a few kilometers away. The aerial blast of that explosion damaged houses but killed no one that night. However, as Orna described, the tents had their own unexpected death toll on children. Furthermore, elderly citizens suffocated to death due to gas masks that were not properly used. The tents were recalled after the war and were replaced by ventilated ones, but Israel has never been the same. Its emergency preparation for chemical warfare improved dramatically.

This intense situation forever changed Orna's perspective on stress. "When someone tells me at work that the meeting was stressful, or the commute was tough, or a decision was really difficult to make, I often think of that split-second moment in my life as a young mother of twenty-four—literally in her house which had become a war zone—who needed to decide what to listen to: the radio, or her heart. What 'stress' is to another is just a curiosity for me, since my scale of stress is vastly different from that of my average colleague. I had to choose—and I chose the heart."

For Orna, her perceptions on how to deal with difficult situations were forever changed. "What is stress? What is strife? What is a 'tough decision to make'?" she asked. "I often think of the bomb attack when I am faced with animosity, dilemma, and claims of impossible choices at work. Strife has a different scale, and so do arguments over right, wrong, devastation, and anger. My demeanor is calm at work, and I do not stress easily, anywhere."

When I met Orna myself, I found a sense of calm assurance surrounding her. She feels that being an immigrant in the United States is a privileged position; that life in California, with its endless opportunities, diverse population, and incredible weather, are a true heaven compared with some of the tough times she endured in Israel.

~ ~ ~

While she was growing up, Orna spoke three languages (Romanian, Yiddish, and Hebrew), and grew to love English at an early age. She discovered she was also good in economics. When she was accepted to the highly competitive Hebrew University of Jerusalem Faculty of Law, she decided not to attend. Instead, she decided to study English literature.

"There is a strong side of me that is emotional, and I love to teach," Orna told me. "These qualities, at that time, guided my decision toward staying close to home, close to my boyfriend (who later became my husband), and to my parents." By foregoing law school, Orna knew that she gave up a lucrative career. "It was tough for my dad to accept that, because all of my family are doctors. It was a bit of a deviation; the medical field surrounded me. I was the only one not choosing a standard professional path. But teaching was my true vocation, and even today, the ability to deconstruct a concept and explain it serves me at work."

Orna studied for a master's degree in English literature and taught in Haifa University and tenth grade at Kiryat Tivon's high school. When she and her husband came to the United States in 1994, she thought about getting a PhD, but instead she started teaching in Silicon Valley. The internet was just emerging at that time, and AOL and Intel were big names in the Valley.

"I was driving on Highway 101, and I said to my husband, 'Maybe one day, I will tap into this whole high-tech world that you are in,' and he mocked me. He asked, 'Where do you think you will work?' and I pointed and said, 'How about here?' That building was just off the 101, it was then Intel's D2 (Development Lab #2). He was quite incredulous as to how I would one day work for Intel. I was an English teacher, don't forget."

Little did Orna and her then-husband know that she would indeed be working there one day. By 1999, she had earned a master's degree in human resource and organizational development from the University of San Francisco. She had a friend at Intel who submitted her resume on her behalf, and they hired her as an instructional designer. This was another big step for her. She had moved not only from Israel to the United States, but also from teaching third grade to working for the largest chip manufacturer at the time. While she was at Intel, her team developed the first process for the Pentium. It was an impressive leap.

During Orna's three years at Intel, she gave birth to a third child, her daughter Noa. The work–life balance was challenging; Intel required shift changes at precisely 6:00 p.m., which was a crucial time for her to be with her family. In 2000, Orna started to look for another opportunity where she could keep her management position and have a life with her family.

"You have dinner, you have kids needing help with homework, you are coming back from work. It was almost impossible for me at that time. Intel felt to me that it wasn't as progressive as it is now, with working remotely or considering women's careers. Rules were rules. My friend Gina—who gave birth before me—actually relinquished her management role. I took over as manager so she didn't have to work during family hours, and then I gave birth. I said, 'Well, I don't want to see my daughter just in pictures and at night.'" One Workplace, a commercial interior design firm, was not high tech, but it was appealing. Orna joined them as a senior manager, and was soon promoted to a director position. One of her motivations in making this move was to go back to her teaching roots and practice organizational development, and One Workplace gave her the opportunity to do both. However, in the down economy of 2000, not many offices were being renovated. Nevertheless, working at One Workplace was an incredible adventure for Orna, because it opened her up to new environments and new people.

"I got to know San Francisco, and I became engaged with the gay and lesbian communities of San Francisco, because our design center was there, and a lot of our designers and salespeople were gay. I was invited places, and I was introduced into a world I had no insight into, with its complexity, challenges, and progressiveness. Being a Jewish immigrant woman, I connected strongly with this other population that has a long journey to reach what most of us just have."

The following year, she moved back to high tech, joining Cadence Design Systems, a CAD design tools company, for an unusual assignment.

"I joined a group that was tasked with rolling out software processes using the stage-gate[63] model in particular, which was a bit rigid for software. Cadence tried hiring outside consultants from McKinsey.[64] Then to complete—or correct—the work and still establish not only a software-defined process but also an open source culture, Cadence management decided to build an internal team with experts in software development, as well as experts in teaching and change management." Orna's background fit all three, so Cadence snapped her up.

After three years of building and refining a flexible software development process, Orna was challenged by a friend and coworker: "Now that you're a consultant telling everyone how to build software, why don't you come to my business group and be a program

---

63   A stage-gate model is a development process of a project that is undertaken in
      several stages.
64   McKinsey is a global consulting company; for an overview, see http://www.
      mckinsey.com/.

manager of a real software project, seeing the day-to-day difficulties, instead of just telling us how it should be done? This will enrich you and will take your theoretical expertise and make it real." Orna felt she would never be as good as she wanted to be if she didn't take this step. "If I don't talk to a customer or an engineer daily at a software bug level, how could I come and consult around processes?" she asked herself. She wanted to experience that challenge, so she made the leap and switched over to project management. Over the next two years with her group, she figured out the many compromises a true release takes, and along the way earned her Project Management Professional certification.

"I stayed a total of five years, until my boss moved to a company called Electronic Arts (EA). He gave me a call and invited me to be the director of development in the games industry," she said, but she was puzzled. EA is a leading publisher of games on consoles, PCs, and mobile devices. "Games, for me, were the thing I had to stop my kids from playing for more than half an hour a day, and I did not play games—I am not a gamer. Why would I be a fit?"

Here is why. The producers at EA had taken over a division called The Sims,[65] and was restructuring its management to improve work conditions for the engineers and artists. To this end, EA brought in a senior level of professional managers who knew how to plan and execute projects, folks who were not necessarily connected to the games industry. Orna was one of those selected.

At EA for five years, Orna learned how to manage technical artists, modelers, animators, concept artists, and engineers. "It was an exciting, amazing adventure, because it combined art and creativity with software development," she said. "I have my name on three game titles, and I was the outsourcing manager of another one."

In those positions, Orna found herself branching into legal, finance, and outsourcing matters due to her negotiation skills. She

---

[65]   Read an EA description of The Sims here: https://www.thesims.com/features/overview.

attributes these skills to her mother, who would "negotiate with grace over every apricot in the Haifa outdoor market." When Orna began dealing with outsourcing, she thought the prices for a 3D art model were outrageous, so it was natural to her to start negotiating to get a better deal for EA. Impressed, her manager asked her to negotiate with other agencies; thus, her role within the company started to expand.

During her final year at EA, Orna decided to move to a new game. That game wasn't brought to market; however, she felt it was a valuable learning experience even though the risk of moving did not pan out. The manager of the game was a fan of agile development[66]—or rather, extreme project management (XPM), an offshoot of agile for which there is no roadmap, with teams developing both goals and software as they go. Orna felt it was chaotic, but through this experience, she discovered both the advantages and dangers of agile development, and the complexity of developing with very large teams.

By this time, Orna had met her second husband, Bill. They wanted to live together and join families, and a difficult decision had to be made: career or a new life with a man who lived more than an hour's commute to EA.

"I made a decision to find a home and start our 'Brady Bunch' family, while changing my work environment. What seemed difficult at the time propelled me to something new, unknown, and exciting. I left the game industry but kept my friends. The move to Nvidia, and later to VMware, brought my career much farther forward and forced me to learn new management styles and industries. I never looked back."

Orna went to Nvidia as a staff program manager. She felt she took a step back in her role, and she vows not to do that again. What

---

66   For a description of the agile software development method, see
https://en.wikipedia.org/wiki/Agile_software_development.
Wikipedia also offers a page about XPM: https://en.wikipedia.org/wiki/
Extreme_project_management.

normally happens when you take a step back is that you have to work your way up again—and that climb is the hardest. "I gave up the director role twice." Beyond the monetary and informational rewards she lost, Orna recognizes this as a gendered issue. Orna feels that men rarely take a step down. Either they make lateral career moves, or they take a step up. "They do not step down," she said. "There is a danger in doing that." When she took that step down at Nvidia, she was making a choice of personal happiness.

"I have a wonderful family, and I will never give that up. I saw it as a choice. I am not sure I had to make that choice; but I made it. I moved close to home—five miles—so close that I could run it if I wanted to in the morning. I did sometimes. Sometimes I biked to work. It was fabulous in terms of the commute and building my new life. I also learned about chip design and graphic processing units, areas I knew little about prior. Remember that every move is a learning opportunity, and eventually every moved propelled me upwards."

Nvidia was a great experience for Orna. With EA, she was accustomed to static games shipping in a box that is delivered to stores. Nvidia software is downloaded millions of times, all the time, because all the gamers in the world want to download the latest and greatest versions to work with, say, World of Warcraft. "This was an unprecedented scale of customers," she said. "If customers hit a bug, or there was a texture missing in World of Warcraft, it was in a matter of minutes that you could see the problem."

In the last of her three years at Nvidia, Orna was responsible for releasing software developed for the Microsoft Surface tablet. Orna found this project exciting, as it was the first version of the tablet. "If anybody thinks there is excitement in high tech, let me tell you, when Surface came out with our chip and our software—I dare to say, my software—inside, we were watching the lines at the Microsoft Store; we wanted to see the adoption! How was it gonna go? We looked at sales, we emailed reviews to each other. It is exciting to see something you created being released."

In 2013, friends who worked at VMware asked her to come and work there.

"I interviewed, and it went extremely well, but they asked me, 'What is the scope of the largest project you have ever managed?' I was thinking maybe the chip software of Nvidia; basically, that was all of the software engineers at Nvidia. I would say that was 700 people, including the quality engineers. They said, 'Okay, that's probably half of what you will deal with here.' I knew I was walking into a different scale of work, and into a new career in a company full of innovation and educational opportunities."

"I didn't know what vSphere[67] was until I walked into one of the largest software releases of all times at VMware, and possibly in the world. I managed the release of vSphere 6.0 for two years, with all of the difficulties it entailed, including standing in front of the executive staff saying, 'This project will never converge to its original schedule.' I was only two months on the job, but getting bad news this early can be fixed with re-planning. They needed to know."

It is amazing that Orna, in a span of three short years at VMware, not only shipped vSphere and NSX[68] products, but she also built an enormous social capital of people who have advocated for, sponsored, and supported her career—something I view as key to one's success, especially for a woman's success. Today, Orna works as director of business operations, building key Dell EMC and VMware development solutions.

~ ~ ~

Orna's hard work and ability to build social capital—the qualities that led her to a colorful career—originated in her family.

"My parents had strife most of their lives, surviving Nazi Germany, then the communist regime in Romania with limitation

---

67   vSphere is VMware's virtualization product suite.
68   NSX is VMware's networking and security product.

of freedoms, all the way to being new immigrants in Israel and acclimating to a new country, language, and professions. They were poorer than dirt when they immigrated to Israel, and they worked harder than imaginable, to not only survive but to thrive. They recycled tea bags, used carton boxes for shelves, and cut shoes to make sandals for the summer. My parents are my teachers as to ethics, perseverance, and compassion."

A critical lesson came from her father, who at the age of nine was forced to quit school and work as a watchmaker's assistant in Romania. He provided the income for his family, and worked in hiding without being able to eat properly, go to school, or play. Five years later, in 1945, after being freed by the Russians, he completed the missing years of school while continuing to work during the day, finishing with perfect grades.

Orna's father would tell her, "One thing, Pontsu, is to not quit; to use every moment of the day and to finish everything you do with excellence. Stand out, be the best you can." As she recalled this, Orna told me, "There is no pedigree, there is no luck, there are no connections—there is only hard work and studying. That's what I grew up on." Eventually, Orna's father finished a master's degree in electrical engineering, and led the group that planned the first Israeli electric power station. He retired as the deputy lead of Israel's power station planning division.

"Studying was the utmost value in our family. My parents were twice robbed, once by the Nazis and then by the Romanian government, which allowed them to take basically nothing when they asked to emigrate to Israel in 1960. They carved a new life in a new country, and money was spent on little but education: books, notebooks, tuition, and the best private school were provided, and the rest you had to work for. We were very self-sufficient. We made our own wine and cheese, my father fixed all that was needed, and we rarely hired contractors or mechanics to fix the cars. Everything he did was with the same striving for excellence."

Orna's mother was a "feminist in hiding," as Orna described her—a woman who challenged the status quo for women by working full-time, raising two children, and guiding her children to equality of sexes. "We all cleaned, we all cooked. Education was for both. Roles were never gender-based." Her mother has a master's degree in chemistry, and worked until she turned seventy. Though a feminist, she relinquished that feminism at home. Orna recalled, "When we were cleaning the house, for example, she would ask my dad to lift his feet up so she could clean the floor underneath him. While she did that, she would whisper to me, 'You are not going to do that, right?'"

Reflecting on how Orna's mother expected work to be divided in the home, I am reminded of a feminist quote by Gloria Steinem, the nationally recognized leader and spokeswoman for the feminist movement in the late 1960s and early 1970s: "Though we have the courage to raise our daughters more like our sons, we've rarely had the courage to raise our sons like our daughters."

This is so true. I come from a family of four kids. I am the youngest of three daughters and a son. All three girls were allowed to step outside traditional roles as women: I studied computer science, one of my sisters became a nationally known cricket player, and my other sister owns her own business. However, my brother was raised as a boy. He didn't have to step outside his comfortable role, never even learning to cook or clean. Steinem is right; we rarely dare to raise our sons and daughters by the same standards, so it was refreshing for me to hear that Orna's family did just that (kudos to her mom). Orna's story was eye-opening for me in another way, as well, as I am raising two boys and a girl.

Orna's mom also taught her the importance of being independent and having your own money. "My mom's biggest lesson was that no matter what you do or what you have, be able to make a living, and persist making a living, even if you give birth, even if your husband is rich, and you don't need to make a living."

In addition to Orna's home influences, one essay shaped her life. "I read, when I was nineteen or twenty, Virginia Woolf's *A Room of One's Own*,[69] and everything clicked." In this essay, Woolf lays out the thesis that a woman should have money of her own if she is to write fiction. She uses fictional characters to develop her theory. For instance, she invents Judith Shakespeare, Shakespeare's sister, who has the same gifts as her brother, but is denied the same legacy because of the doors that were closed to women at the time. Woolf talks about how Judith was not sent to school like her brother, which is similar to what happened to Woolf herself. She had to stay home while her brothers were sent off to school, trapped within the confines of the expectations placed on women. Judith finally kills herself and the world doesn't get to see the genius she is. Woolf ends the essay urging women to have a room of their own where they can become who they are meant to be. Orna grew up on these values of independence and being true to yourself.

~ ~ ~

As we talked about Orna's values and her parents' importance to her own education, I was curious about how Orna fared in school when it came to subjects like math and science. "They were quite challenging for me. My brother had to help me during the summer." Even though Orna is one of the few women in this book who found math and science challenging, she has still had a successful career in tech. She attributes this to her love of learning, even if it is outside formal education. And coding is not the only option—there is a wide array of additional key roles in high tech that are not engineering, per se. "If you learn what engineers do and how they work, you can weave that with program management, product marketing, corporate litigation, and release management or marketing."

---

[69] Virginia Woolf, *A Room of One's Own* (New York: Harcourt, Brace and Company, 1929).

Nevertheless, while it's not her natural area of expertise, Orna does believe in learning about the tools and products engineers build. "I think it is important to understand what 'compile' means, the basic structure of what it takes to check in code, and the process an engineer goes through to check in their code—the software development cycle. If you understand that, you can shine in all the supporting roles around engineering. I eventually got an engineering certificate at Stanford, since it was key to have the education as well."

When asked about imposter syndrome, Orna admits she experiences it at times. "'When feeling it, I dive right in. You can learn anything. I immerse myself in topics, read specs, study spreadsheets until I feel I can master a dialogue in the area. Then I 'meet the expert.' That's my tactic when I have those moments. This way you not only learn but also expand your social network and rely on experts to educate you. What could be better than that?"

Perhaps her imposter syndrome is a blessing in disguise, because it means Orna is constantly learning in order to keep that feeling at bay. I think this is exactly what Sarah Clatterbuck meant when she described imposter syndrome in chapter 14; she said it is part of your growth and development. Orna says, "I constantly try to learn something completely new. When I don't have that, I feel very restless."

When it comes to making decisions, Orna bases hers on three things: "Bravery, risk-taking, and change. Make those moves—without change, there is no progress. Without risk, there is no reward, it is the *only* way to progress. You learn from the failures as much as successes," she said.

From an objective stance, her decision strategy has clearly led to significant success. I wondered, how does she define success for herself? "For me, success is that all the balls in the air are at a reasonable place." The "balls in the air" refer to her children, her husband, her career, and her health. As long as they are reasonably okay—they don't have to be "stellar"—she feels successful. "All of these matter, and if one of them falls behind—if your relationship suffers, or you are neglecting your body, or your kids are failing and alone—then everything else is murky and nothing else matters. All of that has to be balanced," she advises.

Success to Orna is a balance of all those ingredients. There was a lesson here for me, because I skew toward work a lot. I am a Type A personality, and I tend to ignore other aspects of my life. I know I am not the only one who does this—many people today are workaholics. In the age of smartphones, we are perpetually *on*. However, for me, the awareness of needing this balance is a first good step to achieving balance in my life.

Mentors throughout her career have been a strong influence on her ability to find balance. Most of Orna's mentors have been her bosses, her friends, and her husband. For two years (2007–2008), she challenged herself to train for the Ironman triathlon. During that time, she had mentors who guided her through that physical ordeal. Her mentors know her well; they know both her shortcomings and her strengths. Her advice on finding mentors is that "you have to find mentors you can be vulnerable in front of. In other words, you can talk about your shortcomings, and that will never be held against you. My mentors must see the yin and yang in me. They must be willing to say the truth." Orna acknowledges that mentors like these are tough to find.

However, she also believes that mentorship goes both ways; you have an important role to play as mentee. "Come prepared, come with a problem, come with a challenge, come with aspiration and questions. Give your mentor something back, don't just come and demand."

Orna's sense of balance and equilibrium has only occasionally been shaken by instances of gender bias. "Recently someone was suggesting a dress analogy to mansplain a concept to me, and I realized for any one progressive boss I have, there are quite a few who are yet to grow beyond their gender bias. I was amused, and not at all angry. I asked him if he could use a pants analogy instead, as I might understand that better. It is important to point out bias in the moment, with compassion and humor. Control your emotions at all costs in those critical moments, stay professional and calm, since the same people are here tomorrow and you will need to work with them after the current crisis is over. If you can channel your anger, or happiness, to move others to action, then the emotional force can propel you forward."

In my own experience, I have come across many men who have outbursts of anger at the workplace. Somehow, they get away with a slap on the wrist. When women show any emotions at work—a breakdown of tears, or an expression of anger—it's hard for their reputation to recover from that. They are labeled as emotional and unstable. The reason women tend to be judged much more harshly when it comes to emotions is that there is an implicit generalization that women are constitutionally too emotional and touchy. But emotions are in fact a powerful tool, and it often is connected to human insight, so use your emotions, don't squelch them.

The research echoes this. The article "Lean In to Crying at Work," published in 2016 in *The Atlantic*, quotes numerous studies that come to the unanimous conclusion that women who cry in the workplace are generally viewed unfavorably, whereas it is seen as okay for men to cry a bit on occasion.

Orna insightfully noted, "I think corporate America expects people to work as robots; you have to check your emotions at the door. The reality is, we are all human." Then Orna made an astute point about emotions and different gender expectations. "I have noticed many men shout, scream, and slam doors at work. Somehow, that behavior is acceptable," she said. But imagine if a woman did that; she would be labeled as hysterical. Women are given harder standards and expectations, and one emotional outburst could land them in hot water.

Orna agrees. "I think what happens is that there is a set of expectations about how you are supposed to behave. I have received comments that I am too assertive, but I don't think I am. Maybe because I am a woman and I behave in a certain way, the expectation is that I should temper my assertiveness. My utmost expression and success recipe is compassion and identification with the others. Calm is second. Passion is third. I am not going to start cursing; I never cursed in my life. My mother will never forgive me. But assertiveness? Tough luck. I speak my mind."

As part of her job, Orna had to make several business trips to India. She felt that in India it is especially hard for women to assert themselves. "It is hard for them to insert themselves assertively into a male dialogue," she said. "They are expected to not interrupt or take over a conversation, when men do that all the time." She feels women in India wait to have promotion discussions with their managers. She went on to say, "They wait for opportunities to come to them, instead of openly seeking the opportunities. I met and coached quite a few employees from India. About 30% of the men asked about promoting their career, and how to get more money and more projects. Women, not so much." She concluded that, in the fight for equality, "there is long journey ahead of us. To stay hopeful, consider that one hundred years ago most of us were not allowed to vote. So, keep pushing forward."

Orna observed that as hard as it is to succeed as an immigrant in the United States, it is harder for women in certain fields to reach top roles. "If you read Virginia Woolf, she insists on us women continuing to strive for that next step. She said that, eventually, we will have a woman Shakespeare. And every small change, along with financial independence, sets a role model."

Orna says that small acts made persistently throughout the years will someday help to break the glass ceiling. "Hillary Clinton would not have been able to go to Wellesley without Virginia Woolf protesting 150 years ago about the ability to go to school. That path had to be carved." Small acts of defiance will create change. "Even when we are tired, even when the kids are sick, do your best and excel, and the glass ceiling will eventually shatter."

~ ~ ~

TAKEAWAYS

- Orna followed her vocation in schooling, and brought her love of teaching to tech.

- She was always interested in women's equality in the workplace and in society.

- She brought her creativity into her tech work while working at Electronic Arts.

- She observed that men change jobs every three years, always taking a step up—as opposed to women, who too often make lateral moves or take a step down.

- Her parents ingrained in her a desire and an ability to work like there is no tomorrow and to do her very best, which she applies daily in her career.

- Passion propels you forward, when used with control. Do not shy away from emotions; use them to connect to others and move your cause forward.

- She maintains a healthy balance throughout her life in her work, health, and relationships, and does all three with strong goals to excel.

- For mentors, she advises finding ones you can be vulnerable with, who fit your needs at the time, and ensure you are giving back as much as you receive.

- She stays calm, keeping watch over her emotions as a means of dealing with gender bias.

- She advises that women use small acts of self-expression and risk-taking every day to break the glass ceiling.

- Love should be part of everything you do, including work.

POSTSCRIPT

Along the journey that writing this book took me on, a new world opened up to me. Through listening to these women's stories, internalizing their advice, and researching various topics, I learned new skills and mindsets to help counter the effects of unconscious bias. I was inspired to teach myself how to advocate, speak up, negotiate, mentor, sponsor, and be a role model for myself and for others. I now constantly question the status quo, and I am keenly aware of bias in hiring, retention, pay, promotions, and growth. Because of what I know today, I am not afraid to call out bias, both in myself and in others.

I want to share a story about a young girl who went on to have a successful tech career. Her journey started with inspiration from her dad, followed by her own grit and determination to fight stereotypes about what women are capable of. Her dad was a contract accountant who worked on the Hubble Space Telescope. Consequently, she became fascinated by outer space. She describes a beautiful, pivotal moment with her dad. "We were sitting in the backyard, and he was explaining how I was looking back in time by virtue of looking at light from the stars that had traveled so far to reach my eye. This made me question the world, and the concept of time and space, in a very different way."

The girl fell in love with "nerdy" things, but kept that hidden because she wanted to pass as a normal kid. Being labeled a nerd "has a really big impact on girls and boys. There was a stigma attached to being the smart kid, or being interested in these areas. This was the headwind against me, but the tailwind was just a true love of mathematics." She persisted, despite the stereotype threat, and went on to have a fulfilling tech career and to become a successful tech executive.

Throughout this book, there are two consistent lessons. First, persist. Regardless of what society expects of you or tells you to do, persist with your own vision of what you want to achieve in your life. The tailwinds of persistence will help you soar. The second lesson is that we all have the power to change the world for someone else. If each one of us makes it a point to intervene in one woman's life, we can get there, slowly but surely—one woman at a time.

My long term hope for the tech world is to have equal representation of men and women as CEOs, board members, executive leaders, middle managers, and engineers. I hope that by telling these women's stories, I will encourage new generations of women to develop the skills and determination to make this a reality. Let's go change the world.

ACKNOWLEDGMENTS

The day I decided to write this book, I received only tremendous support and encouragement. I have so many people to thank because I could not have written this book on my own. My husband, Jay, was my rock during this process. He watched our young kids on nights and weekends while I wrote. He was also my first editor. Although it wasn't always easy to help me edit the book, I appreciate the care that he put into improving my rough manuscript. The inspiration and the valuable career advice he gleaned from the stories helped him with his own career changes. After seven years of being a stay-at-home dad to our kids (a choice he made), he decided to go back to work. He felt just like the countless women who take a break in their careers and then go back to work. The switch wasn't always smooth, but he internalized the stories from the book, which helped propel him into a career he loves.

I want to thank Jambu Guruswami. When I reached out to people in my network for support and advice on this project, Jambu was incredibly supportive and opened many doors for me. I am so sincerely appreciative that he connected me to women I wanted to interview.

I had several other editors on this journey whom I want to thank. Erika DeSimone assisted me when I first started to write the stories. Her feminist views and thoughtful insights were invaluable. I benefited greatly from our long, lovely conversations. My next editor, Haley Evans, was just wonderful. My first draft of the manuscript came together because of her prompting, prodding, and deadlines. Her comments helped me organize my thoughts around the stories.

My fourth editor, Linda Jay, was endearing and experienced. Back in the 1980s, she wrote two articles for *Woman Engineer*, a national magazine published out of New York. Because she has previously published work on women in technology, she understood what I was trying to do. Next and most importantly, I want to thank Pm[70] Weizenbaum, who did the heavy lifting and crafty editing to get my manuscript ready for publication. She came in at the twenty-mile mark of a marathon and helped me get to the 26.2-mile finish line. She walked and ran side by side with me. I feel like she worked harder than I did on this book and put such passion and clarity of thought into editing the stories. I can't thank her enough. And if it wasn't for Holly Alexander, who connected me to Pm, I'd still be looking for an editor to round off my project. So, thank you, Holly. Finally, I want to thank Judi Heidel for editing my final few essays.

On cover design of the book, I want to thank a few people who helped along the way: Bryan Crowe, Kaori Ikeda Chun for their initial reviews and Dahlia Yuen for designing my vision. A job well done!

For connecting me to the amazing women featured in this publication, I want to thank the following people: Alison McCormack, Anne Holler, Ana Pinczuk, Brendan Kelley, Dana Kramer, Ellen Cohen, Kate Peters, Lily Chang, Mimi Hills, Orna Berryman, Prashanth Ponnachath, Patrick McCormack and Tal Briller.

I also want to thank Alexis Bjorlin, Jana Van Greunen, Jocelyn Goldfein, Komal Mangtani, Natasha Gude, and Vicky Xu for their time. I want to thank Krystal Deaton—the "Gas Girl"—for her amazing story. Krystal introduced me to a variety of topics that were the foundation of the research for this book.

All the women featured in this book gave me so much of their time with interviews and reviews of their material. I can't thank them enough.

To my mentors Mimi Hills, Orna Berryman, and Sridhar Reddy, I've learned so much from each of you. I am a better leader because of

---

70   http://www.weizenbaumeditor.com/aboutmyname.html

you. And to Shane Lowry, under whom I first stepped into a leadership role. Transitioning from an engineer to a manager is never easy. I intentionally chose Shane's team to ensure that I was surrounded by leaders I could learn from. He built teams that had diversity of thought and opinion, as well as being gender, age, and culture blind. This experience was very meaningful to me; his team was one of the best I ever worked in. As I lead and build my own teams, I aspire to lead as he does.

To my dear friends Aastha Bharadwaj, Keith Johnston, Margaret Petrus, and Tea LiukkonenOlmiala, thanks for being my cheerleaders. I want to thank all the people on the legal, and public relations teams at VMware, where I work, who took time to review the material in this book and approve it for publication. But let me make it clear that the content and views expressed in this book are my own, and not those of VMware.

Thank you to Ann Schlegel, who connected me to Friesen Press. A shout-out to this amazing publishing team at Friesen Press: Astra Crompton, Dahlia Yuen, Genevieve Penny, Jamie Ollivier, Jessica Feser, Oriana Varas, Tammara Kennelly, and Valerie Trenholm. And to my patient, dedicated transcribing team: Alison McCormack, Gomathi Krishnan, and Tom Michael.

To Miriam Ohman and Ravi Soundararajan who reviewed the book with an eye to detail. I am indebted to them.

Finally, to my young kids Kian, Kyla, and Zev, who had to bear with two years of an unavailable mommy who worked all day and wrote all evening. Thank you.

BIBLIOGRAPHY

Babcock, Linda and Sarah Laschever. *Women Don't Ask: Negotiation and the Gender Divide* (Princeton University Press, 2003).

CodeChix. http://codechix.org/.

Eagly, Alice H., and Linda L. Carli. *Through the Labyrinth: The Truth About How Women Become Leaders* (Boston, MA: Harvard Business School Press, 2007), p 191.

Girls Who Code. https://girlswhocode.com/.

Glassdoor. https://www.glassdoor.com/blog/companies-equal-pay/.

Goleman, Daniel. *Emotional Intelligence: Why It Can Matter More Than IQ* (Bantam Books, 1995).

Harvard case study. http://www.nytimes.com/2013/09/08/education/harvard-case-study-gender-equity.html?pagewanted=all.

Harvey Mudd. https://qz.com/730290/harvey-mudd-college-took-on-gender-bias-and-now-more-than-half-its-computer-science-majors-are-women/.

Ibarra, Herminia, Nancy M Carter, and Christine Silva. "Why Men Still Get More Promotions Than Women" in *Harvard Business Review* 88, no. 9 (September 2010).

Inventory Test. http://careerassessmentsite.com/tests/strong-tests/about-the-strong-interest-inventory/.

Kanellos, Michael. "General Magic: The Most Important Dead Company in Silicon Valley?" *Forbes*, September 18, 2011. https://www.forbes.com/sites/michaelkanellos/2011/09/18/general-magic-the-most-important-dead-company-in-silicon-valley/#547f3e444d8c.

Krendl, Anna C., Richeson JA, Kelley WM, Heatherton TF. "The Negative Consequences of Threat," *Psychological Science* 19, no. 2 (February 2008): 168-75.

Leigh-Hazzard, Tracy. "If You Want to Be a Successful Woman, Find the Right Life Partner" https://journal.thriveglobal.com/if-you-want-to-be-a-successful-woman-marry-well-592d80e04315.

Maker Faire. https://makerfaire.com/makerfairehistory/.

McKellar, Jessica. "How the Internet works," filmed March 15, 2013 at PyCon US 2013, video, 29:34, http://pyvideo.org/pycon-us-2013/how-the-internet-works.html.

Myers Briggs. http://www.myersbriggs.org/my-mbti-personality-type/mbti-basics/home.htm?bhcp=1.

Nadella, Satya. https://www.theguardian.com/technology/2014/oct/10/microsoft-ceo-satya-nadella-women-dont-ask-for-a-raise.

Nadella, Satya. GHC Keynote https://www.youtube.com/watch?v=Ev6RjaM6rXw.

O'Connor, Cailin. "Are Women Worse at Math? It's Time to Stop Asking," *Huffpost* (February 3, 2015), http://www.huffingtonpost.com/cailin-oconnor/women-math-and-science_b_6573074.html.

Olson, Elizabeth. "Shown the Door, Older Workers Find Bias Hard to Prove," *New York Times*, August 7, 2017, https://www.nytimes.com/2017/08/07/business/dealbook/shown-the-door-older-workers-find-bias-hard-to-prove.html.

Paige, Scott. *The Difference: How the Power of Diversity Creates Better Groups, Firms, Schools, and Societies* (Princeton University Press, 2007).

Pearson, Catherine. "What 15 Female Leaders Really Think About Crying at Work". https://www.huffingtonpost.com/2014/05/28/crying-at-work-women_n_5365872.html.

Sandberg, Sheryl. *Lean In: Women, Work and the Will to Lead* (New York: Knopf, 2013).

Sanz, Carolina Perez,. "Emotional Discipline, Presence, and Leadership." http://templaradvisors.com/blog/emotional-discipline-presence-leadership.

Scott, Kim. *Radical Candor: Be a Kick-Ass Boss Without Losing Your Humanity* (New York: St. Martin's Press, 2017).

Slaughter, Anne-Marie. "Why Women Still Can't Have It All," *The Atlantic* (July/August 2012): 84–102.

Stereotype Threat. http://www.apa.org/research/action/stereotype.aspx.

The Linux Information Project. www.linfo.org.

Victor, Dennis. "'Nevertheless, She Persisted': How Senate's Silencing of Warren Became a Meme," *New York Times*, February 8, 2017, https://www.nytimes.com/2017/02/08/us/politics/elizabeth-warren-republicans-facebook-twitter.html.

Whiston, Susan C., and David L. Blustein. *"The Impact of Career Interventions: Preparing our Citizens for 21st Century Jobs."* https://www.ncda.org/aws/NCDA/asset_manager/get_file/63826?ver=167.

Woolf, Virginia. *A Room of One's Own* (New York: Harcourt, Brace and Company, 1929).

Women Who Code. https://www.womenwhocode.com/.

```
01010100 01101000 01110010 01101111 01110101 01100111 01101000 01101111 01110101
01110100 00100000 01110100 01101000 01101001 01110011 00100000 01100010 01101111
01101111 01101011 00101100 00100000 01110100 01101000 01100101 01110010 01100101
00100000 01100001 01110010 01100101 00100000 01110100 01110111 01101111 00100000
01100011 01101111 01101110 01110011 01101001 01110011 01110100 01100101 01101110
01110100 00100000 01101100 01100101 01110011 01110011 01101111 01101110 01110011
00101110 00100000 01000110 01101001 01110010 01110011 01110100 00101100 00100000
01110000 01100101 01110010 01110011 01101001 01110011 01110100 00101110 00100000
01010010 01100101 01100111 01100001 01110010 01100100 01101100 01100101 01110011
01110011 00100000 01101111 01100110 00100000 01110111 01101000 01100001 01110100
00100000 01110011 01101111 01100011 01101001 01100101 01110100 01111001 00100000
01100101 01111000 01110000 01100101 01100011 01110100 01110011 00100000 01101111
01100110 00100000 01111001 01101111 01110101 00100000 01101111 01110010 00100000
01110100 01100101 01101100 01101100 01110011 00100000 01111001 01101111 01110101
00100000 01110100 01101111 00100000 01100100 01101111 00101100 00100000 01110000
01100101 01110010 01110011 01101001 01110011 01110100 00100000 01110111 01101001
01110100 01101000 00100000 01111001 01101111 01110101 01110010 00100000 01101111
01110111 01101110 00100000 01110110 01101001 01110011 01101001 01101111 01101110
00100000 01101111 01100110 00100000 01110111 01101000 01100001 01110100 00100000
01111001 01101111 01110101 00100000 01110111 01100001 01101110 01110100 00100000
01110100 01101111 00100000 01100001 01100011 01101000 01101001 01100101 01110110
01100101 00100000 01101001 01101110 00100000 01111001 01101111 01110101 01110010
00100000 01101100 01101001 01100110 01100101 00101110 00100000 01010100 01101000
01100101 00100000 01110100 01100001 01101001 01101100 01110111 01101001 01101110
01100100 01110011 00100000 01101111 01100110 00100000 01110000 01100101 01110010
01110011 01101001 01110011 01110100 01100101 01101110 01100011 01100101 00100000
01110111 01101001 01101100 01101100 00100000 01101000 01100101 01101100 01110000
00100000 01111001 01101111 01110101 00100000 01110011 01101111 01100001 01110010
00101110 00100000 01010100 01101000 01100101 00100000 01110011 01100101 01100011
01101111 01101110 01100100 00100000 01101100 01100101 01110011 01110011 01101111
01101110 00100000 01101001 01110011 00100000 01110100 01101000 01100001 01110100
00100000 01110111 01100101 00100000 01100001 01101100 01101100 00100000 01101000
01100001 01110110 01100101 00100000 01110101 01101110 01101001 01110001 01110101
01100101 00100000 01100111 01101001 01100110 01110100 01110011 00101110 00100000
01001001 01100110 00100000 01100101 01100001 01100011 01101000 00100000 01101111
01100110 00100000 01110101 01110011 00100000 01100011 01101000 01101111 01101111
01110011 01100101 00100000 01110100 01101111 00100000 01101000 01101111 01101110
01101111 01110010 00100000 01100001 01101110 01100100 00100000 01100001 01100011
01110100 00100000 01101111 01101110 00100000 01110100 01101000 01101111 01110011
01100101 00100000 01100111 01101001 01100110 01110100 01110011 00101100 00100000
01110111 01100101 00100000 01100011 01100001 01101110 00100000 01101101 01100001
01101011 01100101 00100000 01100001 00100000 01110000 01101111 01110011 01101001
01110100 01101001 01110110 01100101 00100000 01100100 01101001 01100110 01100110
01100101 01110010 01100101 01101110 01100011 01100101 00100000 01101001 01101110
00100000 01110011 01101111 01101101 01100101 01101111 01101110 01100101 00100000
01101111 01110010 00100000 01110011 01101111 01101101 01100101 00100000 01110111
01101111 01101101 01100001 01101110 11100010 10000000 10011001 01110011 00100000
01101100 01101001 01100110 01100101 00101100 00100000 01110111 01100101 00100000
```

can get there, slowly but surely— one woman at a time.

My long term hope for the tech world is to have equal representation of men and women as CEOs, board members, executive leaders, middle managers, and engineers. I hope that by telling these women's stories, I will encourage new generations of women to develop the skills and determination to make this a reality. Let's go change the world.